POPULAR MUSIC CENSORSHIP IN AFRICA

This book is dedicated to the work of Freemuse

Popular Music Censorship in Africa

Edited by

MICHAEL DREWETT
Rhodes University, South Africa

MARTIN CLOONAN
University of Glasgow, UK

ASHGATE

Published by
Ashgate Publishing Limited
Gower House
Croft Road
Aldershot
Hampshire GU11 3HR
England

Ashgate Publishing Company
Suite 420
101 Cherry Street
Burlington, VT 05401-4405
USA

Ashgate website: http://www.ashgate.com

British Library Cataloguing in Publication Data
Popular music censorship in Africa. – (Ashgate popular and folk music series)
　　1.Music - Censorship – Africa – History 2.Music and state – Africa 3.Music – Social aspects – Africa 4.Popular music – Africa – History and criticism
　　I.Drewett, Michael II.Cloonan, Martin
　　303.3'76'096

Library of Congress Cataloging-in-Publication Data
Popular music censorship in Africa / Edited by Michael Drewett and Martin Cloonan.
　　p. cm. – (Ashgate popular and folk music series)
　ISBN 0-7546-5291-2 (alk. paper)
　1. Popular music—Censorship—Africa. 2. Popular music—Political aspects—Africa. I. Drewett, Michael. II. Cloonan, Martin. III. Series.

　ML3917.A4P6 2006
　363.31096—dc22

2006002161

ISBN-13: 978-0-7546-5291-5
ISBB-10: 0-7546-5291-2

Printed and bound in Great Britain by MPG Books Ltd. Bodmin, Cornwall.

Contents

List of Abbreviations

AAA	Artists Against Apartheid
AAM	Anti-Apartheid Movement
AIS	Islamic Salvation Army
ANC	African National Congress
ASP	Afro-Shirazi Party
AZAPO	Azanian People's Organization
BASATA	National Arts Council of Tanzania
BBC	British Broadcasting Corporation (BBC)
BCCSA	Broadcasting Complaints Commission of South Africa
BMU	British Musicians' Union
BSA	Broadcasting Services Act
CASA	Culture in Another South Africa
CCM	Chama cha Mapinduzi
CID	Criminal Investigation Department
COSAS	Congress of South African Students
CPP	Convention Peoples Party
FBI	Federal Bureau for Investigation
FIDA	International Federation of the Women Lawyers
FIS	Islamic Salvation Front
FXI	Freedom of Expression Institute
GCB	Government Censorship Board
GILC	Global Internet Liberty Campaign
HIFA	Harare International Festival of the Arts
ICTR	International Criminal Tribunal for Rwanda
IDASA	Institute for Democracy in South Africa
JMPR	Jeune Mouvement Populaire de la Révolution
KANU	Kenya African National Union
KBC	Kenyan Broadcasting Corporation
MAFREMO	Malawi Freedom Movement
MASS	Movement Against Second Slavery
MBC	Malawi Broadcasting Corporation
MCP	Malawi Congress Party
MDC	Movement for Democratic Change
MRND	National Revolutionary Movement for Development
MYP	Malawi Young Pioneers

MISA	Media Institute of South Africa
MPR	Mouvement Populaire de la Revolution
MTV	Music Television
MUSIGA	Musicians Union of Ghana
NBC	National Broadcasting Commission
NCA	National Constitutional Assembly
NDLEA	Nigerian Drug Law Enforcement Agency
NGO	Non government organisation
NLC	National Liberation Council
NLF	National Liberation Front
NTA	Nigerian Television Authority
OAU	Organization for African Unity
PAC	Pan Africanist Congress
PDG	President Directeur-General
PMAN	Performing Musicians Association of Nigeria
RBC	Rhodesian Broadcasting Corporation
RCB	Rhodesian Censorship Board
RPF	Rwandan Patriotic Front
RTD	Radio Tanzania Dar es Salaam
RTLM	Radio-Télévision Libre des Mille Collines
SABC	South African Broadcasting Corporation
SAHRC	South African Human Rights Commission
SAMA	South African Musicians' Alliance
SSS	State Security Service
STZ	Sauti ya Tanzania Zanzibar
TAA	Tanganyika African Association
TANU	Tanganyika African National Union
TFC	Tanzania Film Company
TNA	Tanzania National Archives
TOT	Tanzania One Theatre
TTACSA	Tanganyika Territory African Civil Service Association
TVZ	Television Zanzibar
UDF	United Democratic Front
UN	United Nations
UNISA	University of South Africa
VOA	Voice of America
VOK	Voice of Kenya
ZANU-PF	Zimbabwe African National Union-Patriotic Front
ZBC	Zimbabwean Broadcasting Corporation
ZCB	Zimbabwe Censorship Board
ZWNEWS	Zimbabwe News

Notes on Contributors

Wilson Akpan, a Ford Foundation/IFP Scholar, obtained his doctorate at Rhodes University, South Africa, in April 2006 and currently lectures in the Department of Sociology, University of Fort Hare, East London, South Africa. He holds an Honours degree from the University of Calabar and a Master's from the University of Ibadan (both in Nigeria). He is also an alumnus of Advocacy Institute, Washington DC, and School for International Training, Vermont, USA. Akpan's research interests cut across environment, oil, social policy, ICT and popular culture. He writes a monthly column for IT & Telecom Digest, and is convenor of the Race, Class and Ethnicity research group of the South African Sociological Association.

Kelly M. Askew is an Associate Professor in the Department of Anthropology and the Center for Afro-American and African Studies at the University of Michigan. She holds a Ph.D. in Anthropology from Harvard University and a BA in Music and Anthropology from Yale University. She is author of *Performing the Nation: Swahili Music and Cultural Production in Tanzania*, (University of Chicago Press, 2002) and co-edited (with Richard R. Wilk) *The Anthropology of Media: A Reader*, (Blackwell Publishers, 2002). Her published articles range in topic from music and politics, music and gender relations, and nationalism, to aesthetics, documentary film, and Hollywood film production.

Gary Baines is an Associate Professor in the History Department, Rhodes University, Grahamstown, South Africa. He holds an MA from Rhodes University and a Doctorate from the University of Cape Town. His areas of research include South African urban history and culture, especially film and music. He has published a monograph and numerous articles on the history of Port Elizabeth where he lived for a decade. He teaches a course on the social history of rock music.

Reuben M. Chirambo is a Lecturer in the English Department at Chancellor College at the University of Malawi. He holds a Ph.D Literature from the University of Minnesota (2005). His previous published papers examine, among other subjects, popular music and politics during the dictatorship of former president for life in Malawi, Dr. H.K. Banda (1964-1994) as well as in the contemporary democratic context. He has also written and published on literature and the democratic transition in Malawi besides co-editing an anthology of short stories and poems from Malawi.

Johnny Clegg has an Honours Degree in Anthropology from the University of the Witwatersrand. He lectured at the University of Natal for three years and at the University of Witwatersrand for one year before he left academia to pursue a full-time career as a musician with Sipho Mchunu and their band Juluka. Clegg went on to release numerous albums and achieve national and international recognition with Juluka, his later band Savuka and as a solo artist.

Martin Cloonan is a Senior Lecturer in Popular Music at the University of Glasgow. He is chair of the international anti-censorship group, Freemuse (www.freemuse.org). Martin is author of *Banned! Censorship of Popular Music in Britain: 1967-1992* (Arena, 1996), the subject of his doctoral thesis, and co-editor (with Reebee Garofalo) of *Policing Pop* (Temple University Press, 1996). He has written numerous articles on the politics of popular music, especially with regard to censorship and is a regular contributor to the Index on Censorship.

John Collins has been active in the Ghanaian/West African music scene since 1969 as a guitarist, band leader, music union activist, recording engineer/producer (Bokoor Studio) and writer. He obtained his BA degree in sociology/archaeology from the University of Ghana in 1972 and his Ph.D in Ethnomusicology from SUNY Buffalo in 1994. He began teaching at the Music Department of the University of Ghana in 1995, obtained a Full Professorship there in 2002, and between 2003-2005 was Head of Department. He is currently Acting Chairman of the BAPMAF African Popular Music Archives NGO, is a consultant for the two Ghana music unions and is co-leader of the Local Dimension highlife band.

Dylan Craig is a second-year Ph.D student at American University's School of International Service (SIS) in Washington, DC. He gained his MA from the University of Cape Town, in 2003. His research interests include the renegotiation of post-Cold War security relationships, the global geopolitics of force, civil-military relations and propaganda, and various transnational phenomena.

Michael Drewett is a Senior Lecturer in the Department of Sociology at Rhodes University, South Africa. He teaches courses in gender and popular culture. His doctoral thesis was on the censorship of popular music in South Africa in the 1980s. He has written various locally and internationally published articles on South African popular music and produced the documentary film *Stopping the Music* about an instance of South African music censorship, for the Danish Film Institute and Freemuse. He is a member of the Freemuse Advisory Board and is on the executive of the International Association for the Study of Popular Music (IASPM).

Graeme Ewens is a freelance writer, editor and photographer who has been involved with African music since the early 1980s. He has written for national newspapers and specialist magazines in the UK, Africa, USA and Europe, and is the author of two books: *Africa O-Ye!*, and *Congo Colossus* - a biography of the legendary Congo-Zairean musician Franco. He was co-producer of a series of music programmes for Radio Africa No 1, has broadcast on BBC World Service and various other radio stations and was a researcher for two TV documentaries. In 1999 he was a member of the pre-selection jury for the KORA All African Music Awards. He has put together several African compilation CDs and is a partner in the RetroAfric record company.

John Francis Kitime was in born in Iringa, a city in the Southern Highlands of Tanzania. He started playing music at an early age as his father was a musician who played guitar, banjo and trumpet. He completed his O level education in 1971 and, after training for two years as a teacher, he taught in different schools in the country for five years before devoting himself to life as a professional musician. He has performed (on guitar and vocals) with some of the best Tanzanian dansi bands, including Chikwala Chikwala (in Iringa), TX Seleleka (1977-79), The Oshekas (1979-80), Orchestra Mambo Bado (1980-83), Orchestra Makassy (1985), Tancut Almasi Orchestra (1986-89), Vijana Jazz (1989-94), Orchestra Magoma Moto (1995-97), and Kilimanjaro Band (1998-present). From 1993 to 1999 he served as Chairman of CHAMUDATA, the Tanzania Musicians' Association.

Malika Mehdid was born in Algeria. She holds a degree from the University of Algiers and an MA and Ph.D from Warwick University in England where she worked in a number of universities teaching French and cultural theory. When in post at Birmingham University in the department of Cultural Studies, she developed courses on postcolonial studies. Her research interests are in Cultural Studies in relation to North Africa and the Middle East. She has published various papers on these subjects and is presently a visiting fellow, attached to the Screen Studies programme at the Drama Department, University of Manchester.

Nomalanga Mkhize is a Junior Lecturer in the Department of History at Rhodes University, Grahamstown. She is currently researching her MA on the subject of heritage and human remains. Her research interests include post-apartheid youth cultures and crime history.

Peter Muhoro Mwangi is the author of several papers and chapters in international journals on music, poetry and society. He holds a Diploma in Education (Music and English), Bachelor of Education (English/Literature), Master of Arts (Literature) and is a Ph.D candidate at Kenyatta University. He is currently a lecturer in the Department of Literature at Kigali Institute of Education, Kigali, Rwanda. Mwangi's Ph.D Thesis is on the poetics of 'Nduumo' poetry and the politics of gender in Kenya. He has been a choirmaster of national repute and is the current coordinator of a CBO on HIV/AIDS - Awareness and Advocacy through music, poetry and drama based in Nairobi.

Diane Thram is Director of the International Library of African Music and co-ordinator of the Ethnomusicology Programme of the Department of Music and Musicology at Rhodes University. Her Ph.D research in Zimbabwe centred on therapeutic dimensions of Shona indigenous religion and the music making attached to its practice. She is currently engaged in similar research on the Amagqirha, healer/diviner tradition among the Xhosa in the Eastern Cape of South Africa. She has published book chapters, numerous articles in academic journals and contributed video footage to the documentary film, *Religions of the World* and the music education text and DVD, *Global Voices* with 'Vinqo' Xhosa music and culture of the Eastern Cape of South Africa.

General Editor's Preface

The upheaval that occurred in musicology during the last two decades of the twentieth century has created a new urgency for the study of popular music alongside the development of new critical and theoretical models. A relativistic outlook has replaced the universal perspective of modernism (the international ambitions of the 12-note style); the grand narrative of the evolution and dissolution of tonality has been challenged, and emphasis has shifted to cultural context, reception and subject position. Together, these have conspired to eat away at the status of canonical composers and categories of high and low in music. A need has arisen, also, to recognize and address the emergence of crossovers, mixed and new genres, to engage in debates concerning the vexed problem of what constitutes authenticity in music and to offer a critique of musical practice as the product of free, individual expression.

Popular musicology is now a vital and exciting area of scholarship, and the Ashgate Popular and Folk Music Series aims to present the best research in the field. Authors will be concerned with locating musical practices, values and meanings in cultural context, and may draw upon methodologies and theories developed in cultural studies, semiotics, poststructuralism, psychology and sociology. The series will focus on popular musics of the twentieth and twenty-first centuries. It is designed to embrace the world's popular musics from Acid Jazz to Zydeco, whether high tech or low tech, commercial or non-commercial, contemporary or traditional.

Professor Derek B. Scott
Chair of Music
University of Salford

PART 1
Censorship Issues

Chapter 1

Popular Music Censorship in Africa: An Overview

Martin Cloonan

Introduction

In recent years various histories of music censorship have been written about a number of places, most notably in the United States (c/f Blecha 2004, Chastenger 1999, Hill 1992, Jones 1991, Kennedy 1990, McDonald 1989, Martin and Segrave 1993, Nuzum 2001, Winfield and Davidson 1999), the UK (Cloonan 1995a, 1995b, 1996) and other western countries (c/f Dümling 1995, Johnson 2003, Sluka 1994, Starr 1985). There have also been attempts to analyse the censorship outside of the Anglophone world (c/f Baily 2001, Cloonan and Garofalo 2003, *Index on Censorship* 1998, Korpe 2004) and to monitor global music censorship (www.freemuse.org). Censorship within particular African countries has also been charted in various places (c/f Cloonan and Garofalo 2003, Drewett 2004a, Eyre 2001, Index on Censorship 1998, Korpe 2004, Servant 2003). However there have hitherto been few attempts to give an account of the experience of music censorship across a continent and this is what *Popular Music Censorship in Africa* attempts.

The rest of this chapter examines the African experience of music censorship, as documented in *Popular Music Censorship in Africa* and elsewhere and locates it within broader censorial trends. It begins by examining the 'norms' of censorship in the west as outlined in previous works and continues by looking at the African experience under colonial and post-colonial rule. It then goes on to examine in more depth the characteristics of African music censorship, before ending by drawing out the implications of that experience for more general theories of music censorship.

Popular Music Censorship in Africa breaks new ground. It is important to note here that only comparatively recently has the history of music censorship been written about in the west[1] in any systematic way. While accounts of individual acts

---

[1] By the 'west' here I primarily mean the 'liberal democracies' of United Kingdom and United States of America, which have produced by far the most detailed accounts of music

of music censorship occasionally made the music and other press, only in the last fifteen years or so have attempts been made to offer overviews.[2] In addition, despite the vital contribution of Afro-American music to popular music and the particular place that music has in African society (c/f Wilson Akpan, Chapter 6 below) the history of African music has not received anything like the coverage of music made in the west. When these factors are combined it comes as little surprise that there are comparatively few accounts of music censorship in Africa. It is in this context that *Popular Music Censorship in Africa* makes its contribution to our understanding of both the power of music and the attempts which are made to restrict that power.

Because of the privileged position of their countries, it has been commentators in the west who have been able to tell their censorial tales and, to an extent, to place them on the international stage. Thus western versions of music censorship have become, via the accounts which exist of them, something of a 'norm'. In this sense the African experience can be seen, as – to use a highly loaded term – 'other'. But rather than seeing things that way, my object here is to show how Africa's experiences of music censorship can give a fuller, more complex, view of music censorship than has hitherto been revealed. While of necessity, this chapter adopts a somewhat broad brush approach which will not always be sensitive to important local differences, it is hoped that this book itself serves at least two purposes: First it begins to redress the balance and secondly, in doing so, it provides further insight into the nature of music censorship.

The perspective of the author – that of an outsider looking in – is important here. In particular, the political implications are profound. As a white northern European living in what is generally referred to as a liberal democracy, I am only too aware of the imperial foundations of my continent's relationship with Africa. Indeed, the politics of two white editors (one an African) editing a book on music censorship in Africa could be debated long and hard.[3] However, my hope is that the outsider's perspective can offer some useful insights. For me the African experiences of music censorship bring new lights to bear. To this outsider they reveal themselves as being simultaneously both familiar *and* different. Importantly there are a range of contexts and a range of censorial agencies which serve to highlight the multi-faceted nature of music censorship. But in order to further

---

censorship and which can thus be seen as something of a 'norm' with which other examples of censorship can be compared. However, the histories of censorship in other 'western' contexts such Nazi Germany, fascist Italy and the Soviet bloc should also be noted.

[2] Thus, for example, my 1996 account of music censorship in the UK spoke of seeking to 'reveal a hidden part of the history of popular music in Britain' (Cloonan 1996: 1).

[3] Of course Michael and I did discuss this. Our aim was to get the broadest possible amount of expert contributors within the constraints of recruiting authors who could to write in English to a high standard and meet various deadlines. We can only hope that we have been at least partially successful.

explore the idea of the outsider looking in, it is necessary to outline the story of the development of censorship closer to home.

Normalizing censorship in the west

Before proceeding it is useful to describe what might be seen as being the 'norm' of censorship in the west. In microcosm this can be described as a story where religion was the most important censor until the emergence of the modern nation-states from the mid-eighteenth century on. There are various examples of the importance of religion as an early censorial force of which perhaps the most famous (and, perhaps, notorious) is the Catholic Church's *Index Librorum Prohibitum*. Importantly, as noted by Annemette Kirkegaard (2004: 62) the Church remains a censorial force in Africa today. More generally organized religion has sought to warn its adherents away from certain cultural artefacts and has not been slow to call for the restriction or outright banning of materials of which it disapproves.

As with organized religion, the nation state also seeks allegiance from its followers (in this case as citizens or subjects) and seeks to guide them in matters of morality. In the case of obscenity this generally meant laying down laws which proscribed certain forms of communication (pornography, racist documents, state secrets, and so on). As technology progressed it also meant regulation (and, often, ownership) of the airwaves also became the domain of the nation state. This frequently meant the formation of state-owned broadcasters whose editorial policies of necessity included forms of censorship. While the starkest examples of state remain those of Nazi Germany (c/f Dümling 1995, Levi 2001) and the Soviet bloc (c/f Starr 1985, Service 2001) western liberal democracies have also censored c/f (Cloonan 1996, Petrie 1997, Travis 2000).

In more recent years states in Western Europe have retreated from a number of their roles. As the availability of satellite television has spread alongside a growth in commercial radio, state broadcasting has been on something of a retreat. One corollary of this is that the observation of censorship has become more complicated. For example, in the UK up until 1973 when local commercial radio arrived, the publicly owned BBC was the only legal broadcaster and thus its music censorship was what any commentator needed to concentrate on. Following the first national commercial radio station, Virgin, in 1992 the UK now has a wide range of music stations with countless others available on the internet. One corollary of all this is to make the observation of music censorship more complex at a time when broadcasting is becoming increasingly important. Similar stories can be found elsewhere in Western Europe, but are just developing in Africa.

Moreover, nation states have found that one of their key strengths – control of their borders – has been complicated by the rise of the internet. Here information, including music, can be transferred across the miles and oceans without the authorities being aware. Thus far concern about this has centred on the use of the internet by criminals (especially paedophiles), but what is important for observers of censorship is that the rules of the game have changed. (Notably none of the chapters here deals with the internet.) In essence what the west is witnessing is a revolution in communications technology which has precipitated a decline in the role of the state as censor and a corresponding rise of the market as censor. One problem this brings is that if state officials can occasionally be held to account for their actions, the market never can.

Thus the history of censorship in the west can be seen as going through stages of religious, state and, now, market censorship. Within this framework the 'norm' of censorship has been that of competing forces trying to influence state policy in order to allow or disallow certain cultural artefacts a market and, in some cases, even the right to exist. In essence what has been at stake is the right to market products which circulate information. In more recent years marketization has proceeded apace and nation states have instituted neo-liberal economic policies which have seen them retreat from intervention in the economy. Where this retreat is arguably less advanced in the field of communications than in other areas, it still raises the possibility of censorial roles being increasingly left to the market, with the state effectively regulating between competing censorial agencies.

Censorship in colonial and post-colonial Africa

The situation in Africa is somewhat different. To begin with religion, while in the west religious groups were often competing for state approval in a political settlement which (with some notable exceptions) the majority of the contending parties accepted, in colonial Africa religion was often a battleground between oppressor and oppressed. The colonialists imported their religious beliefs and often sought to impose them on the indigenous populations, as John Collins shows here in the case of Ghana. As Ole Reitov and Marie Korpe (2004: 74) note, this often has censorial implications. The resistance to this process meant that frequently religion came to be not about different ways of living morally within a given political structure, but about competing versions of the political settlement. Resistance to colonialism often involved religion, while colonial rule often involved importing and trying to impose the religion of the colonialist.

Into this battle came musical forms which had the potential to offend traditionalists (who were often resisting colonial rule), the colonialists (who, as Collins illustrates, used music such as military bands, classical concerts, music theatre and Christian hymns to enforce imperial rule) and those leading liberation struggles (who used music as part of their struggle against that rule). In essence African music could be caught in a triple knot of censorship. Thus in their chapter on Tanzania, Kelly Askew and John Kitime show how colonialists disapproved of *ngoma* dances which confused traditional sex roles, while Collins' chapter reveals that those involved in the liberation struggle in Ghana disapproved of any songs betraying the 'foreign' influence of the colonialists. It is also clear that traditionalists in many countries sought to control overt sexuality in music. In sum the traditionalists, colonialists and liberationists all had censorial agendas.

The legacy of colonial rule can also be seen in struggles over the role of Islam across the globe, but also particularly in Africa. Islam's attitude towards music is contested (see Otterbeck 2004), but the potency of Islam as a censorial force has been most vividly illustrated in the (non-African) case of the Taliban regime in Afghanistan (see Baily 2001). It is also obviously an important influence in such places as Algeria (Morgan 2004, Mehdid Chapter 13 below) and Nigeria (Servant 2003). Additionally the influences of religion as a censor can be seen dramatically in the case of South Africa where Paul Erasmus, an ex-policeman who used to intimidate the political musician Roger Lucey and Cecile Pracher (who worked for the Censor Board Committee of South African Broadcasting Corporation under the apartheid regime) have both spoken of the influence of Afrikaner churches in their actions (Erasmus 2004, Pracher 1988).

If the role of religion has a particularly African twist, then so does the role of the nation state. The structure of many of today's African states has arisen through colonial rule, rather than any geographic, ethnic or political logic. As one music commentator has noted, nation states in Africa are 'often carelessly cobbled together from a chaotic patchwork of tribes and ethnicities by civil servants in the oak-panelled ministries of Paris or London' (Morgan 2004: 107). This gathering together of disparate ethnic groups into one nation across a highly variegated land mass often meant that post-colonial regimes had to undertake nation-building projects. In this process those who stood outside the project or who critiqued it ran the risk of both censure and censorship. Examples of this are found throughout *Popular Music Censorship in Africa*.

Possibly the most vibrant example of this in contemporary Africa is post-apartheid South Africa and the complications and censorial implications of this have been brought to the fore in the example of Mbongeni Ngema's song 'AmaNdiya' which Gary Baines discusses in Chapter 4. Here an attempt to build a new nation united across cultural and ethnic diversity was deemed to be undermined by a music attack on one ethnic group by a member of another. For the critics of 'AmaNdiya' criticisms of other ethnic groups have to be circumspect if national unity is to be preserved. Here it seems that a form of 'political correctness' is seeking to silence a dissenting (if arguably unpleasant) voice. As Baines (op cit) notes what is at stake here is membership of the nation, of who 'belongs'. Moreover, while the motivation might be different, there are clear parallels here with the authenticity programme carried out by President Mobutu in Zaire in the early 1970s, as documented by Graeme Ewens in Chapter 12 below. In both cases populations were being urged to take up particular sets of values. In the case of modern South Africa, this is multiculturalism; in the case of Zaire it was a mono-cultural Africanism. In both cases the result was forms of censorship.

The nations which existed in colonial Africa were also different from the 'norm' of the west. In effect the role of the state was assumed by the 'home' imperial nation state and its legal systems were imported to a greater or lesser extent. The legacy of this can still be seen by the fact that UK Commonwealth countries such as Jamaica and Belize have Britain's Privy Council as their final court of appeal (see http://www.privy-council.org.uk/output/Page32.asp). While the depth of colonization varied across the continent, the colonial experience meant that to varying degrees the colonists sought to impose imported moral, as well as legal, codes on indigenous populations.

Inevitably the experience of colonialism shaped the post-colonial era. Many regimes appeared to have learned well from their imperial masters about the need to control their populations. Thus Africa witnessed (and continues to witness) a series of authoritarian regimes in which political dissent was often harshly punished and moral codes strictly enforced. As is illustrated perhaps most vividly by Zimbabwe today (Thram below, Eyre 2001, 2004, Palmberg 2004), liberation from colonial rule did not always imply personal liberation.

Naturally music was far from immune from these processes. Under colonial rule, the battle was two-pronged. The first battle was to preserve local cultures from dominance by imperial power. Within this struggle debate inevitably took place over what was worth preserving. For example, in Ghana Collins shows how in the 1920s dances which encouraged mixed couples to touch were frowned upon by elders, as was music which was influenced by western styles. The second battle was to use that culture to critique the colonial power and, subsequently, to assist in the battle for national liberation. Thus the famous Nigerian singer and songwriter Fela Kuti pledged that he wanted to achieve 'the emancipation of all Africans from colonial mentality' (cited in Santorri 1998: 67). The role of music in liberation struggles was to see it censored under both colonialism and post-colonial rule and the legacy of both these struggles are apparent throughout this book. One legacy of colonialism is that, as Akpan shows in his chapter on Nigeria, Africa today suffers from the disadvantage of having to try to get a global audience for its music in competition with powerful, entrenched, music forms from the west. Another legacy is that the sorts of political critiques which supporters of national liberation movements penned, were not always welcomed by those same national liberation movements once they had assumed power, as will be shown below.

Having thus far examined the 'norms' of censorship from a western perspective and sought to locate the African experience as being removed from that 'norm', I now wish to further explore the notion of an African experience of music censorship.

Characteristics of music censorship in Africa

The evidence presented in *Popular Music Censorship in Africa* suggests that there are five main areas in which particular characteristics can be identified within music censorship in Africa. These are censorship and resistance in colonial times, censorship in post-colonial times, the relative importance of overtly political censorship (including the role of praise songs), the role of broadcasting and particular differences with the western 'norms'. These areas should not, of course, be seen as discrete but rather as overlapping with, and sometimes reinforcing, one another.

Colonialism, resistance and music censorship

With regard to censorship and resistance in colonial times, three things are apparent in this book. The first is that the colonialists had their own forms of censorship. For example, in the case of Kenya, Peter Muhoro Mwangi's chapter shows how the colonialists brought the first systematic forms of censorship. Askew and Kitime document similar events in Tanzania and Collins shows how music, along with religion and the controlling of depictions of sex, was used by the imperial power in Ghana as part of the colonization process. In her chapter on Algeria, Malika Mehdid notes that censorship in Africa must be understood as part of broader colonial policies. Importantly, as will be shown below, one legacy of imperial rule was that once the colonialists were no longer in political power, successor regimes were able to use the tools of their erstwhile rulers for their own censorial ends.

The second part of colonial censorship is that liberation struggles are cultural as well as political (Cabral 1979, 1982, Fanon, 1970, Flulo 2004: 175). In the case of music once resistance to colonial rule was articulated in song, attempts were made by the colonial power to censor those songs. This is shown here in cases such as Ghana, Kenya, Tanzania and Zimbabwe and has been well documented in the case of the liberation struggle in South Africa (Drewett 2003, 2004a, 2004b). To a certain extent this is part of what I have previously (Cloonan 1996: 115) referred to as a 'censorial climate' linked to current events where music is more likely to be censored in times of political turmoil. The banning of Thomas Mapfumo's music at the height of the guerrilla war in Rhodesia, alluded to by Diane Thram (Chapter 5 below) provides just one example of this. It also means, as Reuben Chirambo notes in the case of Malawi (Chapter 7 below) that songs which were previously deemed to be innocent can *become* controversial.

The third characteristic of colonial censorship was that resistance to colonial rule also involved acceptance of some forms of censorship. Perhaps the most vivid example of this here comes from Tanzania where Askew and Kitime note how rivalries within the ngoma scene were perceived as advantageous to imperial rule and six months before independence the Tanganyika African National Union (TANU) issued instructions to musicians that they must stop insulting or ridiculing one another. It is little surprise, therefore, to learn in the same chapter that in 1975 foreign music was banned from national radio in an effort to promote traditional music.

It should also be noted that, as Collins shows in the case of Ghana, traditional indigenous values could be simultaneously part of the liberation struggle and a source of calls for censorship. This could again contribute to forms of post-colonial censorship as Chirambo shows how important promotion of traditional music was in censorship in Malawi and Ewens shows how traditionalists in Zaire moved against sexually explicit material. In sum, traditionalists, liberationists and colonialists all had censorial agendas which came to be played out further in the post-colonial era. However, in an interesting alternate take, Thram's chapter suggests that in Zimbabwe it is the breaking down of one traditional value – that of the musician being accepted as a social commentator – which is fuelling censorship.

Post-colonial music censorship

The most striking characteristic of post-colonial censorship is that one recurrent issue for post-colonial governments was what to do with overtly political musicians whose music had been used in the liberation struggle, but who now used their music to criticize the post-colonial governments. For example, Collins notes that following independence in Ghana the critical songs of some political musicians 'were directed away from the colonial authorities towards their own Ghanaian governments' (p. 179 below).

This was seldom welcomed by the new regimes and the cases documented in *The Censorship of Music in Africa* suggest that there were a number of results of such moves. First, once in power national liberation movements sanctioned forms of censorship which had previously been the domain of the colonists. National unity now replaced loyalty to the home nation as a reason to silence musicians. For example in the case of Zimbabwe, Banning Eyre has noted that: 'Long depended upon to express the suffering, hopes, fears and aspirations of their people, Zimbabwean musicians have now endured years of government scrutiny, intimidation, unofficial censorship and, most recently pressure – both carrot and stick – to distort and transform their art from free expression to outright state propaganda' (Eyre 2004: 94). Diane Thram explains that this situation still exists and that: 'Musicians who prefer to be apolitical and those who refuse to work for the regime on moral grounds face the threat of no work and no airplay, plus the fear of more serious repercussions if their music is viewed as critical of ruling-party politics' (p. 85 below). One prominent example of this in the contemporary era is Thomas Mapfumo who fell foul of the Mugabe government in Zimbabwe and went into exile despite his service to the liberation struggle (Eyre 2004, Thram Chapter 5 below).

In Tanzania the Sukuma artist Kalikali was jailed in 1965 for singing songs about political corruption, despite his longstanding support for the nationalist cause (Askew and Kitime Chapter 9 below). A similar fate befell Tabu Ley Rochereau in Zaire in 1997 when, despite the fact that he had returned to the country to support the new regime of Laurent-Desiré Kabila and take part in his country's cultural life, he still found that his song 'Mil Mi Nef Sa' was condemned by the authorities for 'morally incorrect language and imagery' by what the government sanctioned press described as an 'obscene musician' (Brown 1998). Ewens notes in Chapter 12 that he was one of a number of Zairian musicians who found that songs they had written praising certain politicians were withdrawn when the politicians fell out of favour with the ruling regime, a phenomenon also found in Kenya (Mwangi Chapter 10 below).

Matters were further exacerbated if the post-independence struggle for national unity was undermined by power struggles between ethnic groups. The examples of Algeria (Mehdid op cit, Morgan 2004) and Rwanda (Craig and Mkhize Chapter 3 below) provide the most extreme examples of this. In such conflicts musicians can find themselves as victims of violence as in the case of Matoub Lounés in Algeria (Mehdid Chapter 13 below) and the popular singer Khogali Osman who was stabbed to death by 'a Muslim fanatic' in Sudan in November 1994 (Reitov and Korpe 2004: 73). They can also be alleged perpetrators as in the case of Simon Bikindi in Rwanda (Craig and Mkhize Chapter 3 below) and Mbongeni Ngema in South Africa (Baines Chapter 4 below).

It is also the case that the post-colonial regimes often used the same tools which the colonialists had used to stifle opposition. Thus Askew and Kitime show that 'Having inherited a tradition of government censorship… the Tanzanian government chose to continue it' (p. 142 below). Furthermore censorship of post-colonial Tanzanian radio was frequently for 'virtually the same issues colonial censors found objectionable' (Askew and Kitime p. 145 below), in Algeria post-colonial censorial policies was 'not too dissimilar in their effect from those associated with former colonial rule' (Mehdid p. 205 below) and in Kenya contemporary censorship has 'its origins in colonial censorship processes' (Mwangi p. 157 below). Indeed one notable aspect of *Popular Music Censorship in Africa* is the frequency with which official Censorship Boards were set up by post-colonial regimes.

In another example Eyre (2004) and Thram (Chapter 5 below) have both shown how the Zimbabwean authorities have used the mechanics of colonial censorship for their own ends. Certainly the case of Kenya outlined below also shows that sexual mores were a reason for both pre- and post-colonial censorship, while the evidence from Malawi (Chirambo Chapter 7 below) suggests that post-colonial rule made censorship legally arbitrary. However the country also shows how difficult it can be to censor if there is a thriving black market in music, as the case of the Kenyan song 'Baba Otonglo' shows (see Mwangi pp. 165-166 below).

Overtly political censorship

Another striking characteristic of music censorship in Africa is how overtly political it is. In the west political censorship tends to be more covert, such as banning the broadcast of music which allegedly support terrorism (Cloonan 1996: 129) or broadcasters issuing guidance about what music is acceptable in times of war or national emergencies (Cloonan 1996: 118-120, Nuzum 2004). Although Wilson Akpan shows in his discussion of Nigeria below that music censorship is by no means the sole prerogative of dictatorial regimes, there is still a sense in which music censorship in Africa is highly politicized in ways which are less common in the west. It is the government and political machinations which are to the fore in *Popular Music Censorship in Africa*. Thus in Africa, musicians' careers could be more subject to the whims of politicians than to commercial pressures – and this is a real difference to the west.

It is clear that the many dictatorial regimes which existed in post-colonial Africa created climates of fear and suspicion. For example, in Banda's Malawi, Chirambo says that 'even a whisper in the dark was dangerous' (p. 120 below) and, according to Thram (p. 74 below) in today's Zimbabwe 'For artists... the prevailing admonition is Be Careful!' Africa is hardly unique in experiencing dictatorships, but that experience has clearly shaped the history of music censorship on the continent. Perhaps the most extreme case of this is Malawi under Dr H.K. Banda where according Chirambo (Chapter 7 below), the population became complicit in its own censorship and citizens exercised extreme forms of self-censorship. Such was the regime's hegemony that it almost did not need to assume the mantle of censor. Importantly music was used to legitimize such rule (ibid.). This similarly had its parallel in Mobutu's Zaire in the 1980s when members of the *Jeune Mouvement Populaire* would listen to practising musicians and report any contentious material to ruling party functionaries (Ewens Chapter 12 below). Chirambo and Collins both use Gramsci's (1971) notion of hegemony to explore music censorship and the cases here provide ample examples of how music can be used in both hegemonic and counter-hegemonic projects.

The authoritarian nature of post-colonial regimes should not really surprise us. Anti-colonial struggles for independence were often drawn out, bloody and brutal affairs. One result of this was that organizations which had struggled long and hard to gain political power, and who were accustomed to ruthlessness from colonial regimes, were similarly ruthless to their political opponents once in power. This was doubly the case if, as again occurred frequently, there was a need to unite often disparate populations. Nation building became a key part of post-colonial regimes and the effect on musicians was often more censorship. In sum, argues Andy Morgan (2004: 108), the leaders of many new nation states found that 'they cannot entertain progressive notions of federalism and live-and-let-live cohabitation for fear that the weak mortar which binds their nation together will just crumble into dust and anarchy'. Thus 'The grail of national unity becomes an end that justifies the most violent and oppressive means' (ibid.). For example, one of the reasons why the Nigerian musician Fela Kuti was attacked by the authorities was because he offered a pan-African (and thus anti-national) vision (Santorri 1998: 68). But it is also important to note that musicians such as Kuti resisted and this is another characteristic which emerges here. Even in the harshest of times, musicians were resisting and/or aiding the resistance of others. At times this might have been subterranean, at other times it was open. But it is, as several examples show here, an ever present.

If resistance through music was apparent, then so was co-option. The most striking example of this is the use of praise songs as a means of uniting populations. Such songs were sometimes about the new nation, but more often appear to have been about rulers who, in the eyes of themselves and their supporters, symbolized those nations. Thus nation-building projects often involved the writing of praise songs for despots. As national liberation leaders took up government and the position of 'father of the nation', musicians were recruited to write in praise of their achievements. Collins notes that praise songs were used in liberation struggles as well, so that in the case of Ghana songs in praise of Kwame Nkrumah were part of the battle for independence. This continued post independence. Similarly Ewens notes that in Zaire under Mobutu (1965-1997) compulsory singing was introduced for many government employees, while in Malawi under Banda praise songs 'explicitly suggested that Banda was a God-given Messiah' (Chirambo p. 112 below) and in Nigeria the military regimes also used praise songs (Akpan Chapter 6 below). Similarly Verney (1988) has reported from contemporary Sudan that the National Islamic Front government also used praise songs, especially for its Popular Defence force, as part of its attempt to instil its own hegemony.

While some musicians were doubtless sincere in their praise, others appear to have carried out what amounts to acts of self-censorship for purely pragmatic reasons. While praise songs have received comparatively little academic attention (but see Howard 2004) it is clear that, at the very least, their existence has implications for freedom of music expression, as do the systems of patronage which surround them. Here some musicians have found themselves 'sponsored' by the government or cajoled into making music in praise of authoritarian regimes, with Zimbabwe also at the forefront of contemporary examples of this (Eyre 2004, Thram op cit). Thram reports that the Mugabe regime has used music as part of its 'openly racist and isolationist ideology' (p. 74 below). This includes the intimidation of perceived (music) opponents and the patronage of musicians who will sing songs in praise of the government. Former Minister of Information, Jonathan Moyo overtly funded musicians who praised the regime. In effect this is a form of censorship in which only those who praise the regime get heard and Palmberg (2004: 33-34) argues that this sort of 'sanctionship' is as important as censorship. In this example the legacy of the liberation struggle is being (mis)used to construct a new nationalism which views the seizure of farmers' land and other government moves a continuation of the original liberation struggle. Within this the regime uses music to disseminate its own version of 'patriotic history'. In places such as Zimbabwe the only officially sanctioned form of political discourse was that in praise of regimes it is little wonder that musicians joined their fellow citizens in exercising self-censorship.

Broadcasting

The starkest example of the power of broadcasting is provided by the case of Rwanda, outlined here by Dylan Craig and Nomalanga Mkhize (Chapter 3 below) who show the role played by *Radio-Télévision Libre des Mille Collines* (RTLM) in inciting genocide against the country's Tutsi population. They conclude that the radio station was a symptom rather than a cause of Rwanda's ethnic strife and suggest that 'successful' censorship (in the sense of curtailing some expressions in order to promote ethnic harmony) can only work in places with established civic society. Nevertheless the events of 1994 were so horrific that even the most ardent supporters of free speech must feel unease at the way in which radio promoted hatred.

The separation of public broadcasting and state policy is far more rare in Africa than in the west and the most contemporary example of the power of broadcasting in (music) censorship in Africa is once again Zimbabwe. Below Thram shows 'unofficial censorship has…. become the status quo' (p. 71 below) following changes in laws on media ownership which cemented the power of state-owned stations and 'served to make private radio or television impossible in Zimbabwe' (Thram pp. 77-78 below). Furthermore an unofficial policy of 100 per cent local content for music on the radio now exists. But while the net effect has been that all the stations sound the same, the evidence she presents, while generally negative, also illustrates that the overall effect has been ambiguous as some musicians have benefited from the quota and 'the recording industry is stronger now than before the 100 per cent local airplay policy was instituted' (Thram p. 82 below). But this does not apply to all. The popular musician Leonard Zhakata has been told by the ZBC that his music, which some view as critical of the government, is not banned. However it receives no airplay – a situation which leaves him in artistic limbo as he says that 'Without media support your career is in trouble' (Thram p. 85 below).

The developments in Zimbabwe have been particularly sinister, especially as most of the censorship is not declared (see also Freemuse 2005). It hardly needs to be as musicians and others have come to know what is and what is not acceptable. Moreover, the media lacks independence and Eyre (2004: 98) writes that the Mugabe regime regards the Zimbabwean Broadcasting Corporation (ZBC) as its mouthpiece. Since the opposition Movement for Democratic Change became a powerful oppositional force in the country, the ZBC has, writes Eyre (2004: 94) 'devoted its entire range of activities to the task of supporting and defending the regime' (ibid.). Under these circumstances the DJs at ZBC know what they can and cannot do, without official censorship ever having to be instigated. Moreover musicians find themselves in a double knot of censorship. Without state support they may not be able to work, but accepting such support has the potential to alienate them from their audiences who may seek revenge, especially after the regime changes. In many ways this parallels the situation which Michael Drewett and Johnny Clegg (Chapters 2 and 8 below) outline in apartheid South Africa where progressive musicians could find themselves censored internally for being anti-apartheid and externally for being South African (and thus a product of apartheid).

The role of the South African Broadcasting Corporation in supporting the apartheid regime is also a scar on the continent's broadcasting history and led one former censor to claim that 'I was just doing a job' (Pracher 1998: 83) – a chilling statement which echoes the idea that Nazi officers were simply 'obeying orders'.[4] Meanwhile the links between government and state broadcaster as shown, for example, in Mwangi's chapter on Kenya, are much closer than generally the case in the west. Similarly Collins (p. 182 below) notes that until the mid-1990s governments in Ghana 'totally controlled the airwaves'. Ironically, it seems that such control might be necessary if traditional African music is to prosper in an era of increased commercial radio. Thus Akpan (Chapter 6 below) notes that while a radio quota system might help to preserve Nigerian music, it also has censorial implications which mean that Nigerians may have to choose their preferred mode of censorship.

Of course broadcasting is a powerful tool in nation building and so close links between government and broadcasting organizations were to be expected in post-colonial Africa. In addition, the story of music censorship on the radio is one which will be familiar to western readers. Yet in other ways the story of music censorship in Africa is very different from that of the west.

Another story?

The first of these is that agencies which have proved to be important in the censorship of music in the west have a comparatively smaller role in music censorship in Africa.[5] For example, the music industries themselves, especially the recording industry, generally appears to play less of a role. In the west the role of the major record companies in shaping musicians' work so that it meets commercial criteria and reported instances of companies' refusal to sign acts which may cause censorship problems is well documented (Cloonan 1996). But this market-based influence is nowhere near as apparent in *Popular Music Censorship in Africa*. On occasion labels have carried out censorship on behalf of governments as Collins documents in Ghana and Akpan in Nigeria. But labels have also produced materials which resisted government policies, as Mwangi notes in the case of Kenya (Chapter 10 below). More generally if there is censorship by record companies it is a censorship of omission whereby much African music still fails to reach the international audiences necessary for high level commercial success (Thorsen 2004). The problems of local music being swamped by transglobal music product is shown here by Akpan, along with the stark choices this brings forth.

Similarly the role of live music venues does not appear to be significant in the way that has been witnessed in the west, perhaps because the combination of local

---

[4] Reitov and Korpe (2004) point out how far this separated censor and censored. For Pracher, censorship *was* simply part of her job, for those she censored the battle could be one of life and death.

[5] One well-documented exception to this here is South Africa. For example Erasmus (2004: 76) shows how WEA was complicit in apartheid censorship and Reitov and Korpe (2004: 84 and 85) cite examples of record company complicity. See also Drewett (2004a).

authorities and commercial chains which contribute to censorship by venues in the west (Cloonan 1996) are less prevalent in Africa. But live performance is a vital part of African musical tradition and has also been censored. The efforts to control performance are crucial to Collins' story in Ghana where the links between dance performance and politics was vitally important. The effect was that an art form which might be seen as apolitical in the west could be subject to censorship in colonial Africa. Meanwhile in contemporary Tanzania the licences needed for live performance have obvious censorial implications (Askew and Kitime Chapter 9 below). Elsewhere official disruption of live performance has been noted in such places as apartheid South Africa (Erasmus 2004) and Sudan (Verney 1998). In this volume it is noted in Nigeria (Akpan Chapter 6) where police raided concert venues during the military dictatorship and in the chilling incidents around live music in Zimbabwe (Thram Chapter 5 below).

Retailers in Africa appear not to have taken on the censorial mantle which has been witnessed in the UK (Cloonan 1996) and by the actions of Wal Mart in the US (www.freemuse.org and www.massmic.com). The role of would-be censors is also different. Because of different political settlements and different civil societies, the role of pressure groups in campaigning for media censorship does not appear to be as developed. Certainly it is possible to scour the pages of this volume in vain looking for an equivalent to the US's Parents Music Resource Center or the UK's National Viewers and Listeners Association (now Media Watch UK). The potential for civil society to censor is thus un-represented here.

In Africa it seems that pressure is often applied in a more sinister way by vigilantes acting on behalf of dictatorial regimes which have used semi-official means to carry out censorship. One example is Zimbabwe where anonymous 'war veterans' and members of the youth brigades have threatened musicians who have performed what have been perceived as anti-government songs (Eyre 2004, Thram below). This parallels the *Jeune Mouvement Populaire* in Zaire noted earlier. Once again unofficial censorship has the capacity to be the most despotic of all.

The use of vigilantes is perhaps the most extreme example of what might be called cultural differences between Africa and the west which have profound implications for music censorship. A more familiar phenomenon is the use of double-meanings as a means by which to avoid censorship. However, once again this appears to have been given a particularly African twist. Broadly speaking, if censorship of *double-entendres* in the west centred on sex, then in Africa the issue of politics was often to the fore. Of course, sexual ambiguity could cause problems as Askew and Kitime show in the case of Tanzania. However the use of double-meanings to hide political content has been commented on by musicians and appears to have been a particularly contentious issue in apartheid South Africa (see Drewett 2003, 2004a, 2004b and Reitov and Korpe 2004). It is also shown here in the cases of Ghana where oblique criticisms were made of Nkrumah (Collins Chapter 11 below), Malawi where ambiguity and innuendo were used against Banda (Chirambo Chapter 7 below) and Zaire where seemingly innocent songs were scrutinized by listeners hoping for political allusions (Ewens Chapter 12 below). What is not in doubt is that the use of *double-entendres* was also part of resistance.

Cases here also show the problematic nature of trying to use censorship for politically progressive causes. Drewett is ultimately ambivalent about the use of a cultural boycott in the battle to end apartheid, seeing it as both a contribution to the cause (of which he approves) but also as a form of censorship (of which he disapproves). He opposes those aspects of it which prevented freedom of musical expression, but is supportive of persuasion being used to dissuade musicians from certain sorts of musical associations and works. He draws the line at the sorts of coercion which others saw as necessary to the struggle. Similarly, an attempt to forge a united, multi-cultural, South Africa is being underpinned by censorship which harks back to a previous era and, as Baines notes (p. 67 below) is 'contrary to the growth of a resilient democracy and vibrant civil society'. Even in the case of the horrors of Rwanda, Craig and Mkhize (Chapter 3 below) do not appear to think that censorship would have helped. All this is not to say that censorship is inevitably regressive, but it does give food for thought for those who want to use it for progressive ends.

Conclusion

The history of music censorship in Africa once again shows how complicated the phenomenon is. It is not simply a matter of offended parties putting blue pencil lines through unacceptable lyrics, but of contending forces using music in power struggles over the nature of the (colonial and post-colonial) political settlement. For example, Collins shows that in Ghana the colonial administration, traditionalists and the liberation movement all had their own censorial agendas, while censorship continued in the post-colonial era. The case of South Africa – where the apartheid regime's censorial system echoed that of Nazi Germany as people simply obeyed orders or did their job – has left a legacy of its confusion about what is permitted under a democratically elected government.[6] The ways in which censorship worked as a hegemonic project in Malawi and Ghana offer fascinating insights into how a population can become complicit in their own censorship. Here a collective right to national unity trumped any individual right to freedom of expression. In general it is clear that Africa has had too many dictatorial regimes – a situation which has left the fate of musicians subject to the whims of politicians and often needing to be politically astute in ways which would be anathema to their western counterparts. These regimes created climates of fear. Once again, this is not a uniquely African experience, but it is a vital part of explaining music censorship on the continent.

---

[6] For a moving account of reconciliation between censor and censored see Lucey (2004) and Erasmus (2004).

Thus Africa offers a rich patchwork of cases and stories which illuminate the power of music and the lengths to which opponents of certain forms of music will go. In all this it is music's power to represent which is at stake. Songs which represent freedom struggles, alternative politics, sexual liberation or which attack religious sensibilities are constantly in danger of suppression. The particular politics of Africa, especially the colonial legacy, give these battles a particular local tinge but echo broader themes. Freedom of artistic expression has been fought over in Africa as elsewhere. Seen from the outside there is much that is familiar and much that is alien.

In what follows the censorship of popular music in Africa is divided into two parts – issues and case studies. The first part deals with issues such as whether censorship can be progressive (the cultural boycott of apartheid South Africa), hate speech (Rwanda), political correctness (in the 'new' South Africa), market censorship (Nigeria) and unofficial censorship (Zimbabwe). Notably these cases concern post-colonial Africa. The second section contains a number of national case studies which span the colonial and post-colonial eras. In total they provide more insights into Africa, popular music and the censorship which can surround it. There is certainly much to learn and it is hoped that *Popular Music Censorship in Africa* acts not only as an historic record of those struggles, but also inspires more musicians and activists to resist oppression.

References

Baily, J. 2001. *Can You Stop The Birds Singing? The Censorship of Music in Afghanistan.* Copenhagen: Freemuse.

Blecha, P. 2004. *Taboo Tunes.* San Francisco: Backbeat.

Brown, D. 1998. 'Dance, dance, wherever you may be', *Index on Censorship*, 27: 6. pp. 79-80.

Cabral, A. 1979. 'National Liberation and Culture', in Cabral, A. *Unity and Struggle: Speeches and Writing.* New York: Monthly Review Press. pp. 138-154.

Cabral, A. 1982. 'Culture, colonization, and national liberation', in A. de Bragança and I. Wallerstein (eds), *The African Liberation Reader Volume 1.* London: Zed Press. pp. 157-166.

Chastenger, C. 1999. 'The Parents' Music Resource Center: from information to censorship', *Popular Music*, 18: 2. pp. 179-192.

Cloonan, M. 1995a. 'I fought the law: Popular music and British obscenity law', *Popular Music*, 14: 3. pp. 377-391.

Cloonan, M. 1995b. 'Popular Music and Censorship in Britain: An overview', *Popular Music and Society*, 19: 3. pp. 75-104.

Cloonan, M. 1996. *Banned!* Aldershot: Arena.

Drewett, M. 2003. 'Music in the struggle to end apartheid: South Africa', in M. Cloonan and R. Garofalo (eds), *Policing Pop*. Philadelphia: Temple University Press. pp. 153-165.

Drewett, M. 2004a. *An analysis of the censorship of popular music within the context of cultural struggle in South Africa during the 1980s*. Grahamstown: Rhodes University, doctoral thesis.

Drewett, M. 2004b. 'Remembering subversion: resisting censorship in apartheid South Africa', in M. Korpe (ed.), *Shoot The Singer! Music Censorship Today*. London: Zed Books. pp. 88-93.

Dümling, A. (ed.) 1995. *Eintarete Musik*. Berlin: City of Berlin Department of Cultural Affairs.

Erasmus, P. 2004. 'Roger, me and the scorpion: working for South African security services during apartheid', in M. Korpe (ed.), *Shoot The Singer! Music Censorship Today*. London: Zed Books. pp.73-81.

Eyre, B. 2001. *Playing With Fire: Fear and Self-Censorship in Zimbabwean Music*. Copenhagen: Freemuse.

Eyre, B. 2004. 'Playing with fire: manipulation of music and musicians in Zimbabwe', in M. Korpe (ed.), *Shoot The Singer! Music Censorship Today*. London: Zed Books. pp. 94-105.

Fanon, F. 1970. *Toward the African revolution*. Harmondsworth: Penguin.

Flolu, J. 2004. 'Music teacher education in Ghana: Training for the churches or the schools?', in S-M Thorsén (ed.), *Sounds of Change – Social and Political Features of Music in Africa*. Stockholm: SIDA. pp. 164-179.

Freemuse. 2005. 'Zimbabwe seminar', www.freemuse.org/sw9601.asp .

Hill, T. 1992. 'The enemy within: Censorship of rock music in the 1950s', in Anthony DeCurtis (ed.), *Present Tense*. Durham, NC: Duke University Press. pp. 39-72.

Howard, K. 2004. 'Music for the great leader', in M. Korpe (ed.), *Shoot The Singer! Music Censorship Today*. London: Zed Books. pp. 29-38.

Index on Censorship. 1998. *Smashed Hits: The Book of Banned Music*. London: Index on Censorship.

Jelavick, P. 2001. 'Nazi Germany 1933-45', in D. Jones (ed.), *Censorship: A World Encyclopaedia*. Chicago: Fitzroy Dearborn. pp. 926-930.

Johnson, B. 2003. 'Two Paulines, two nations: An Australian case study of the intersection of popular music and politics', *Popular Music and Society*, 26: 1. pp. 53-72.

Jones, S. 1991. 'Banned in the USA: Popular music and censorship', *Journal of Communications*, 15: 1. pp. 71-87.

Kennedy, D. 1990. 'Frankenchrist versus the state', *Journal of Popular Culture*, 24: 1. pp. 131-148.

Kirkegaard, A. 2004. 'Remmy Ongala – Moderating through music' in S-M. Thorsén (ed.), *Sounds of Change – Social and Political Features of Music in Africa*. Stockholm: SIDA. pp. 57-69.

Korpe, M. (ed.). 2004. *Shoot The Singer! Music Censorship Today.* London: Zed Books.

Levi, E. 2001. 'Degenerate music', in D. Jones (ed.), *Censorship: A World Encyclopaedia.* Chicago: Fitzroy Dearborn. pp.2082-2087.

Lucey, R. (2004). 'Stopping the music; censorship in apartheid South Afirca', in M. Korpe (ed.), *Shoot the Singer! Music Censorship Today.* London: Zed Books. pp.67-72.

McDonald, J. 1989. 'Censoring rock lyrics: An historical analysis', *Youth and Society,* 19: 3. pp. 294-313.

Malm, K. 2004. 'Intellectual property rights and unfair exploitation of traditional music and other traditional knowledge in Africa', in S-M Thorsén (ed.), *Sounds of Change – Social and Political Features of Music in Africa.* Stockholm: SIDA. pp.120-134.

Martin, L. and Segrave, K. 1993. *Anti-Rock.* De Capo Press: New York.

Morgan, A. 2004. 'Guerrilla of pop: Matoub Lounés and the struggle for Berber identity in Algeria', in M. Korpe (ed.), *Shoot The Singer! Music Censorship Today.* London: Zed Books. pp. 106-126.

Nuzum, E. 2001. *Parental Advisory: Music Censorship in America.* New York: Perennial.

Nuzum, E. 2004. 'Crash into me baby: America's implicit censorship since 11 September', in M. Korpe, (ed.), *Shoot The Singer! Music Censorship Today* London: Zed Books. pp.149-159.

Palmberg, M. 2004. 'Music in Zimbabwe's crisis', in S-M Thorsén. (ed.), *Sounds of Change – Social and Political Features of Music in Africa.* Stockholm: SIDA. pp.18-46.

Petrie, R. 1997. *Film and Censorship: The Index on Censorship Reader.* London: Cassell.

Pracher, C. 1988. 'Only doing my duty', in *Index on Censorship Smashed Hits: The Book of Banned Music.* London: Index on Censorship. pp. 83-85.

Reitov, O. and Korpe, M. 2004. 'Not to be broadcast', in S-M Thorsén (ed.), *Sounds of Change – Social and Political Features of Music in Africa.* Stockholm: SIDA. pp. 70-86.

Santorri, R. 1998. 'From praise to protest', *Index on Censorship,* 27: 6. pp. 67-70.

Servant, J-C. 2003. *Which Way Nigeria? Music Under Threat: Question of Money, Morality, Self-Censorship and the Sharia.* Copenhagen: Freemuse.

Shuker, R. 1994. *Understanding Popular Music.* London: Routledge.

Sluka, J. 1994. 'Censorship and the politics of rock', *Sites,* 29. pp. 45-70.

Starr, S. 1985. *Red and Hot.* New York: Limelight.

Thorsén, S-M. (ed.) 2004. *Sounds of Change – Social and Political Features of Music in Africa.* Stockholm: SIDA.

Travis, A. 2000. *Bound and Gagged: A Secret History of Obscenity in Britain.* London: Profile.

Verney, P. 1998. 'Does Allah like music?', Index on Censorship, 27: 6. pp. 75-78.

Winfield, B.H. and Davidson, S. (eds) 1999. *Bleep! Censoring Rock and Rap Music*. London: Greenwood Press.

Chapter 2

The Cultural Boycott against Apartheid South Africa: A Case of Defensible Censorship?

Michael Drewett

Introduction

In 1948 the Nationalist Government came to power in South Africa, and immediately set about consolidating a system of racial inequality and separation inherited from previous colonial governments. The injustice of this 'apartheid' system, together with the zealousness with which the new government implemented it, resulted in international condemnation and a steady growth in anti-apartheid resistance. One of the strategies devised to oppose the apartheid government was the cultural boycott.

It is argued in this chapter that the formalized boycott strategy as practised against apartheid South Africa incorporated core aspects of censorship, defined as:

> a wide variety of inter-related practices (both legal and extra-legal) which combine to explicitly interfere with the freedom of expression, association and movement of popular musicians to ensure that the articulation of certain facts, opinions or means of expression are stifled, altered and/or prohibited. (Drewett 2004b: 14)

In the ensuing discussion, a general history of the boycott is provided, documenting both arguments for and against specific forms of the boycott strategy. It is argued that although the boycott was adopted for progressive reasons, aspects thereof nevertheless constituted forms of censorship, preventing the performance of music in particular contexts. In some cases the prohibition was based on extremely strong moral restraints, whilst in other cases performance was actually prohibited outright. The paper proceeds to consider whether the boycott might be regarded as a form of 'defensible censorship' (McGuigan 1992) because it attempted to undermine the apartheid state. It is concluded that as a blanket strategy aimed at all musicians, the boycott was debilitating, removing a key area of resistance from the cultural terrain.

The implementation of a cultural boycott against apartheid

In 1954 Anglican clergyman and anti-apartheid activist, Father Trevor Huddleston, made a call for a cultural boycott of South Africa according to which cultural performers would refuse to play in apartheid South Africa (Nixon 1994: 157). In 1957 the British Musicians' Union (BMU) followed the lead set a year earlier by the British Actors' Union – Equity – who decided that its members would not perform before segregated audiences in South Africa. The effect of the BMU's stance was clearly seen in 1964 for example, when the Rolling Stones called off their scheduled tour of South Africa (Braam and Geerlings 1989: 174) and in 1968 when Gram Parsons quit the Byrds after the other members of the group refused to call off their planned trip to South Africa (Denselow 1989: 58-59). The boycott began to gain international recognition when, in December 1968, the United Nations General Assembly accepted Resolution 2396, according to which all member states and organizations were asked to cut 'cultural, educational and sporting ties with the racist regime' (Willemse 1991: 24). Attempts to actually impose the cultural boycott intensified after the Soweto uprising of June 1976. The exiled African National Congress (ANC) and the South African-based Azanian People's Organization (AZAPO) were the primary advocates of the cultural boycott (Stewart 1986: 4). By December 1980 the call had been stepped up (in terms of UN General Assembly Resolution 35/206E) through the establishment of a 'Register of Artists, Actors and Others who have performed in South Africa'. In the early 1980s the strongest support for the boycott within South Africa came from AZAPO. Although AZAPO was a minority oppositional group in South Africa, it was the most influential representative of black consciousness orthodoxy, and it did, to some extent, influence the political landscape at the time, especially through its wholehearted support of the cultural boycott (Lodge 1983: 344-346).

The boycott issue came to the fore in October 1980 when Ray Charles proposed a concert in Soweto on the third anniversary of the banning of a variety of black consciousness organizations, which took place in the wake of the Soweto uprising in 1976 and the death of Steve Biko in 1977. The Congress of South African Students (COSAS) and AZAPO called for the concert to be cancelled. A spokesperson said, 'we are not willing to accept Ray's noise. We are in mourning' (*Anti-Apartheid News* June 1981: 11). Charles ignored AZAPO's call and became the first artist to be placed on their boycott list when it was compiled in March 1981 (ibid.).

AZAPO's approach was to seek meetings with artists planning to tour South Africa in an attempt to dissuade them from doing so while apartheid still remained intact. For AZAPO the boycott strategy was one of the few strategies available to anti-apartheid activists. In a press statement AZAPO called upon black South Africans 'to make the sacrifice of boycotting performances by foreign artists', arguing that 'no nation has or ever will achieve liberation without lifting a finger. Certain pleasures must thus be sacrificed for the greater goal of liberation' (ibid.).

And in an appeal to overseas musicians in April 1981, AZAPO (in *Anti-Apartheid News* September 1982: 6) stated that:

> We are doing our spring cleaning and we do not want people to be moving in and out of this country. We want our black brothers in America to come back when we have cleaned the house. Right now the country stinks, it is full of muck and filth. Granted, most of them are talented in the field of music and are regarded as heroes by our people, but must they stoop so low by siding with the enemy of humanity?

Overseas organizations (most notably the Anti-Apartheid Movement, [AAM]) were eager to embrace any South African anti-apartheid organization which endorsed and thereby legitimized their own support for a boycott strategy. Therefore AZAPO's stance was promoted and supported by pro-boycott organizations, regardless of AZAPO's limited support base within South Africa.

The form of cultural boycott that developed out of the efforts of lobby groups including AAM, AZAPO, the ANC and Pan Africanist Congress (PAC) in the early 1980s was a blanket one. It strongly discouraged foreign musicians from playing in South Africa and prevented South African musicians from performing, recording or releasing their music outside of South Africa unless they went into exile or no longer performed in South Africa. The AAM was one of the organizations to call for a total boycott, based on the argument that the success of total boycotts lies in their very consistency. Selective boycotts required the adoption of criteria that are not easily understood by the public. Furthermore, selective boycotts would lead to political wrangling over who was permitted to perform and under what conditions. Interestingly, the AAM thought this would lead to 'numerous accusations of political censorship' (*Anti-Apartheid News* April 1987: 11), as if a blanket boycott somehow did not constitute censorship. Nevertheless, the AAM's underlying argument, held by most proponents of a total boycott, was that a selective approach would lead to a weakening of the campaign to totally isolate apartheid South Africa (ibid.). In further support of a blanket boycott, Lewis Nkosi (cited in Hanlon and Omond 1987: 124) argued that overseas musicians should not be allowed into South Africa, even if they were prepared to challenge the apartheid state. He argued that: 'Apart from their skill with song, they actually take their *bodies* there. By so doing, they lend their immense prestige and glamour to the propaganda of those who wish to create an impression of a sunny South Africa'. Furthermore, Nkosi seriously doubted the ability of music to affect change. He argued that: 'It is difficult to see how a state as powerful as South Africa can be brought down by a rhyming couplet' (Ibid.). The pro-blanket boycott view prevailed and until 1987 the blanket boycott remained in place, as it was easier to administer and simpler to explain.

The Sun City boycott

Support for the boycott in the west grew with the release of the *Sun City* (1985) album recorded by a collective of musicians calling themselves Artists United Against Apartheid. Given that most top musicians were not prepared to perform in South Africa, the Sun City holiday resort in Bophutatswana exploited the homeland's 'independence' to attract a host of international musicians to perform in South Africa.[1] The album was an attempt to create awareness about apartheid and in particular to call for a boycott of performances by musicians at the Sun City holiday complex in the 'phoney homeland' of Bophutatswana.

The significance of the Sun City resort to the apartheid government must not be downplayed. With the growing international isolation of South Africa the resort became a crucial tool in the fight against the cultural boycott. In the early 1980s when it was increasingly difficult to attract musicians to South Africa, Bophutatswana's fake independence and Southern Sun Hotel's large sums of money were used to lure overseas musicians to perform in a part of South Africa. The regular appearance of top international musicians at Sun City in the early 1980s prevented complete isolation of South Africa and was a serious blow to the effectiveness of the cultural boycott. Musicians appearing at Sun City between 1980 and 1985 included Elton John, Leo Sayer, Cliff Richard, Gloria Gaynor, Chicago, Rick Wakeman, Cher, Kenny Rogers, Dolly Parton, George Benson, Frank Sinatra, Queen, Shirley Bassey, Barry Manilow, David Essex and Rod Stewart (Wilkinson 1990: 12-13).

In an attempt to stem this flow, (Little) Steven Van Zandt[2] (of Bruce Springsteen's E-Street Band) initiated the *Sun City* album. The purpose of the album was to educate musicians and audiences, particularly through the title track '(I ain't gonna play) Sun City' (1985) on which a variety of top international singers participated, including Bob Dylan, Pete Townshend, David Ruffin, Bruce Springsteen, Bobby Womack, Nona Hendryx, Miles Davis, Linton Kwesi Johnson, Peter Gabriel, Kurtis Blow and Jimmy Cliff. In the first verse the singers introduced the purpose of the song, saying that they disapproved of what was going on in South Africa. They called for justice and truth, claiming that the only thing

---

[1] In attempting to give credence to its policy of separate development, the South African government established separate homelands for South Africa's African ethnic groups. The plan was for these to be granted independence, so that Africans could gain full citizenship in these 'independent states' only, allowing South Africa to remain 'white'. In a perpetuation of the notion of African as 'other' they were then treated as foreigners within 'white' South Africa (which constituted 87 per cent of the land). In the face of resistance, just four of the nine homelands were ever granted 'independence'. These were Transkei (1976), Bophutatswana (1977), Ciskei (1980) and Venda (1981). With the granting of this independence by the South African government (not recognized internationally), puppet governments were allowed to practise self-rule, but under the scrutiny of the South African government who controlled the purse strings in the form of 'foreign aid'.

[2] Also known as Steve 'Miami' Van Zandt, a solo musician in his own right.

they could do was to refuse to play at Sun City. Later in the song they claimed that to do so would be to stab 'our brothers and sisters in the back' (Artists United Against Apartheid 1985).

The album included other anti-apartheid songs performed by the likes of Peter Gabriel, Bono and Gil Scott-Heron. Following the release of the album, and to add to its momentum, Dali Tambo (son of the then ANC President, Oliver Tambo) and Jerry Dammers (of the Specials and Special AKA[3]) founded a United Kingdom-based organization called Artists Against Apartheid (AAA) in April 1986. The purpose behind AAA was to specifically focus on the role played by those working in the entertainment industry in propping up apartheid. AAA pushed for the complete cultural isolation of South Africa (including Sun City). Tambo was quoted as saying: 'White South Africans are desperate for things like European pop records which make them feel that their way of life is normal. Pop music and similar leisure products help keep the minority's heads in the sand. Don't help them keep their morale up' (*Anti-Apartheid News* June 1986: 11).

The effect of the *Sun City* (1985) title track and album and related initiatives was almost immediate, with far fewer musicians playing in Sun City in the latter half of the decade, and many of those who previously had done so pledged not to do so again (and thereby had their names removed from the UN list). For example, in early 1986 *Anti-Apartheid News* (January/February 1986: 10) reported that: 'The trickle of boycott-busting stars applying to have their names removed from the UN cultural register is likely to become a flood now that Elton John has made a clear statement that he will never return to South Africa while the apartheid system remains'. Others to have their names removed after making similar pledges included Dolly Parton, Rod Stewart and the members of Queen (*Anti-Apartheid News* May 1987: 11; Denselow 1989: 193).

Those who did perform at Sun City were heavily criticized, especially within the press. Black Sabbath were banned from a Dutch concert hall in Tilburg when the owner heard that they had played at Sun City in 1987 (*Anti-Apartheid News* December 1987: 15). In 1988 Modern Talking and Laura Branigan were the only overseas musicians to perform at Sun City, and in 1989 the only musicians to do so were Irene Cara and (once again) Laura Branigan. The Sun City campaign, with the support of groups such as AAA and the Special Committee Against Apartheid of the United Nations, had successfully ended the steady flow of musicians to South Africa.

On the surface it appears that the Sun City campaign as engaged by the Artists United Against Apartheid constituted self-censorship by musicians, given that the campaign could be construed as a call for a limitation on musicians' (and audiences') freedom of movement. However, the Sun City project itself did not constitute censorship. As mentioned, it was merely an attempt to educate people, not to censor them. It drew to people's attention the fact that visiting the Sun City

---

[3] In 1984 Dammers wrote The Special AKA's '(Free) Nelson Mandela' (1984), which reached number nine in the UK seven singles charts.

resort involved tacit support of the apartheid system, but did not outlaw them from going there. The argument here is that not all boycott calls constitute censorship. In this regard it is useful to employ Peter Blecha's (2004: 120) distinction between censorship and 'citizenship in action'. For Blecha, a boycott call is a necessary strategy for civil rights supporters, as a method 'of taking principled and public stands against what they consider to be offensive ideas' (Blecha 2004: 120). It is the right of every musician (and member of public more generally) to call on others to make political and moral stands. This is not censorship. If a boycott call involves no coercive repercussions it is not censorship. However, as soon as it involves threats, blacklisting, penalties, punishment, prohibitions and coercion it is censorship. The Sun City campaign would have constituted censorship had musicians been barred from actually performing there in the first place, or if musicians who performed there received some form of legal sanction or physical harassment on their return. Sanctions practised against people who performed there were in accordance with additional pressure in terms of the cultural boycott itself, for example performers who were barred from performing in particular venues. This was the case with British musicians who were members of Equity, which imposed its own sanctions on its members who performed in South Africa. In most instances anti-apartheid activists simply picketed and boycotted these musicians, but did not call on them or their music to be banned altogether (acts which would have constituted a call for censorship).

The introduction of a selective cultural boycott

Notwithstanding the success of the Sun City campaign, some musicians and activists began to question the strategic purpose of a blanket boycott. Johnny Clegg (Interview 1998), himself a victim of the cultural boycott (as discussed below), was among those who argued that there was 'a difference between the culture of the oppressed masses and the culture of the ruling elite'. Accordingly, it did not make sense to apply the boycott to the culture of the masses. Clegg argued that only the culture of the ruling elite should be boycotted. This position is itself not without problems. For example did the music of Peter Gabriel (who sang 'Biko'[1980] and 'No More Apartheid' [1985]) and U2 (who sang the anti-apartheid 'Silver and Gold' [1988]) belong to the culture of the masses or the elite? Certainly when U2 performed in South Africa in the late 1990s the audiences comprised predominantly middle-class whites. This would not have been different in the 1980s. Nevertheless, if allowed to perform in the country (and assuming they would have wanted to) these musicians could have directly challenged the audiences, transforming the concert arena into a contested terrain. However, it is doubtful whether the government would have permitted this. This point is interestingly illustrated by an incident involving Cliff Richard, who repeatedly performed in South Africa, 'to bring Jesus into people's hearts and thus change them and society' (*Anti-Apartheid News* October 1984: 10). At a protest against

Richard's boycott-breaking in England in July 1986, one protester asked him if he would ask for the release of Nelson Mandela during his forthcoming visit to South Africa in January 1985, Richard responded, 'I couldn't do that because then I wouldn't be allowed to return to South Africa any more' (ibid.).

Paul Simon also went to South Africa, where he recorded part of his *Graceland* (1986) album. Simon's decision to do so was highly controversial, and led to a rethinking of the total boycott strategy. Simon was criticized for going to South Africa without clearance from the relevant monitoring organizations such as the UN and the ANC (although he did consult prominent anti-apartheid musicians such as Harry Belafonte and Miriam Makeba). He argued that he had not strictly broken the boycott because he had not performed in South Africa. Simon's refusal to condemn apartheid in the lyrics or in a message on the album cover further angered many anti-apartheid activists and academics (see for example Hamm 1989). Simon tried to squirm his way out of his apolitical stance by arguing that:

> I am not a South African and cannot choose, as a public personality, a specific political party in South Africa. There are so many that I cannot really endorse any one in particular. The only sentiment I really feel I should express on the issue is that as far as all political parties are concerned ... they should not tell me how I should play or write my music. (Rathbone and Talbot 1987: 6-8)

Simon's response demonstrates his attempt to dismiss political pressure. He blocked out the protests, the image of the political censor, and did what he wanted to because of his privileged position, both as a wealthy musician and as a non-South African. The option of breaking the boycott in this way was not readily available to most South African musicians.

Whatever the problems with the *Graceland* album, it further added to the chaos associated with the implementation of the cultural boycott. It allowed participating South African musicians such as Stimela and Ladysmith Black Mambazo to receive international airplay, something not supposedly possible under the terms of the cultural boycott. Yet it was the very nature of the blanket boycott that made it necessary for South African musicians to rely on such collaborations for exposure and economic survival.

Although Simon continually insisted that he had not broken the boycott, the UN Special Committee Against Apartheid announced that anyone buying the album was violating the embargo on South Africa (Meintjes 1990: 65). A clear sign of the anti-apartheid lobby's ability to keep musicians in line is seen in a statement released by Stimela and Ladysmith Black Mambazo in which they apologized:

> For anything we may have said or done which may be construed as a slight, insult or disregard for the cultural boycott, the people's movement and their leaders ...After consulting with the mass democratic movement it became clear that the differences that have arisen were clearly as a result of our own interpretation and understanding of the boycott itself. We reiterate our commitment to consulting and working with democratic

and progressive structures in the community and being accountable to these structures. (*Anti-Apartheid News* December 1987: 15)

There is no doubt that Ray Phiri (of Stimela), Ladysmith Black Mambazo and others who participated on the *Graceland* album and/or subsequent promotional tour benefited from their involvement, but the debate concerning Simon and the South African musicians who participated in the album and/or subsequent tour emphasized the controversial nature of the total boycott strategy. This led the ANC in particular to reconsider its position.

Despite reservations from the likes of BMU and AAM who wanted to preserve the blanket boycott for reasons previously discussed, some organizations (for example the ANC, by 1987) did agree with the argument put forward by Johnny Clegg. The ANC and its internal South African wing – the United Democratic Front (UDF) – believed that the political credentials of each South African group/performer should be taken into account when deciding whether or not they should be allowed to perform outside of the country. The interpretation of this, as well as other aspects of the boycott, was nevertheless shrouded in disagreement. For example, in 1988 Johnny Clegg and Savuka were barred by the BMU from playing at the Nelson Mandela 70th birthday tribute at Wembley despite being given the go ahead by the UDF, the internal wing of the ANC. The BMU banned Clegg because he lived and worked in South Africa (Bell 1988:12).

Within South Africa the UDF set up a cultural desk in 1988 to deliberate over the application of the boycott. But the desk was soon regarded as a more severe censor than the state itself. As Rob Nixon (1994:169) noted, 'Ironically, it was the easing of the boycott that brought about the charge of censorship to the fore'. Many musicians resented the style of the desk, believing that it was trying to promulgate culture by decree. Amampondo, for example, were boycotted in South Africa after performing at the aforementioned Mandela birthday tribute without the desk's clearance. Band member, Dizu Plaatjies (Interview 1999), expressed the band's position: 'That really frustrated us because you do a gig for somebody that is well respected by the world, and then at the end of the day you are boycotted by the very same people who support this man. You know, it was like "man, what can you do?"'

In an extreme statement indicative of the close association between anti-apartheid and socialist ideas, the UDF's cultural desk insisted that in order to receive UDF backing, artists had to 'support the principles and politics of the UDF and COSATU, and…acknowledge the struggle is led by the workers' (cited in Press 1990: 39-40). The UDF's approach clearly amounted to political censorial practice, not allowing musicians freedom of expression or movement. In a debate on the cultural boycott at the First Conference on South African English Literature in Bad Boll, Germany in 1986 one participant asked: 'If we are going to … continue to tell people not to come and continue to tell people you are allowed to go there, aren't we then playing the role exactly that which is currently happening at home? Being sort of censors? … Aren't we going to that danger of being censors?' (in Kriger [ed.] 1987: 199). Lewis Nkosi (in Kriger [ed.] 1987: 200) acknowledged this perception. In response he said he was: 'extremely worried about any idea of setting up a board of censors or whatever we want to call it, that says so and so should not go; and if he/she goes, we are going to arrange solidarity groups to boycott the person abroad'.

Yet this is exactly what happened. Those fighting apartheid increasingly used similar strategies to those of conservative forces. However, the cultural boycott was premised on a distinction between strategies of resistance and strategies of oppression. In this sense the boycott was qualitatively different to apartheid censorship, because it was employed as a means of overcoming racial oppression. The censorship of musicians was insignificant compared to the lack of freedom experienced by black South Africans living within the context of apartheid. Importantly, this approach accepts firstly, that censorship is not necessarily a bad thing, and secondly, that politically speaking, there are different levels of censorship in line with Jim McGuigan's (1992: 202) distinction between defensible and indefensible censorship. Defensible forms of censorship prevent expressions which undermine certain respected freedoms of others. Accordingly, forms of censorship linked to the struggle *against* apartheid were defensible insofar as they were introduced, not so much to protect certain rights of individuals, but to oppose the oppressive apartheid system. Nevertheless, on an analytical level it is important to consider the similarities in the opposing strategies. The apartheid state did not allow musicians to play wherever they wanted to, nor did organizers of the cultural boycott permit musicians to play wherever they wanted to. While the former was attempting to maintain separate development and minimize radical musical influences, the latter attempted 'to create among white South Africans powerful feelings of resentment at their isolation' which would hopefully 'be directed at the regime itself or its hated policy of apartheid' (Nkosi in Hanlon and Omond 1987: 124). The apartheid state banned albums, intimidated and imprisoned musicians, while in opposition to the state, anti-apartheid groups blacklisted musicians, cancelled their shows, refused them permission to play where they wanted to and also intimidated and harassed them (for example the houses of Abigail Kubeka and Steve Kekana were burnt down when they participated in a government propaganda song). The strategies of both sides affected the creativity of musicians, putting doubts into their minds as to what could be performed, where it could be performed, and under what conditions.

South African musicians and the cultural boycott

Most South African musicians supported the boycott insofar as they refused to perform at Sun City, although there were a few exceptions such as Ella Mental and Leslie Rae Dowling. However, few musicians agreed with the ban on South African groups from performing and releasing their music overseas, either because they were not sufficiently politically involved or because they were, and wanted their message to be heard by foreign audiences. Furthermore, and crucially, the cultural boycott made it very difficult for South African musicians to make a living from their music, especially those whose music had been banned in South Africa (at distribution and/or broadcast level). Musicians were caught in a double bind of censorship, from within and outside the country. For example, successful South African band Via Afrika went over to the United States in 1985 to promote their music and were very popular: their performances were sold out, they received strong interest from record companies and were interviewed on CNN. In one of the many contradictions of the boycott they also appeared (along with another South African band, the Malapoets) on the *Sun City* album. Yet, as band member Renee Veldsman (Interview 1998) explained:

> The record companies came around, and said 'This is great, but we can't actually help you because of the policy of your country, you could wait', ...but our record company couldn't help us and well, nobody could help us at that point. So that's actually why Via Afrika dissolved really, because we wanted to push forward, but we did hit walls all the time.

One of the effects of the cultural boycott was indeed to isolate white South African musicians. Musician Jonathan Handley (Interview 1998) expressed the bleakness of the situation most severely:

> We were white apologists. Definitely. Going overseas, going to England, if you said you were South African it was immediately a sort of unclean thing to say, you know: 'I've got leprosy or I've got a contagious disease and I'm a white South African and we oppress blacks'. And DJs couldn't play our music, so the one trend was towards increasing isolation.

This was even the case for white bands such as the Cherry Faced Lurchers who were strongly anti-apartheid in their stance, in terms of supporting anti-apartheid festivals and in their overt lyrics – and they recorded on the progressive Shifty label. The band were hoping to perform at the Culture in Another South Africa (CASA) anti-apartheid conference in Amsterdam in 1987, but were turned down in favour of black bands such as the Genuines and the less politically overt African Jazz Pioneers. Black musicians and crossover bands had easier access to overseas performances than did white bands. Musicians such as Savuka, Mango Groove, Steve Kekana and Amampondo performed overseas regularly while Sipho Mabuse even secured a recording contract with Virgin Records in the mid-1980s and Rounder Records released Mzwakhe Mbuli's music overseas.

Some white musicians, although frustrated by international rejection, nevertheless accepted their situation. Gary Rathbone (Interview 1998) outlined the pro-cultural boycott position in the strongest terms:

> Sure it was a shit deal for us. But the bigger picture was much more worth it than any sort of problems that we might have had, like some people whining and saying 'Oh I lost

my career because of it'. You say, well jeez some people, a lot of people, lost their lives and their families. Never mind your bloody career for God's sakes. Most of those people who whined about how they lost their music careers are probably now comfortably ensconced in comfortable advertising executive jobs and things like that. So I don't know what the fuck they were whining about.

Although the bigger picture was undoubtedly more important and far more sobering, musicians looking for creative outlets did feel frustrated when they were deprived of opportunities to at least perform overseas. Certainly, the fact that some anti-apartheid bands were prohibited from performing outside the country, and overseas protest musicians were strongly discouraged from performing in South Africa, essentially removed an important aspect of cultural struggle from the political contest. Musician Warrick Sony of the Kalahari Surfers (Interview 1998) argued that:

> I didn't really support the whole idea of a cultural boycott... I supported the sports boycott because I think that hurt, but ... I think of how much I've learnt from listening to records. For people like Billy Bragg not to have had their records available in South Africa is ridiculous. It is. He's not a huge seller but his ideas needed to come here.

South African Musicians' Alliance (SAMA) President, Mara Louw (Interview 2001) agreed that overseas musicians should not always have been unilaterally shut out:

> I would have preferred if any artist who came over here, would come, go into the township and go and teach, spend a month at a school and contribute somehow, but not come here and take the bucks and go like Millie Jackson, you know: 'I've just come for the gold'. But people like Jimmy Cliff.[4] He went to Soweto. He went right inside the township and he wanted to perform for the people in the township, not in some posh theatre in town. So that's why I thought something's not right.

Notwithstanding Nkosi's views about the inefficacy of rhyming couplets (above), Peter Stewart (1986: 5) agreed with Louw's view regarding the critical challenge of culture. He argued that the potential for culture to challenge the state had not been entirely eradicated by state repression and censorship, but that there was a danger that the additional effects of the cultural boycott could cripple South African culture.

Furthermore, the attempt to use the cultural boycott to undermine the apartheid state's propaganda view of South Africa as a normal society was largely unsuccessful because it failed to prevent international music from being sold and broadcast in South Africa. The fact that controversial political music was either

---

[4] In 1980 Jimmy Cliff was the last musician invited to perform (and conduct workshops) in Soweto by black political groups before the implementation of a blanket cultural boycott (Denselow 1989: 187-189).

banned at some level or another or was never released in South Africa in the first place, meant that music that challenged or encouraged the audience did not get through to most South Africans. Almost all that remained of overseas music was music which made South Africans feel that society was normal: the mostly entertainment-oriented music that dominates the Western popular culture industry. Supporters of apartheid were able to listen to the very same music as United States of American and British fans; they could watch the music videos on television and read about the performers in international and local magazines. Even before the arrival of the Internet, the ease with which South Africans could access this music almost completely normalized South African music consumption (so what if they could not see the musicians live in South Africa? Wealthy South Africans simply went to see them in neighbouring countries or overseas anyway). Musicians such as Peter Gabriel and Dire Straits claimed that their music was not available in South Africa,[5] yet this was not the case. Major labels including EMI and WEA remained in the country and most of those who were not located in South Africa organized licensing deals with companies in South Africa. Record companies that did not distribute in South Africa, such as Earthworks, Rounder and Rough Trade, were exceptions. Even so, it was possible to obtain almost anything as an import. This made it even more difficult for South African musicians, who not only were prohibited from selling their music outside the country, but internally they had to compete with international releases. Those who recorded counter-hegemonic music had to deal with the additional problem of the censorship of their music, and the consequent loss of airplay and sales (see Drewett 2003).

Conclusion

Although the cultural boycott can, in some ways, be seen to have contributed to the demise of apartheid, aspects of the boycott did nevertheless constitute forms of censorship. The prohibition of performances by South African musicians in foreign countries constituted censorship given that it curtailed those musicians' freedom of movement, a process cemented by the setting up of formal structures to decide which South Africans could perform outside of South Africa. Furthermore, the decision to call for a boycott (especially a total boycott) imposed a particular strategy on all progressive musicians, regardless of their particular approach to fighting apartheid. Those who disagreed with the total boycott strategy felt under immense moral and political pressure to conform, lest they be regarded as condoning apartheid.

---

[5] In fact at Nelson Mandela's 70th birthday gig at Wembley, Mark Knopfler, carried away by the tide of the occasion, fallaciously claimed that he was 'happy to say' that the first Dire Straits album was banned in South Africa. On the contrary, the album (like all other Dire Straits albums) was not banned, was available in shops, and was popular and sold well. Even the single and video of 'Brothers in arms' (1985) were played on SABC.

Some practices associated with the cultural boycott can therefore be seen to fit into the general definition of censorship as interfering with the freedom of expression, association and movement of musicians. The blacklists, committees and other forms of pressure used by the UN and various anti-apartheid organizations comply with this description and therefore constitute forms of censorship.

Nevertheless, the cultural boycott effectively achieved progressive goals when it specifically targeted initiatives which bolstered apartheid, such as inviting musicians to perform at Sun City and to participate in government propaganda songs. These boycott calls were specifically designed to undermine apartheid in the form of the homeland policy and the government's hearts and minds campaign, using songs to propagate the view that the government was on the side of all South Africans. By exposing these government initiatives as attempts at propaganda, boycotters successfully undermined the government's attempts to maintain its hegemony. On these selective levels the cultural boycott was a successful counter-hegemonic strategy and worthy of progressive support, insofar as musicians were educated about and discouraged from participating in certain highly problematic arenas.

However, as argued by Sony (above), the cultural boycott as a whole (especially as a blanket boycott) was less defensible considering the way it restricted the cultural field, rather than transformed it. Instead of using culture to challenge South African audiences, the boycott strategy effectively added to the silencing effect of apartheid censorship, making it even more difficult for resistant voices to be heard. By removing resistant voices from the cultural contest in this manner, it was easier for the apartheid discourse to dominate the cultural field. For musicians engaged in counter-hegemonic struggle a blanket (and in cases selective) cultural boycott was counterproductive. Spaces needed to be found within which cultural struggle could take place, rather than simply close doors on musicians. The rationale behind the boycott was never to encourage a more direct cultural struggle on the part of foreign musicians – allowing foreign resistant music to be sold, distributed and performed in South Africa. If this led to banning at least an attempt would have been made to challenge the dominant discourse. Just as local musicians found ways to successfully voice their resistance (See Drewett 2003; Drewett 2004a), so too could international anti-apartheid supporters have devised means of taking forward the cultural struggle within South Africa.[6] South African musicians, if permitted to perform outside South Africa could have educated audiences and thereby taken forward an aspect of anti-apartheid struggle. Audiences in return could have financially supported these musicians through attending their shows.

---

[6] For example, musicians such as U2 (1988) and Phil Collins (1989) included anti-apartheid statements on their albums covers which, when sold in South Africa, challenged or reassured those who bought their albums.

The fact that the cultural boycott denied progressive musicians the opportunity to decide how best to participate in anti-apartheid struggle means that the boycott strategy as practised against apartheid South Africa constituted censorship. Just because a strategy opposes an oppressive system does not exempt it from progressive criticism (as opposed to a value-free liberal critique). As a strategy imposed on all musicians by a select few, the cultural boycott amounted to a form of vanguard censorship and as such it denied musicians freedom of movement, association and expression which could have led to important attacks on the apartheid system. Those aspects of the boycott which prevented musicians from exercising such freedoms constituted censorship. This does not include attempts by musicians and others to educate and convince people of the problems involved in certain musical associations and forms of expression: calling for a boycott in which people have the right and freedom to choose. The choice, however, must always lie with the musician him/herself.

References

Anti-Apartheid News. 1981. 'Black Musicians Say: No! to Apartheid'. June. p. 11.
Anti-Apartheid News. 1982. 'Statement on Foreign Artists Issued by the Azanian People's Organisation'. September. p. 6.
Anti-Apartheid News. 1984. October. p. 10.
Anti-Apartheid News. 1986. 'Elton John Sets a Trend'. January/February. p. 10.
Anti-Apartheid News. 1986. 'Sun City is no Fun City'. June. p. 11.
Anti-Apartheid News. 1987. 'Cultural Boycott: Why it Must Be Total'. April. p. 11.
Anti-Apartheid News. 1987. May. p. 11.
Anti-Apartheid News. 1987. December. p. 15.
Bell, A. 1988. 'Musical Discord'. *Time Out* (London edition). June 29-July 6, p. 12.
Blecha, P. 2004. *Taboo Tunes: A History of Banned Bands and Censored Songs*. San Francisco: Backbeat Books.
Braam, C. and Geerlings, F. 1989. 'Towards New Cultural Relations: A Reflection on the Cultural Boycott', in W. Campschreur and J. Divendal (eds), *Culture in Another South Africa*. London: Zed Books. pp. 170-181.
Denselow, R. 1989. *When the Music's Over: The Story of Political Pop*. London: Faber and Faber.
Drewett, M. 2003. 'Music in the Struggle to End Apartheid: South Africa', in M. Cloonan and R. Garofalo (eds), *Policing Pop*. Philadelphia: Temple University Press. pp. 153-165.
Drewett, M. 2004a. 'Aesopian Strategies of Textual Resistance in the Struggle to Overcome the Censorship of Popular Music in Apartheid South Africa', in B. Müller (ed.), *Censorship and Cultural Regulation in the Modern Age*. Amsterdam: Rodopi Press. pp. 189-207.

Drewett, M. 2004b. *An analysis of the Censorship of Popular Music within a Context of Cultural Struggle in South Africa During the 1980s*. PhD thesis. Grahamstown: Rhodes University.

Hamm, C. 1989. 'Graceland Revisited'. *Popular Music* Volume 8 Number 3. pp. 229-304.

Hanlon, J. and Omond, R. 1987. *The Sanctions Handbook*. Harmondsworth: Penguin.

Kriger, R. (ed.) 1988. *South African Literature*. Bad Boll: Evangelische Akademie.

Lodge, T. 1983. *Black Politics in South Africa Since 1945*. Johannesburg: Ravan Press.

McGuigan, J. 1992. *Cultural Populism*. London: Routledge.

Meintjes, L. 1990. 'Paul Simon's Graceland, South Africa and the Mediation of Musical Meaning'. *Ethnomusicology.* Winter. pp. 37-73.

Nixon, R. 1994. *Homelands, Harlem and Hollywood*. London: Routledge.

Press, K. 1990. 'Towards a Revolutionary Artistic Practice in South Africa', in K. Press and M. van Graan *Popular and Political Culture for South Africa*. Cape Town: University of Cape Town Centre for African Studies. pp. 1-70.

Rathbone, G. and Talbot, C. 1987. 'Gracelands'. *Bits* Number 3, March. pp. 6-8.

Stewart, P. 1986. 'On the Cultural Boycott'. *Reality* Volume 18 Number 6. pp. 3-5.

Wilkinson, A. 1990. 'South African Music Explosion?', in N. Johnson et al. (eds), *Top Forty Musical Annual: The First Decade*. Johannesburg: Top Forty Publishers. pp. 11-27.

Willemse, H. 1991. 'Censorship or Strategy', in D. Smuts and S. Westcott (eds), *The Purple Shall Govern*. Cape Town: Oxford University Press. pp. 24-25.

Discography

Artists United Against Apartheid. 1985. *Sun City*. EMI.

Collins, Phil. 1989. *...But Seriously*. WEA.

Dire Straits. 1985. *Brothers in arms*. Vertigo.

Gabriel, Peter. 1980. *Peter Gabriel* (3rd album). Charisma Records.

Gabriel, Peter. 1985. 'No More Apartheid'. Artists United Against Apartheid. *Sun City*. EMI.

Simon, Paul. 1986. *Graceland*. WEA.

Special AKA. 1984. 'Free Nelson Mandela'. 2 Tone Records.

U2. 1988. *Rattle and Hum*. Island.

Interviews with the author

Clegg, Johnny   Johannesburg, 20 April 1998.
Handley, Jonathan   Klerksdorp, 18 April 1998.
Louw, Mara   Johannesburg, 29 August 2001.

Plaatjies, Dizu   Cape Town, 4 February 1999.
Rathbone, Gary   Johannesburg, 14 September 1998.
Sony, Warrick   Cape Town, 17 July 1998.
Veldsman, Rene   Johannesburg, 16 April 1998.

Chapter 3

Vocal Killers, Silent Killers: Popular Media, Genocide, and the call for Benevolent Censorship in Rwanda

Dylan Craig and Nomalanga Mkhize

Introduction

In the wake of the Rwandan genocide of 1994, a number of attempts have been made (and are continuing to be made) to decode the significance of statements such as these, which were both made as the slaughter in Rwanda reached its peak:

> You [Hutu] cockroaches must know you are made of flesh! We will not let you kill! We will kill you! (Rwandan radio announcer, quoted in Metzl 1997: 633)

> Hutus should know who the enemy is and that the enemy is the Tutsi. (Rwandan folk musician Simon Bikindi, quoted in Unknown 2001)

Judicially, such investigations have focused on determining what constitutes a clear incitement to genocide; academically, they have instead focused on the provision of suitable explanations of the causes of sentiments such as those quoted above and the eventual genocide – in other words, how did ordinary people come to participate in what one writer calls 'the horrible, savage, numbing details of what millions of Rwandans did, or had done to them' (Diamond 2005: 328).

In what follows, an analysis of the role of popular music within the Rwandan media, with particular reference to the role of Rwandan folk singer Simon Bikindi, and radio station *Radio-Télévision Libre des Mille Collines* (RTLM), is conducted.

What is not at issue here is the status of hate speech or incitement to genocide as pressing challenges to the human rights culture of our times; clearly, these are ills which must be attended to, and the intricacies of such analyses are left to other writers here and elsewhere.[1] Furthermore, as will be shown in what follows, the *overall* culpability of both RTLM and a figure such as Simon Bikindi, is without

---

[1] Specifically, the chapter by Gary Baines in this volume ('Racist Hate Speech In South Africa's Fragile Democracy: Censoring Ngema's "*AmaNdiya*"').

question as such. What *is* at issue, however, are the deeper historical, political and economic fault lines which render elements of a society – in this case, Rwandan Hutu extremists – capable of issuing the call to genocide, and society at large capable of responding to this; thus, the difference between *cause* and *symptom*.

In this chapter, it will be argued that RTLM and Bikindi are best read as expressions of problems which have a longer history than either party, and which, indeed, have survived the genocide in a new, more internationally palatable, form. To respond to this with calls for censorship, even in a 'benevolent' form aimed at silencing those who may (or do still) call for mass violence, is thus an error. Beyond the fact that such initiatives, conducted 'in the best interests' of at-risk populations, ignore (or fail to appreciate) a variety of factors which demonstrably contributed to the outbreak of mass violence, they also run the risk of concretizing an uneven global standard for who may control 'free speech', as well as *how* and *when*. Hate speech is a problem, to be sure, but what needs to be carefully considered is whether pathologizing African identity-discourse, and seeking to dictate its terms in external forums, is a good solution to the problem – or whether others must be found.

Background to RTLM and Bikindi

The role played by RTLM is prominent in many discussions of the genocides (Snyder and Ballentine 1996: 30-34; Unknown, 2003b). RTLM's name ('The free radio of the thousand hills') makes clear its claim to the status of an authentic voice issuing, as it were, from the Rwandan countryside itself. However, while ostensibly 'private' (in terms of having been founded by private investors), the strong links between RTLM's owners and operators, and the inner circles of the Habyarimana government meant that RTLM effectively operated as a mouthpiece of the Hutu power ideology – thus, issuing not from the many, but from the few.

Three factors can be considered to have assisted in the transmission of RTLM's divisionist agenda to the populace. First, the station's prominence and claim to 'authenticity', which were intricately linked to its position as the sole rival to the more moderate state-run radio service, and stretched back to its creation in 1993, when pressure from civil opposition groups forced the Radio Rwanda to tone down its anti-Tutsi message (Fuiji 2002). Secondly, RTLM's casual, unstructured format and its reliance on popular music, colloquial speech, and topical discussion which ensured a large and loyal listener base who were used to tuning in and receiving accessible and 'honest' information (Li 2004). Thirdly, the prominence of radio in the lives of ordinary Rwandans – through sets installed in bars, cafes, and rural village squares, or distributed by the government – which allowed radio in general (and thus RTLM in particular, once it began to be more popular than Radio Rwanda) to outstrip the printed word as the primary means of extending ideological links between extremist groups, such as RTLM's backers, and groups of Rwandan civilians (Chalk 1999: 95).

Around the time of the genocide, the solid links established between RTLM's staff and their listeners became an operational framework for mass murder. Inflammatory broadcasts made on RTLM were clearly linked to attacks on Tutsis and Hutu moderates alike; within the course of everyday operations, RTLM staff provided the militias with lists of prominent 'enemies' (who were then targeted for assassination), co-ordinated offensive and defensive deployments against civilians and the advancing Rwandan Patriotic Front (RPF) forces alike (Metzl 1997: 631-2), and provided a steady supply of anti-Tutsi folk music by popular artists such as Simon Bikindi's.

Bikindi hails from Gisenyi Prefecture, the heartland of extremist anti-Tutsi sentiment since the colonial era and the home province of many prominent Hutu politicians including President Juvenal Habyarimana (Corfield 2001: 10). He rose to popularity through the catchiness of his songs and his inventive blend of English, French and Kinyarwanda lyrics (Temple-Raston 2002), which further strengthened his appeal for RTLM listeners. However, the lyrics of Bikindi's songs were not only anti-Tutsi, but also anti-coexistence. One of his most popular songs, 'Naga abaHutu' ('I hate these Hutu') lashed out at moderate Hutus for being 'naïve' and allowing outsiders to 'manipulate' them:

I hate these Hutu, the arrogant Hutus,
Braggarts, who scorn other Hutus,
Dear comrades, I hate these Hutus, the de-Hutuized Hutus
Who have disowned their identity dear comrades.
(quoted in Gourevitch 1998: 100)

Elsewhere, Bikindi's lyrics vilified Tutsis, portraying them as animalistic and evil:

The Tutsi are ferocious beasts, the most vicious hyenas, more cunning than the rhino … the Tutsi inyenzi [cockroaches] are bloodthirsty murderers. They dissect their victims, extracting vital organs, the heart, liver and stomach. (quoted in Berkeley 2001: 2)

Bikindi's anti-Tutsi stance made him, like many other RTLM stalwarts, a clear target for prosecution in the wake of the genocides. In March 2003, Bikindi stood in front of the UN's International Criminal Tribunal for Rwanda (ICTR) and pleaded 'not guilty' to six counts of genocide-related crimes (Foundation Hirondelle 2003a). Bikindi's involvement was held to be threefold; first, in terms of his songs, due to lyrics such as those reprinted above; secondly, in terms of his connections to RTLM (as a primary shareholder) and various prominent pro-genocide public figures such as Minister of Youth and Sports Callixte Nzabonimana, RTLM co-founder Ferdinand Nahimana, and President Habyarimana himself; and, thirdly, in terms of his direct participation in *Interahamwe* (Hutu militia) activities, rallies, and educational sessions through Irindiro Ballet, his theatrical troupe.

The last of these – Bikindi's actions in support of the *Interahamwe* – leaves little doubt as to his personal sympathies. An active recruiter and mobilizer at the grassroots level, he exhibited the drive and authority of a government official; working alongside the *Interahamwe*, Bikindi was alleged to have driven a vehicle fitted with loudspeakers, from which he made public announcements denouncing the Tutsis and calling for their extermination (Unknown 2003a). In mid-1994, for example, he is reported to have addressed a meeting in Gisenyi where he categorically stated that 'Hutus should know who the enemy is and that the enemy is the Tutsi' (Unknown 2001). Again in June 1994, he allegedly drove around the Kimuvu and Kavoye communes in Gisenyi with a group of *Interahamwe* stalwarts in tow, declaring to Hutus that, 'The majority population, it's you, the Hutu I am talking to. You know the minority population is the Tutsi' (Unknown 2001).

If these well-supported accusations are indeed correct, Bikindi is clearly guilty of inciting genocide through his *actions*. What is important here, however, is not Bikindi's overall guilt, but rather his relationship to a Hutu audience who had already been primed to receive his message. Bikindi's first big hit was in 1987 with 'Twasezereye' ('We said goodbye to the feudal regime'). However, despite predating the outbreak of genocide by several years, 'Twasezereye', was to make a powerful comeback in 1992-93, when it became an anthem for Hutus dissatisfied with the strictures of the Arusha Accords[2] (the Organization of African Unity [OAU]-sponsored peace agreement signed in Arusha, Tanzania, which ended the first Rwandan Civil War), joining Bikindi's other hits as part of the anti-Tutsi playlist repeated by RTLM up to fifteen times a day. 'Twasezereye' thus exists on either side of even the most elastic definition of the period of the mass killings in Rwanda (1990 to 1994); the same goes for several other Bikindi songs which now form part of the case of incitement to genocidal action levelled against him. The significance of this dislocation between the songs and the genocide is discussed below.

The origins of a divided Rwanda

Rwanda's ethnic identities, as they are understood at the time of writing, are a product of the drive to map, name, describe and order groups of people which formed part of the colonial expansion into Africa. When the Germans, and later the Belgians, colonized Rwanda in the late nineteenth century, they identified what they construed as two distinct 'tribes' – the Hutu and the Tutsi.[3] However, this

---

[2] These accords provided for the establishment of a coalition government, and thus constituted a direct threat to 'Hutu power'.
[3] The existence of the Twa minority, the smallest of Rwanda's ethnic groupings, was also acknowledged. However, the Twa's minority status and their existence outside the cattle-based agriculturalist lifestyle of the Hutu and Tutsi resulted in their absence from the ascriptive process undertaken by the colonists with regard to the two other groups.

distinction was not as rigid as it must have appeared to outsiders. The geographical origins and precise date of arrival of the Hutu and Tutsi people in the Great Lakes area remain the subject of debate amongst historians. Irrespective of this, however, it appears that in pre-colonial Rwandan society these identities signified relative social status, wealth and class position rather than fixed ethnic identity, with Tutsis holding more cattle (and therefore wealth) along with some form of legal jurisdiction over Rwandan society. Hutus, in contrast, were predominantly cultivators of land, but could rise in social rank if they attained wealth and livestock. Hence, while colonialism did not introduce the connection between 'Tutsis' and 'privilege', it concretized it (Mamdani 2002a: 143; Kellow and Steeves 1998: 113). Under colonial rule, these previously flexible Hutu and Tutsi identities were reified. In 1933 for example, identity documents classifying Rwandans as belonging to one group or the other were introduced by the Belgian authorities (Hintjens 1999: 253).

A further impact of the Belgian imposition of strict tribal identities in Rwanda was to effectively de-indigenize the Tutsis, associating them with exogenous mythologies while Hutu identity narratives were wholly endogenous. The motivation behind this de-indigenization was the 'Hamitic myth', which conceived of the Tutsi as a discrete racial group separate from the Hutu, originating from the north, closer to the mythical Ethiopian root-stock, and even endowed with semi-European physiognomic features. The Hamitic myth provided a justification for what the colonizers saw as a fundamental division between the rich and powerful Tutsi and the poor and powerless Hutu; by interpreting this divide in racial terms, such a disparity could be easily reconciled with their own race-supremacist views. Inasmuch as these 'invented truths' were seen to reappear as anti-Tutsi slogans following the post-colonial revolution against the (initially) Belgian-sponsored Tutsi monarchy,[4] the effect of this particular colonial project was, indeed, an assimilation of a racialized 'other' by many of the Hutu revolutionaries. This assimilation was to form a central aspect of the extremist views responsible for the actions of the 1994 *genocidaires*; even Bikindi wove his songs around these mythologies, speaking obliquely by addressing his songs to the *mbira abumva* ('those who can understand') and calling on the colonial-era stereotypes of Hutu and Tutsi identity in songs such as 'Bene Sebahinzi' ('Sons of the cultivators'[5]) and the previously mentioned 'Twasezereye'.

---

[4] This 'revolution' is better described as a series of social upsets between 1959 and 1962, which culminated in the electoral defeat of the Tutsi-dominated post-colonial government by the populist Parmehutu party (later, the MNRD of the Habyarimana administration). This 'revolution' sparked a wide-scale flight of Tutsis into neighbouring countries – the exile population numbering 600 000 by the mid-1980s – where the RPF was formed to champion the cause of a Tutsi return to Rwanda.

[5] As distinct from the '*bene sabatunzi*' or 'sons of the pastoralists' – that is, the Tutsi. See Berkeley, 2001, p.2.

However, Rwanda's colonial and early post-colonial difficulties do not yet explain, satisfactorily, why the 1994 genocides occurred. For most of Rwanda's post-independent history, and well into the late 1980s, 'Hutu power' was a far less extreme ideology than it would later become; the Tutsi minority were able, despite pervasive discrimination against them within the Rwandan government and army, to continue a relatively trouble-free existence, attain mid-level career posts, and intermarry with their Hutu neighbours. This delicate balance, however, was upset by the ongoing regional turmoil in the Great Lakes area in the last few decades of the twentieth century, as well as Rwanda's integration into the competitive global capitalist economy following independence (Unknown 2000). A worldwide collapse in coffee prices in 1989, combined with a severe drought and domestic pressures for political reform, empowered radical factions within the Habyarimana administration at the same time as it swelled the ranks of the army and filled the urban and rural areas with the young, unemployed men who would later provide the foot soldiers of the *Interahamwe* genocide squads. Simultaneously, the plight of Tutsi refugees in Uganda – who had been refused re-entry to Rwanda on the grounds that the country was 'overpopulated' – enabled a similar hardening of attitudes within the RPF leadership, leading to a declaration in 1990 affirming not only the right of the refugees to return by force if necessary, but also stating the RPF's intention of ousting Habyarimana and returning Rwanda to 'democracy' (Otunnu 1999: 31-49).

When the RPF made good on its threat in October 1990, the invasion served to validate Hutu extremist propaganda which, drawing on the rhetoric of Hutu 'authenticity' opposing Tutsi 'foreign-ness', commanded Hutus to defend themselves against the invading aliens. This ideology, seen at work during the invasion and the three-year civil war that followed it, motivated several unsettling foreshadowings of the genocide to come, as isolated groups of Tutsi civilians and moderate Hutu were killed across the country in what appear to have been government-sponsored covert exercises (Article 19 1996). Simultaneously, credible rumours began to emerge that a general attack on the tiny UN peacekeeping force (inserted after the Arusha Peace Accords in 1993) was being planned by government forces (Ngesi and Villa-Vicencio 2003:13-14).

These events suggest that, by 1994, Rwandan society was primed for genocide to such a degree that the peace process launched at Arusha may have been unworkable even before the Accords were signed. Over the course of two centuries, Rwanda had become a nation driven not only to construct and identify 'aliens', but also possessed of a population vulnerable to ethno-nationalist rhetoric and socialized to accept the command to fear, revile, and even kill the 'other'. This socialization existed in a context of explosive instability – local and regional, political and economic – and became a weapon wielded by political elites, both within Habyarimana's National Revolutionary Movement for Development (MRND) and the RPF itself.

RTLM and Bikindi as symptoms

As mentioned previously, a distinction must be drawn between Bikindi's active and physical participation in *Interahamwe* activities, and the role fulfilled by his songs as incitement to genocide. It is tempting to run these two charges together, given that the actor in both cases is the same person and given the clearly divisionist tone of Bikindi's songs throughout his period of popularity. This, however, ignores variations in demonstrable *intent* and *causality* (as required by criminal law) between the former charge and the latter.[6] The 1948 Convention on the Prevention and Punishment of the Crime of Genocide not only defines and criminalizes ethnic cleansing but also includes 'conspiracy to commit genocide, direct and public incitement to commit genocide, attempts to commit genocide and complicity in genocide' as punishable crimes (Vetlesen 2000: 519); thus while international law is clear on the role of ideological manipulation in a genocidal environment, this clarity is tempered by an insistence that a specific and direct link must be established between the alleged incitement and the genocidal acts themselves. In the case of Bikindi, such a link has never been hard to establish, owing to his physical proximity to several slayings, as well as his complicity in murders committed by his associates. This link, however, is far less plausible in the case of Bikindi-as-musician, where his role is entirely long-distance.

This distinction is well illustrated by the events surrounding Bikindi's 'Twasezereye'. Given that this song was first performed in 1987, with Rwanda in a state of relative internal peace, it seems more reasonable to attribute to it the status of social commentary – albeit of a bigoted and divisionist nature – than of a call to genocide. However, when this song was revived in 1992-93 and specifically co-opted to focus popular dissent against the peace plan being developed in Arusha, this status was replaced by a new set of objectives. At this point 'Twasezereye', like several of Bikindi's songs, must be thought of as beginning a new career, turning from simple hate speech to a demonstrable element of a consciously deployed call to genocide; but this was a career no longer incontestably tied to the intention of the author, and this prompts a shift in culpability from Bikindi to the medium of radio broadcast and RTLM in particular. By this argument, then, Bikindi-as-musician (as opposed to Bikindi-as-*genocidaire*) takes on the role of a

---

[6] The issue of demonstrable intent was clearly referred to in the recent indictment of former Rwandan Finance Minister Emmanuel Ndindabahizi, on similar charges as Bikindi. The ICTR's press release regarding Ndindabahizi's case states: 'By his words and deeds, the Accused manifested an intent that [Tutsi] … should be attacked and killed. Further, the Accused was *well aware that his remarks and actions were part of a wider context of ethnic violence, killing and massacres in Rwanda during this period*. The Chamber found that the Accused intended to destroy, in whole or in part, the Tutsi ethnic group and convicted him for genocide' (ICTR Press Release 2004, emphasis added).

'conduit' of a particular message rather than a perpetrator.[7] If this is true, it requires a closer examination of the organization who did seek to perpetrate violence via the lyrics of Bikindi's songs: RTLM itself, and its backers.

RTLM not only expressed and disseminated the message of deep and ideologically-sustained ethno-nationalist divisions within Rwandan society, but also focused the attentions of its listeners on what to do about these divisions. However, while radio provided an effective means to co-ordinate a particular style of genocide in Rwanda – what Mamdani (2002b: 6) calls the 'intimate affair' of neighbour killing neighbour – the presence of a station such as RTLM neither explains the *desire* of extremists to call for the genocide, nor the *ability* of ordinary civilians to respond. This gap, between the call to genocide and the genocide itself, motivates the question behind innumerable examinations of the Rwandan genocides: 'how were ordinary civilians transformed into functionaries of a policy of hands-on extermination?' It is also an appreciation of this gap that underlies the present emphasis on the necessity of *reading* RTLM and Bikindi's roles more deeply.

In fact, and as argued above, the existence of such profound potential for violence can only be understood through an examination of the source of the divisionist discourse which led to the civil war and genocide: the experiences of the colonial and post-colonial era. These events, which significantly predate the genocides, are the only means by which the depth of ideological manipulation required to turn neighbour against neighbour, can be understood and in this regard, the relatively short histories of Radio Rwanda and RTLM are significant in arguing *against* assigning them a formative role in the genocide. However, in terms of the propagation of the genocidal project, Bikindi, RTLM and the power of the 'electronic tom-tom' (Heisbourg 1997: 2) certainly featured as symptoms, or sustaining voices, of the social fractures – such as land scarcity and related ills – which turned the Rwandan situation into one of chronic and escalating conflict between families, neighbours, the young and old, poor and rich, and of course different ethnic groups. This highlights a critical element of the story of the Rwandan genocides which dispels the pervasive blurring of boundaries between the pre-existing pro-genocide socialization applied to the Rwandan Hutu population and the social/material conditions effecting all Rwandans not included in or benefiting from the elite's hold over power, and the specific and focused injunctions and vocalizations of hate provided by RTLM, Bikindi, and others. The pertinent question thus becomes: if RTLM served as a crucial permissive factor in

---

[7] It was on this distinction that the foundation cases against Nazi propagandists Julius Streicher and Hans Fritzscher in the Nuremberg courts rested, setting the precedent on which subsequent examinations of incitement to genocide have rested. On the basis of a demonstrable link between elements of his publication (*Die Sturmer*) and specific acts of genocide on the eastern front, Streicher was executed; Fritzscher, despite a far more prolific hate-speech career, was not (Metzl 1997:636-7).

the Rwandan genocide, could efforts to control the medium (or, indeed, the message) have served to head off the crisis?

Control and the media

Before, during, and after the genocide, a variety of efforts were made to wrest control of the Rwandan airwaves from the *genocidaires*. However, in the absence of an understanding of the relationship between the messengers (such as Bikindi and RTLM, with their relatively short careers), the message (of ethnic division, the older roots of this in pre-colonial society, and the present land and resource distribution crises), and the eventual genocide, most of these efforts would now appear to have been misdirected. In what follows, three episodes are used to support this statement: the abortive UN attempt to contest the call to genocide, the various initiatives directed at taking RTLM off the air during the genocide, and the RPF government's promotion of politically correct but nonetheless divisive 'right thinking' in Rwanda after 1994. Furthermore, following these failures, and at the very moment when the future of a post-genocide Rwanda is at stake, world attention (and thus interest in the Rwandan media environment) has shifted elsewhere, in a final demonstration of the superficiality of the analysis which has informed international concern.

Contesting the message

Following the 6 April 1994 rocket attack which brought down President Habyarimana's plane and sparked off the genocides,[8] the UN intervention force attempted to use the radio network for its own purposes. General Romeo Dallaire convinced a Hutu moderate, Prime Minister Agathe Uwilingiyimana, to make a public broadcast calling for calm on Radio Rwanda. Rather than allow this, unknown assailants attacked and killed Uwilingiyimana (along with her UN bodyguards) in the grounds of the main military camp in Kigali (Unknown 2004b). Dallaire has blamed Theoneste Bagosora, a senior defence minister at the time (and allegedly the man behind the actions of the Interahamwe *genocidaires*), for Uwilingiyimana's death; although this has not yet been proven, it remains clear that elements of the Rwandan government, if not Bagosora himself, were responsible.

Thus, the idea of a moderate voice gaining access to the ears of the Rwandan people was seen as unacceptable by these elements, but it was not the *content* of an

---

[8] Speculation continues as to the origins of the ground-launched rockets which destroyed Habyarimana's aircraft. Clearly, the obvious suspects are anti-government forces such as the RPF, but this has been denied; indeed, given the moderate-vs.-extremist struggles, the existence of a hardliner faction bent on seizing power after Habyarimana's death is not inconceivable.

RTLM broadcast – or, indeed, any single media source – that convinced Uwilingiyimana's assassins to strike. Rather, it was their adherence to a pre-existing set of ethno-nationalist agendas in whose terms the very act of moderacy was unacceptable; an adherence formed by ideological conditioning and scarcity of resources stretching back far further than RTLM and well into the present (Diamond 2005).

Taking RTLM off the air

In parallel with the genocide and the RPF's return to military operations in Rwanda, calls for RTLM broadcasts to be jammed or shut down were made in several forums – within the US government, and before the UN – in late 1994. The apparent military and/or humanitarian utility in such a move was clear; as mentioned previously, RTLM had become a *de facto* source of co-ordination for the various *genocidaire* groups, making it an obvious target for those forces aimed at ending the conflict. While the RPF's artillery was attempting to take the station off the air by shelling its antennae in Kigali, the US Committee for Refugees had joined human rights groups and journalistic sources in recommending that US military resources be deployed to interdict or otherwise interfere with RTLM broadcasts. This recommendation was not acted on, largely due to the US's powerful commitment to broadcast freedom (aimed at protecting its own propaganda stations, such as Radio Free Europe during the Cold War, and Radio Martí which broadcasts into Cuba), as well as a general unwillingness on the part of Western states to endure the expense of airborne jamming operations or the risk of ground-based ones (Metzl 1997: 628-30). In addition, direct action aimed at the RTLM infrastructure merely prompted the station to move its base of operations, first to a mobile transmitter somewhere in Kigali, then to the extremist-held Gisenyi Prefecture, and finally into exile in Zaire. The station was knocked off the air three times; each time it promptly resumed broadcasts (Metzl 1997: 628-52).

Once again, the presence of a powerful ethno-nationalist *will* behind the RTLM phenomenon is visible; large numbers of Rwandans, not all of whom can have been active *genocidaires*, were willing to work long and hard to keep the station broadcasting, and their motivations are not easily explicable in terms of the station's broadcasts alone. This clearly speaks to the station's status as a 'voice' possessing substantial legitimacy for many ordinary Rwandans.

Ongoing divisive talk

In the wake of the RPF's seizure of power in 1994, the media's interactions with the Rwandan people have once again become the site of government intervention:

> To a casual visitor, Rwanda does not seem oppressive … [but] there is no freedom of the press, because that might allow 'divisionists' to spread once more their foul ideology…Having once been the victims of media-coordinated violence, it could be

argued that Kagame government is simply clamping down on the possibility of a re-occurrence of such events. However, the article cited above goes on to say: *There is no freedom of association, either. Anyone who tries to set up a serious opposition party is subject to harassment, arrest and threats that Rwandans take seriously because they know their government can be ruthless when the occasion demands.* (Unknown 2004c: 27)

The RPF's relationship with the legacy of meaning left behind by the massacres is thus more complex than a simple aversion to past horrors. Specifically, the government's tendency to label any outspoken critic of the regime a 'divisionist' or genocide-sympathizer (given the ongoing tensions in Rwandan society following the massacres) has contributed to a pervasive atmosphere of 'right thinking' in which the refrain, 'We are all Rwandans now' is often repeated but not necessarily felt by all (Walker 2004: 31).[9] This suggests that rather than simply attempting to negate, or replace, the negotiations of meaning and creations of ideology expressed through and sustained by RTLM between 1993 and 1994, the RPF government has simply reconfigured a divided society in which 'Rwandans' oppose 'Divisionists' much in the same way as 'Hutu power' once faced the 'alien Tutsis'. The fear experienced by the Rwandan public in 1994 has thus not only persisted but become concretized in post-massacre government policy, perpetuating popular media's potential as a source of re-destabilization.

This examination of failed attempts to address the role of the media in Rwanda once again emphasizes the need for better-informed analyses in the case of Rwanda. Such analyses can now, ten years after the genocide, draw on an enormous body of work on the Rwandan experience. This is of interest *at least* because the Rwandan case seems to represent so many of the challenges facing Africa as a whole and the UN (and international community in general) as an intervening power, but also because it can be used to inform debates around not only what *should have been done* but also what *should be done in future.*[10]

Conclusion

It has been argued above that Rwandan popular media (specifically, RTLM and the folk songs of Simon Bikindi) were symptoms of causes which simple censorship cannot fix. More particularly; the deeply rooted divisions in Rwandan society, with their long history intricately connected to local power structures and regional and international instabilities (which were in turn occasioned by various economic and

---

[9] This article is primarily concerned with the *gacaca* (village court) hearings through which attempts at uncovering the truth of the '100 days' are being made.

[10] Indeed, the Rwandan case has become a point of reference for those who argue in favour of 'benevolent censorship' to oppose hate radio. See 'The Sound of Hatred', *BBC News*, 30 March 1998, archived at http://www.hartford-hwp.com/ archives/35/180.html.

political factors), were certainly articulated and focused through the popular media, but RTLM and Bikindi-as-musician can still not be regarded as *causes* of the 1994 genocide. It is in order to address these causes effectively that this chapter urges a more historically-informed understanding of the challenges embedded in modern Rwandan society, specifically, challenges pertaining to the role of the media.

In societies without deep ethnic, class, or other divisions, and without population pressure, and human environmental impacts and droughts leading to a scarcity of resources and widespread poverty, the products of a specific sector of the popular media might very well resemble the material presented on RTLM (and performed by artists such as Simon Bikindi) so closely that they can barely be distinguished from one another – and yet not result in genocide. A case in point is Denmark's neo-Nazi *Radio Oasen* (Radio Oasis), which not only broadcast without incident for several years in the late 1990s, but in fact received a monetary allowance commensurate with its status as a non-commercial radio station from the Danish Department of Culture (Unknown 2004a). Such a position is supported by the ongoing difficulty in establishing anything but the most tenuous of links between the broadcast of recorded music, and ensuing acts of violence by everyday listeners (Temple-Raston 2002). In contrast, in a Rwandan society gripped by divisions (where listeners had ceased to be 'everyday', and were rather primed from above and below, so to speak, for violence), genocide resulted with what appears to be an actualizing call in the form of RTLM and Bikindi. But were these *really* the call to genocide? Or were they simply one of many routes the call could have taken?

What has not been addressed in this chapter is the potential for other media forms as transmitters for genocide – did it have to be radio, in this case? We feel that the answer is no. Certainly, radio was a powerful conduit in the Rwandan genocides, but larger massacres have taken place without identifiable media prompting (such as the ongoing violence in the Democratic Republic of the Congo, which has already resulted in the deaths of 3-4 *million* people to date). Furthermore, the fact that even RPF soldiers preferred listening to RTLM over their 'own' propaganda station (Li 2004), and this without displaying a marked inclination to switch sides or abandon the Tutsi cause, suggests that the issue at stake is not the message but the education of the mind which hears it. Given this, we would argue that it is the creators and exploiters of divided societies – politicians and power-brokers who use anything they can lay their hands on (including the media) to remain in power – that we should be concerning ourselves with if something effective is to be done. To act otherwise is simply to shoot the messenger.

References

Article 19. 1996. *Broadcasting Genocide: Censorship, Propaganda and State-Sponsored Violence in Rwanda 1990-1994.* London: Article 19.

Berkeley, B. 2001. *The Graves Are Not Yet Full: Race, Tribe, and Power in the Heart of Africa*. USA: Perseus Publishing.

Chalk, F. 1999. 'Hate Radio in Rwanda' in H. Adelman and A. Suhrke (eds), *The Path of a Genocide*. New Jersey: Transaction Publishers.

Corfield, A. 2001. 'The Creation of Myths in Rwandan Society – 1990-94. A Study of Propaganda and its role in the Genocide'. MA thesis, Rhodes University.

Diamond, J. 2005. *Collapse. How societies choose to fail or succeed*. New York: Viking.

Fuiji, LA. 2002. 'The diffusion of a genocidal norm in Rwanda', http://www.isanet.org/noarchive/rwanda.html.

Gourevitch, P. 1998. *We Wish to Inform You That Tomorrow We Will Be Killed With Our Families: Stories From Rwanda*. New York: Farrar Straus Giroux.

Heisbourg, F. 1997. *Predictions: The Future of Warfare*. London: Phoenix ICTR Press Release Number ICTR/INFO-9-2-396.EN. 2004. 'Tribunal Sentences Ndindabahizi to Life Imprisonment for Genocide.' http://www.ictr.org/ENGLISH/PRESSREL/2004/396.htm.

Hintjens, H. 1999. 'Explaining the 1994 Genocide in Rwanda', *Journal of Modern African Studies*, 37, pp. 241-86.

Kellow, C. and Steeves, H. 1998. 'The Role of Radio in the Rwandan Genocide', *Journal of Communication*, 48:3, pp. 107-28.

Li, D. 2004. 'Echoes of violence: considerations on radio and genocide in Rwanda'. *Journal of Genocide Research* 6:1 (March): 9-27.

Mamdani, M. 2002a. 'Making Sense of Political Violence in Post-Colonial Africa', in *Fighting Identities: Race, Religion and Ethno-Nationalism: Socialist Register 2003* in L. Panitch and C. Leys (eds), London: Merlin Press, pp. 132-51.

Mamdani, M. 2002b. *When Victims Become Killers: Colonialism, Nativism and Genocide in Rwanda*. Princeton: Princeton University Press.

Metzl, J.F. 1997. 'Rwandan Genocide and the International Law of Radio Jamming', *The American Journal of International Law*, 91,4: 631-2.

Ngesi, S. and Villa-Vicencio, S. 2003. 'Rwanda: Balancing the Weight of History', in E. Doxtader and C. Villa-Vicencio, *Through Fire with Water: The Roots of Division and the Potential for Reconciliation in Africa*. Cape Town: David Philip, pp. 1-36.

Otunnu, O. 1999. 'An Historical Analysis of the Invasion by the Rwanda Patriotic Army (RPA)', in *The Path of Genocide: The Rwanda Crisis from Uganda to Zaire*. Howard Adelman and Astri Suhrke (eds), New Brunswick: Transaction Publishers, pp. 31-49.

Snyder, J. and Ballentine, K. 1996. 'Nationalism and the Marketplace of Ideas', *International Security*, 21, 2: pp. 30-34.

Temple-Raston, D. 2002. "Radio Hate". http://www.legalaffairs.org/issues/September-October-2002/feature_raston_sepoct2002.html.

Unknown. 2000. 'Debt and the Rwandan Genocide', *Jubilee2000*.

Unknown. 2001. International Criminal Tribunal for Rwanda case no. ICTR- 2001-72-I, Indictment against Simon Bikindi. ICTR Archives, http://157.150.221.3/ProcessLogin.asp.

Unknown. 2003a. 'Musician Again Pleads "Not Guilty" to Genocide', *Foundation Hirondelle*,
http://www.hirondelle.org/hirondelle.nsf/0/4fc571f5e3e9dd55c1256a8a00 006e75?OpenDocument.

Unknown. 2003b. 'Case Study - Rwanda', *Media in Conflict* series at Internews, http://www.internews.org/mediainconflict/mic_rwanda.html
http://www.jubilee2000uk.org/jubilee2000/news/rwanda.html.

Unknown. 2004a. 'Hate Radio: Europe', *Radio Netherlands Wereldomroep*. http://www.rnw.nl/fearradio/dossiers/num/hateradioeur.html.

Unknown. 2004b. 'The Devil's Work', *Weekly Mail and Guardian*, 19 March 2004.

Unknown. 2004c. 'The road out of hell', *The Economist*, March 27, p.27.

Vetlesen, A. 2000. 'Genocide: A Case for the Responsibility of the Bystander', *Journal of Peace Research Special Issue on Ethics of War and Peace*, 37:4.

Walker, R. 2004. 'People's Justice', *BBC Focus on Africa*, April, pp. 30-31.

Chapter 4

Racist Hate Speech in South Africa's Fragile Democracy: The Case of Ngema's 'AmaNdiya'

Gary Baines

Introduction

The right to freedom of expression was regularly violated by South Africa's apartheid regime. Censorship was used to silence those voices that variously: criticized the regime; questioned moral and religious values which the regime (in partnership with the Dutch Reformed Church) sought to uphold; were deemed blasphemous, sexually explicit, used swear words, or simply mixed languages. When it came to the censorship of popular music, the Directorate of Publications responded largely to public complaints, whilst the South African Broadcasting Corporation (SABC) acted of its own accord to exclude 'undesirable' songs from the airwaves over which it exercised a monopoly. Consequently, a relatively small but significant number of musical recordings and performances were either banned outright or subjected to some sort of restrictions by the authorities (Drewett 2004a).

The first song to be censored in post-apartheid South Africa was Mbongeni Ngema's 'AmaNdiya'. It was banned from airplay (except under certain conditions) by the Broadcasting Complaints Commission of South Africa (BCCSA) on the grounds that it amounted to hate speech. Sales of the album called *Madlokuvu Jive* (Ngema 2002) on which the song featured, were subsequently restricted to those who were eighteen years and older by the Film and Publication Board. These acts of censorship met with mixed reactions. The pro-censorship lobby argued (somewhat paradoxically) that the country's fragile democracy should not be sacrificed for the sake of freedom of expression. Those who believed that the liberation struggle was fought to entrench the right to freedom of expression found this argument unconvincing. Ngema himself commented that:

> It was an eye-opener to a lot of people that the song was banned. Because people thought that censorship was gone. It has made people very wary of the fact that it now means that they cannot criticize this government. The very government that was fighting for the liberation of the press – free press, free expression, free everything. Can this be

the government...that will condone censorship? I don't know why the censorship is still there. And I think it should be dismantled. (cited in Drewett 2004b: 1)

Others held that hate speech should be tolerated as a necessary price to pay for freedom of expression. Thus the 'AmaNdiya' controversy proved to be something of a test case in which the value of freedom of expression was weighed against other rights and interests in the new political/constitutional dispensation of post-apartheid South Africa. This chapter examines the 'AmaNdiya' case in order to explore whether curbs on freedom of expression and artistic creativity can be justified in a potentially volatile situation, and whether censorship can safeguard a fragile socio-political order.

The 'AmaNdiya' affair

Unlike the white minority regime which used race and ethnicity to divide and rule, the post-apartheid government has sought to promote tolerance of cultural diversity. The new constitution acknowledges that the country is a multicultural society and a nation-building project which seeks to construct South Africa as the 'rainbow nation' was given official sanction (during the Mandela years, at least). However, these efforts have not been able to mask the deep fault lines in the society that have been manifest in the particularism of identity politics. This much was clear from the response to Ngema's song 'AmaNdiya' that highlighted latent tensions that existed in KwaZulu-Natal, a region well known for political intolerance and periodic outbreaks of violence. Coplan (2003: 10) notes that 'this strain of tension and resentment which, since the violent riots of 1949,[1] has threatened to burst into open confrontation on various occasions, is commonly acknowledged in social discourse in KwaZulu-Natal'. Certainly, the controversy sparked by Ngema's song served to highlight Zulu-Indian tensions in the region.

Mbongeni Ngema, an acclaimed but controversial songwriter and playwright, holds strong Zulu and African nationalist views. Ngema's song 'AmaNdiya' ('the Indians') opens with an introductory voice-over in English stating that: 'This song represents the way many African people feel about the behaviour of Indians in this country. It is intended to begin a constructive discussion that will lead to a true

---

[1] Following an altercation in an Indian-owned shop after which the trader inflicted injury on an African youth, Africans attacked Indian traders throughout the city in January 1949. By the time the cycle of violence and recrimination and police intervention had been played out, 142 people had been killed and over a thousand injured. The incident was invoked by the Nationalist government to justify its argument that different ethnic groups could not co-exist peacefully. See Davenport, (1987: 367-8).

reconciliation between Indians and Africans'. The lyrics themselves are in Zulu and have been translated as follows:[2]

Oh men!
Oh virulent men!
We need a courageous man
to delegate to the Indians
For this 'indaba ' (matter) is complicated and now needs to be reported to men
Indians don't want to change even Mandela has failed to convince them
It was better with whites we knew then it was a racial conflict

Even our leadership is not keen to get involved in this situation
Your buds are watering for roti and bettlenuts
Indians are not interested to cast their vote but when they do so they vote for whites
And their numbers fill up the Parliament and in the Government mould

What do you say, Buthelezi, you're so quiet
  yet the children of (your) Ngqengelele kaMnyamana (Buthelezi's Clan Hierarchy)
Being turned into clowns by Indians
Zulus do not have money and are squatting in shacks as chattels of Indians

Where's Sbu Ndebele? Where's Prince Gideon Zulu?
Hawu Ndabezitha wakaDabulamanzi!
I have never seen Dlamini relocating to India
Yet here is Gumede in Durban being homeless
We struggle so much here in Durban, as we, have been dispossessed by Indians
Who in turn are suppressing our people.

Mkhize is moaning, as he wants to open a business in West Street
Indians block him saying there is no place to open up a business or to rent it out
Our people are patronizing Indian businesses
What are you saying Mbeki? You are silent
Indians are playing the fool with us!

It's like that, brethren! Yeah men of men
[Fanakalo excerpts]: 'Hhayi, listen, I tell you that you must give people money,
Black folk buy from Indian shops in Isipingo, at Clairwood, in Durban and Verulam black people
Buy from Indians yet Indians do not even like to build schools for black children
They don't even like children of black people

I have never seen, Dlamini, emigrating to Bombay, India
Yet, Indians, arrive everyday in Durban – they are packing the Airport full

---

[2] These English lyrics are sourced from the BCCSA, Case No: 2002/31 SABC-'Ngema Song', Human Rights Commission of South Africa (Complainant) vs SABC (Ukhozi FM) (Respondent).

It's so my men; it's so my men! But no Indian wants to see a black-owned shop

In the song Ngema expressed rather bluntly the strong sense of grievance that many Zulu feel at what they consider their marginalization by the Indian community in the KwaZulu-Natal region. They feel exploited by Indian merchants and landlords, and many who work in the textile industry where many factories are Indian-owned, consider themselves underpaid. Moreover, Africans also perceive themselves excluded from jobs in local government because most positions in the Durban Metropolitan Council were filled by Indians (Boyte 2004: 45). This added up to a widespread – but mistaken – impression that all Indians were wealthy and were benefiting more than Africans from the end of apartheid. Ngema claimed that 'AmaNdiya' expressed the views of 'Black Africans throughout the country, at taxi ranks, soccer matches and shebeens'. Ngema presumed to speak for Africans 'because of the lack of authentic voices that articulate the sentiments of the people on the ground' (Memela 2002). Moreover, he castigated the new ruling elite for their lack of political will in addressing the plight of Africans. But what really made 'AmaNdiya' both audacious and politically incorrect was that Ngema voiced these sentiments openly in spite of the government's efforts to promote the project of reconciliation and nation building.

A chorus of voices demanded an apology from Ngema for maligning the character of the South African Indian community. Ngema's claim to have merely reflected 'the inescapable reality of Indian racism' (*Mail & Guardian*, 28 June 2002) appears to have been substantiated by acknowledgments that 'widespread racist ideas [are] still held by significant sections of the Indian population' (Raman 2003). In their defence, Indians could point to the role of eminent leaders in the liberation movement, and to their community's significant contributions to the development of the country. It is apparent from such statements that Ngema's song raised questions about who 'belonged' and was committed to the 'new South Africa'. And it is significant that such questions should have been raised precisely at a time when Indian South Africans were grappling with the issue of being part of a wider diasporic community. Some seem to be reclaiming their Indian cultural heritage while others have disavowed it; some have turned their gaze to the sub-continent whereas others consider Africa their home. But however religion, regional origin, or political orientation framed their identity, the Indian community shares a fear, fuelled by the memory of the 1949 Durban riots, that slurs against them might lead to attacks or even calls for their expulsion from the country. They, too, have been victimized and react partly out of a sense of insecurity.

If Ngema initially responded to his critics by justifying his song, he was soon pressurized to change his tune and concede that it was harmful to race relations. Former President Nelson Mandela, a figure of moral authority, met with Ngema and 'shamed' him with his statement that 'AmaNdiya' did not deal appropriately with the problem of racism in South Africa. Ngema thereupon maintained that his intention 'was to break the silence rather than air racial hatred' (*New York City News*, 2002). This validation was accompanied by a pledge to engage in a process of debate with interested parties around the problems and barriers that obstruct the process of reconciliation and nation building. A symposium facilitated by the Institute for Democracy in South Africa (IDASA) was held in Durban between 26 and 27 June 2002. It was aimed at promoting dialogue between Indian and African leaders from across the political spectrum by giving serious consideration to the song's claims and to what could be done to defuse the tensions between the two communities. Ngema boasted that his aim of getting both communities to 'talk frankly and openly' had been achieved. However self-serving and disingenuous this statement, Ngema was to some degree vindicated. In the aftermath of the initial outrage, both Indian and Zulu spokespersons endorsed Ngema's call for 'constructive discussion' in the interests of reconciliation (Boyte 2004: 46).

If the song 'AmaNdiya' caused offence in some quarters, it also provided further ammunition for opportunistic politicians to gain some mileage and lobby groups to press for legislation which would make it easier to prosecute propagators of hate speech. Complaints regarding the song's lyrics were lodged with the South African Human Rights Commission (SAHRC). The SAHRC is the national institution established to entrench constitutional democracy. According to its mission statement, the SAHRC is committed to promoting respect for, observance of and protection of human rights for everyone without fear or favour. The SAHRC speaks for those bodies which place a premium on upholding those clauses of the Constitution which protect the dignity of a person or group from defamation, loss of self-esteem and physical harm. The organization issued a statement that as South Africa was a 'young democracy…grappling…with the challenge of nation building', the song:

> Has the potential to polarize rather than bring together people in social dialogue that is so necessary. While the Commission has noted that [Ngema's] stated intention was to promote and encourage dialogue on an important social matter, we have also noted that nowhere in the lyrics of the song is such a call made. (SAHRC 2002)

In spite of Ngema's repeated assertions that the song was intended to facilitate constructive discussion about African-Indian relations, the SAHRC remained sceptical about the artist's sincerity. Whilst it acknowledged the need for robust and open debate on matters pertaining to identity politics, the SAHRC asserted that 'AmaNdiya' was an act of provocation that was likely to exacerbate an already tense situation. Consequently, it referred the song to the BCCSA to test whether it amounted to hate speech.

The Broadcasting Complaints Commission ruling on 'AmaNdiya'

The BCCSA plays a watchdog role over the broadcast media. This regulatory body was established by the National Association of Broadcasters of Southern Africa in 1993 'in order to promote freedom of speech, the free flow of information and the maintenance of high standards of broadcasting in South Africa' (BCCSA Constitution). Its brief is to adjudicate and mediate complaints against broadcasters who had voluntarily signed its Code of Conduct. Radio and television stations that were found to have violated the BCCSA Code can be subjected to a range of sanctions from a reprimand to a stiff fine.

The SAHRC initiated a complaint against the SABC which had broadcast Ngema's 'AmaNdiya' during a current affairs programme on its Zulu-language radio station Ukhozi FM. In its findings, the BCCSA recognized that the song should be afforded the protection of section 16(1) of the Constitution that guaranteed freedom of artistic creativity. On the other hand, it noted that the Constitution did not, in any way, rule out the possibility that artistic creations can also advocate hatred. However, this did not necessarily condone such work nor ameliorate the song's message. In fact, it was asserted that 'when the words accuse Indians in a sweeping manner of oppression, they are pronounced by the medium of song'. It added that 'the medium of song is likely to enhance the effect of the words on those who are targeted' (BCCSA Case No. 2002/31: 10). It further noted that the words of the song were inflammatory, not least of all in its assertion that life was better under apartheid than it was in the current dispensation. It exceeded freedom of expression allowed by the broadcasting code because it 'promoted hate in sweeping, emotive language against Indians as a race', and caused Indians to fear for their safety. Accordingly, the BCCSA ruled that under the broadcasting code the song constituted racial hate speech with incitement to harm.

The BCCSA noted in its ruling that 'harm' is not limited to physical harm and if likely that words could lead to fear or a related psychological state, it would justify a finding of hate speech. It added that 'harm must, in the interests of free speech, be interpreted to mean serious harm and would not simply be found to be present where the complainant exhibits a lack of tolerance or over-sensitiveness'. As the complainant was the SAHRC and not representatives of the Indian community or 'wronged' party, the BCCSA treated the case as if a matter of principle was at stake. So the ruling was not a legal precedent for the courts which still had to grapple with the problem of defining harm, as we shall see below.

Based on previous judgments by the Constitutional Court, the BCCSA ruled that freedom of expression should not be allowed to impair the rights of minority groups (in this case, Indians), nor impinge on state interests, and the pursuit of national unity and reconciliation. The ruling refers to these precedents in order:

> to accentuate the importance and the recognition of diversity and the protection of a minority in the pursuit of national unity and reconciliation. The dignity and vulnerability of members of any minority must, at all times, be protected against explicit (*in casu*) implied threats and/or derogatory language. (ibid., p. 11)

In citing other judgments on minority rights, the BCCSA ruling appears to invoke the liberal democratic discourse of the South African constitution's founders and interpreters; a discourse which privileges the recognition of cultural difference under the guise of tolerance. It meant, in effect, endorsing the view that in certain instances freedom of expression should be subordinated to the protection of minorities against hate speech, and that priority should be accorded to the nation-building project rather than the protection of individual rights – in this case that of Ngema.

The BCCSA ruling accepted at face value Ngema's claimed intention of stimulating discussion on the negative impressions some Africans have of Indians. It stated:

> An argument could be made that the song is likely to act as a catharsis for those Zulus who feel prejudiced by the economic position of the Indian businessmen...We also accept in favour of the writer, that he intended to begin a constructive discussion that could lead to reconciliation, as stated in the opening words by the writer. (BCCSA Case No. 2002/31: 10)

But this did not let Ngema off the hook entirely. For the statement included the rider that 'the song amounts to hate speech, in spite of the reconciliatory introduction of the writer' [as] 'the song itself does not convey the same message'. As with the SAHRC, the BCCSA identified a disjuncture between Ngema's stated intentions and the lyrical content of 'AmaNdiya'.

Finally, the BCCSA judgment upheld the view that offensive or derogatory material such as songs are allowed if they are broadcast in the context of analysis and discussion of its contents, and also in the context of bona fide artistic, scientific, documentary, or religious programmes. While 'banning' the song from general broadcast on the airwaves, the BCCSA accepted that the SABC was acting within its right to broadcast 'AmaNdiya' in the context of a current affairs programme. But the BCCSA made no ruling about the distribution and ownership of the song. This was the brief of the Film and Publication Board which deemed the song unsuitable for consumption by those under eighteen years of age and ruled that a warning sticker was to be attached to CDs and cassettes displayed in retail stores. This ruling was made in terms of Section 29 of the Films and Publications Act of 1996 which forbids the knowing distribution of hate speech in publications and the broadcast, distribution and exhibition of films in public, where the content amounts to hate speech.

The public debate about 'AmaNdiya'

The 'AmaNdiya' affair captured the attention of the South African media and public, and even made it on to the pages of *The Times of India*.[3] SABC TV broadcast a programme in the current affairs format which solicited opinion from

---

[3] *The Times of India*, 20 June 2002, 25 July 2002, 28 July 2002, 2 Sept. 2002, 1 Nov. 2002. http://timesofindia.indiatimes.com/articleshow/26947997.cms

'people in the street' and 'experts' alike. The input was generally accusatory and emotive rather than level-headed and the discussion tended to short circuit rather than engage meaningfully with the issues sparked by the controversy. Many from whom opinions were solicited expressed strong views regardless of whether they had actually heard the song or not. With a view to addressing what I would identify as some of the key issues, this section will critically examine a selection of media comments, especially statements issued by NGOs, academics, and other interested parties in respect of the Ngema song.

In its reaction to the BCCSA ruling, the SAHRC said that the judgment was significant in that it clarified the limits of freedom of expression in a constitutional democracy based on the values of equality and human dignity in a climate of contested speech. In other words, the BCCSA ruling confirmed its standpoint and vindicated its decision to brand 'AmaNdiya' as hate speech. It also claimed that the BCCSA ruling represented closure of the debate about whether the song constituted hate speech and called for parties involved in the controversy to move on (South African Human Rights Commission, 2002b). But this was obviously premature for the ruling had been confined to issues that had a bearing on the regulatory framework of broadcasting. The BCCSA could hardly have been expected to address the underlying causes of the controversy. Nor can it have reasonably been expected that a verdict by a regulatory body which had no influence in the framing of policy matters would satisfy those sectors of the public which appeared to want to outlaw hate speech in post-apartheid South Africa.

The Freedom of Expression Institute (FXI), an organization that seeks to uphold rights of individuals, including artists, to express their opinions without restriction, also entered the public debate. The FXI regards unwarranted limits on freedom of expression as a violation of the Constitution. It was critical of the BCCSA judgment on numerous grounds, both technical and substantive. The organization's Executive Director, Jane Duncan (2003: 5) held that:

> The logic that the judgment follows is that 'minorities' need to be wrapped up in cotton wool to protect them against 'hate speech' of the majority. The judgment set a dangerous precedent where historically advantaged groups could seek banning orders against speech they find offensive on the grounds that they feel threatened by criticisms of their position of privilege.

It is a moot point whether the South African Indian community can be regarded as [relatively] 'historically advantaged'. But there can be little doubt that power relations impact on the determination of what constitutes hate speech. Duncan inferred from another episode that:

> A person's ability to act on their subjective understanding of hate speech depends on their access to power and privilege, leading to the propagators of hate speech often being defined as parties other than the ruling elite, and individuals marginalized by the current political establishment. (Ibid.)

She concluded that the implication for South Africa was that: 'Those most vulnerable to charges of hate speech are the growing numbers of unemployed and independent social movements who are increasingly expressing their dissatisfaction with the current economic and political order' (ibid.). However, this did not mean that the FXI was not critical of the contents of the song, but it held that this alone was not sufficient basis for it to be banned for what it termed 'reactionary reasons'. The FXI argued that the era of banning or censoring expression simply because certain sectors of the public found it offensive was over. Rather than take its lead from the apartheid legal system which severely proscribed expression and violated basic human rights, the FXI believed that South Africa would do better to follow the example of the American courts which have generally not been convinced by attempts to establish a causal connection between hate speech by one party and the actions of others.

A researcher at the Centre for the Study of Violence and Reconciliation, Bronwyn Harris, provided a perspicacious analysis of the lyrics of 'AmaNdiya' (http://www.csvr.org.za/articles/aarthar3.html). She expressed the view that 'the song plays a divisive role, repeating old racial stereotypes and introducing new ways of fostering prejudice'. She rejected the view that 'AmaNdiya' merely reflects a social reality and that it is innocent of intent. Indeed, realism is often a pretext for propagating racist, sexist and other reactionary views (Cloonan 1995). Harris asserted that the rhetoric of the song reified existing prejudicial and negative stereotypes of the 'Other' which were fashioned during the apartheid era. By portraying Africans and Indians in monolithic terms, the song 'denies the audience an opportunity to confront the complex dynamics that create and sustain prejudice'. Harris added that:

> 'AmaNdiya' does not only portray negative stereotypes that are drawn on racial lines. It also creates prejudice through the language of xenophobia. By presenting 'Indians' as outsiders from India, the song raises questions about belonging within South Africa. This moves beyond race alone because it introduces concepts of citizenship and nationality. It implies that 'Indians' are not South African and therefore have less legitimate claim to their citizenship than others. (Ibid.)

This reading was presumably derived from the reference to the line of 'AmaNdiya' which refers to Indians 'arriving everyday in Durban...packing the airport full'. Harris notes that:

> Foreigners have become handy scapegoats for South Africa's ills, particularly crime and unemployment. 'AmaNdiya' extends this xenophobic discourse to 'Indians' and so conflates a race-group with a national-group. This is a divisive trick. Not only does it challenge the idea of racial inclusiveness and unity, it also suggests that South African nationality is racially exclusive. (Ibid.)

In fact, xenophobic discourse has been employed as an exclusionary nation-building device. I have no argument with Harris's analysis of the content of

Ngema's song, nor do I deny that it constitutes hate speech. Yet, as with most commentaries, it begs the question of whether 'AmaNdiya' can be shown to have incited acts of harm or violence. The causal relationship between expression and action is notoriously difficult to determine and most opinions skirt this issue altogether. While expression – including songs – can prompt action it is not a foregone conclusion that it will do so.

Another who ventured an opinion on this matter was the legal columnist for the Johannesburg *Sunday Independent*. Rob Amato (2002: 7) wrote:

> AmaNdiya's tone is ironic rather than hateful. It makes no character attack on Indians, although it says they are oppressive and don't help the Zulu poor. It calls for political, not violent, responses to social inequity. It might be right or wrong, but it is not unconstitutional...

I cannot concur with the view that Ngema does not attack the collective character of Indians. Yet the song can hardly be regarded as a 'call to arms' by Zulus against Indians. Although the journalist Max du Preez claimed that 'AmaNdiya' created a climate in KwaZulu-Natal which was similar to that in Rwanda where the Hutus had sung racist songs as a prelude to the genocide of Tutsis (*Daily News*, 2002), this analogy is spurious. As contributors to this volume show, the broadcast of Simon Bikindi's song 'Bene Sebahinzi' was appropriated by those with murderous intent, but the song itself did not spark the genocide. Du Preez was also critical of the ruling African National Congress and government for their silence on the 'AmaNdiya' affair when its spokespersons are quick to condemn the racism of its detractors. He opined that '[b]lack African arrogance and chauvinism can develop into something as ugly as white racism' (*Daily News* 2002). This may be so. But the language of 'AmaNdiya' is quite moderate when compared with misogynistic American gangsta rap or South Africa's own hip-hop idioms which masquerade as expressions of ghetto and Cape Flats culture, respectively. Although this music advocates violence against women, there has been no concerted campaign to remove it from the airwaves or the shelves of music outlets. Even if we do not buy the 'social realism' defence that rap is an art form which 'tells it like it is', there is no evidence to substantiate the claim that Ngema's 'AmaNdiya' was responsible for the killings of Indians by Africans in the aftermath of the furore.[4]

One of the most contentious pieces on the 'AmaNdiya' affair appeared in the *City Press* under the name of Sandile Memela (2002: 1). This writer asserted that the ruling elite is out of touch with the person in the street and closed ranks to suppress the voices of 'pro-African radicalism' which might subvert the rhetoric of the rainbow nation. Memela holds that Ngema's 'dream to get South Africa talking lies shattered on the pavement of political correctness and pseudo non-racialism'.

---

[4] A number of such claims were made. In one such instance, it was reported that the killers had actually invoked 'AmaNdiya' whilst attacking their victims. See http://www.rediff.com/news/2002/aug/30spec.htm

Memela may well have accepted Ngema's claim to represent the voice of the marginalized at face value and misrepresented the efficacy of his intervention in regional politics which produced yet another talk shop rather than solutions to intractable problems. He may well have overstated the case for the difference one person – who happens to be a musician – can make to changing long-standing perceptions about other groups. But he may be correct if he means to imply that there is far greater risk to sidelining such populist voices than there is to ignoring them in the public debate. The 'AmaNdiya' affair might be unusual inasmuch as it involved the medium of song for voicing the racism of Africans. But the numerous other reports of 'hate speech' and 'race hate crimes' by the media since 1994 suggest that this was not an isolated event.

Racism and hate speech in post-apartheid South Africa

Race might be a social construct but it is still lived as 'real'. This implies that the commonsense understanding of race in South African society is essentialist. In fact, race remains the primary marker of social identity. In the realm of public discourse race and racism tend to be employed as catch-all terms. It is not surprising, then, that Ngema's song 'AmaNdiya' framed the Zulu-Indian tensions in KwaZulu-Natal as a 'racial conflict' although it clearly had class and ethnic dimensions.

The ending of apartheid and the establishment of democracy in South Africa obviously did not also bring about the end of racism within the country. The formal, institutionalized racial order with its system of legalized discrimination may have been dismantled, but racist attitudes and behaviour have persisted. Racism cannot simply be repealed. Nor is racism the preserve of the formerly powerful and privileged white ruling elite. Indeed, racism rears its ugly head between and within groups which the apartheid ideologues had defined as 'non-white'. It is also a highly emotive issue – alleging racism can become a potent political weapon to discredit opponents, a polemical device, or a defence mechanism to deflect criticism (Maylam 2001: 1). For instance, certain of President Thabo Mbeki's critics have asserted that the re-racialization of the public sphere during his presidency has contributed to rising levels of intolerance, and that Mbeki himself has come dangerously close to racist hate speech. Whether or not this is the case, racism is still very much alive in the new South Africa.

Racism is socially learned, and discourse is essential in the process of its ideological production and reproduction (van Dijk in Whillock and Slayden 1995: 3). Whilst South Africa's new ruling elite may be committed to the creation of a non-racist and non-sexist society, its ability to control public discourse is not unlimited. Because of its unassailable parliamentary majority and public mandate, the African National Congress (ANC) sets the agenda for transformation and the tone for much of the public debate around issues pertaining to race (for example, affirmative action, quotas, and so on). But there is some space in the public sphere for dissenting voices to be heard. Sometimes these voices may be heard directly in radio talk shows, letters to newspaper editors, and so on. Otherwise, public discourse may be indirectly mediated by politicians, journalists, and even musicians. Whilst the SAHRC found 'no evidence of the mainstream media indulging in blatant advocacy of racial hatred or incitement to racial violence', it did characterize South African media as 'racist institutions' (SAHRC 2000: 89-90). Ironically, it is the same media that have highlighted the pervasiveness of racism and the prevalence of hate speech in society at large.

In the past decade or so, the prevailing social characterization of racist expressions has been reduced to the category of hate. Smith (in Whillock and Slayden 1995: 259) sees hate as a manifestation of the emotion of fear, created by economic insecurity, relative status deprivation, lack of education, feelings of powerlessness, sexual insecurity, or a more general fear of all differences as disconfirming the validity of one's own personal security. Whillock and Slayden (1995: ix-x) argue that hate should not necessarily be seen as 'an extreme expression that arises only in moments of cultural tension [as this] encourages us to ignore its role in the subtle negotiations that take place daily in complex, modern society'. Instead, they hold that 'hate is an integral part of society, that it has numerous functions within the public and private discourses by which society discovers and comments on itself.' Acknowledging that hate is naturalized, that it finds subtle as well as extreme expression, that it is not simply irrational, enables us to explore more thoroughly its uses within society and to recognize that it is culturally bound. Admitting hate as part of a culture rather than extraneous to it brings us more clearly in touch with its uses. In practice hate becomes an essential tool for the construction of identity and the acquisition or negotiation of power. Hate exerts its influence in a wide range of power relations. It is used by those in power as well as by the disenfranchised or marginalized. Whillock and Slayden (1995: xiii) observe that '[f]ar from the notion that [hatred] is used only as a propaganda technique in state-controlled cultures, any culture (and any group, dominant or subordinate) can and does use hate speech to establish in-groups and out-groups'.

Even when directed at individuals, hate speech targets whole classes of persons or a people. This is a circular process, for hatred functions by denying individuality and practising objectification based on generic descriptions of the 'Other'. This is a form of stereotyping. Strong negative emotions such as hate are used to polarize particular groups in order to organize opposition, solidify support, and marshal resources towards tackling a perceived problem. This polarization predisposes audiences to disregard the claims of others as deserving of equitable treatment, rendering them instead as symbolic objects of hatred at which anger is focused. The practice of assigning blame to or scapegoating others has, as its corollary, the assumption of victimhood status oneself. Those who believe hate speech hear the affirmation that something is wrong and that the something that is wrong is not their fault (Whillock and Slayden 1995: xv). Accordingly, if the fault lies elsewhere, then there is no need for self-evaluation and transformation.

Hate speech exists because it articulates and resonates with certain needs, especially the felt conditions of people's lives. Hate speech expresses the anger/rage of individuals, but it looks for justification to patterns of behaviour and belief that permeate the rest of society in less extreme form. If its logic is faulty (and it is), its visceral appeal is credible. For this reason it must be allowed and listened to and admitted as a form of public discourse. We should not try to eradicate it but should instead ask why it exists and examine critically what is being said and why (Whillock and Slayden 1995: xv). However, the case of 'AmaNdiya' suggests that South Africa is likely to follow the lead of those countries which would seek to outlaw hate speech altogether.

The constitutional/legal status of hate speech in South Africa

South Africa has only recently joined the fold of liberal democracies. As with its more established counterparts it has to grapple with whether to make freedom of expression an article of faith or a constitutional principle subject to qualifications. Most liberal democracies impose some restrictions on the market place of ideas, especially where state security is thought to be at risk. Some states (for example, Germany) prohibit hate speech and incitement to violence primarily in order to preserve law and order, or to protect minority groups from victimization. South Africa's new constitutional dispensation entrenched the importance of the values of human dignity, equality and freedom as the cornerstones of the country's newfound democracy. Freedom of expression is safeguarded by Section 16(1) of the Constitution which, *inter alia*, guarantees 'freedom of artistic creativity'. Whilst the Constitution attaches importance to freedom of expression, this right is not absolute nor does it have pre-eminence over the right to dignity or equality. In other words, there is no hierarchy of rights. Rights of free expression will have to be weighed up against other rights (in the event that such disputes are referred to the courts). And there are restrictions attached to these rights. Section 16(2)(c) of the Constitution stipulates that the right to freedom of expression does not extend to 'advocacy of hatred based on race, ethnicity, gender or religion, and that which constitutes incitement to cause harm'. This so-called 'hate speech clause' does *not* outlaw hate speech *per se*. Hate speech is, by and large, constitutionally protected, except for the narrow category of such speech that may result in harm being caused (Duncan 2003: 2). This brings us (back) to the question: what is harm?

The issue has been contested ever since the nineteenth-century philosopher John Stuart Mill (1975 [1859]: 1) articulated the classic liberal standpoint that state encroachment upon the freedom of individuals is only warranted in order to prevent harm to others. But how is the 'harm principle' to be applied? Is it confined to physical harm or does it include mental and psychological anguish, loss of material income and so on? As we have seen, the BCCSA proposed a wide-ranging definition of 'harm'. However, Duncan (2003: 7) argues that '[t]he problem with this approach is that the broader the definition of harm becomes, the more difficult it becomes to verify, opening up the problem of subjective interpretation/application of the relevant [constitutional] clause'. Until such time as the courts are asked to provide a statutory definition, or the legislature passes laws that elaborate a definition of harm, the question will not be resolved satisfactorily.

This is apparent from an examination of Section 10(1) of the Promotion of Equality and Prevention of Unfair Discrimination Act (No 4 of 2000) which provides that:

> no person may publish, propagate, advocate or communicate words based on one or more of the prohibited grounds, against any person, that could reasonably be construed to demonstrate a clear intention to be hurtful; be harmful or to incite harm; promote or propagate hatred.

This is subject to Section 12 of the Act which does not preclude *bona fide* engagement in artistic creativity. Provision is made to refer a hate speech complaint to the Director of Public Prosecutions for the possible institution of criminal proceedings. The Act requires a test that hate speech must 'reasonably be construed to demonstrate a clear intention' on the part of the accused to cause harm. Thus prosecution under the Equality Act requires the state to prove an advocacy of hatred as well as the incitement to cause harm (SAHRC 2002: 4). This remains problematic so long as there is no constitutional/legal definition of harm.

As no provision yet exists by which hate speech can be prosecuted in terms of general criminal law, perpetrators of crimes motivated by racism, sexism or xenophobia can only be charged with assault, grievous bodily harm and other acts involving physical violence. Some commentators see this as a loophole in the law and lobbied the government to either amend existing legislation or introduce new legislation to deal more effectively with hate speech and related crimes. The portfolio Committee on Justice then asked the Minister of Justice to draft legislation to deal with the criminalization of hate speech. It is envisaged that the Prohibition of Hate Speech Bill will be tabled during the forthcoming session of Parliament. Section 2(1) of the Bill seeks to define more specifically the offences that may be prosecuted. However, it 'clearly exceeds the general limitations of freedom of expression as allowed for by the Constitution especially where these pertain to defining hate speech'. The provisions could criminalize anything remotely construed as hate speech and inhibit public discourse (Media Institute of Southern Africa 2004: 2, 3). If passed in its present form there is every likelihood that this will see a shift in emphasis from the educational/remedial to the deterrent/punitive function of the law. If the greatest advantage of the law as a moral exemplar is that it communicates a clear message of acceptable and unacceptable behaviour in society, then it serves a useful and constructive role when providing the social foundations required for altering social attitudes and value systems rather than simply punishing offenders (SAHRC n.d.).

With the legislative process in limbo, the courts are bound to have to take the lead in interpreting the provisions protecting freedom of expression in the constitution. The interpretations of the courts might establish useful precedents for the legislature in defining hate speech. On the one hand, certain court judgments would seem to suggest that there is a need to 'bend over backwards' to create a culture of respect for human rights which the country fought so hard to win. On the other hand, other judgments appear to be premised on the view that South Africa's special circumstances require particularly firm – some might say censorious – treatment of racism and hate speech. In such instances, rulings tend to be based not only on the merits of legal/constitutional arguments of the case but on the bigger picture, especially the quest for reconciliation and nation building (SAHRC 2000: 75). Such judgments invoke South Africa's status as a young and fragile democracy as extenuating circumstances for diluting freedom of expression. In other words, political expediency can be said to trump human rights enshrined in the constitution. This does not bode well for the preservation of constitutionally-guaranteed freedoms for it establishes a dangerous precedent whereby all forms of expression that the ruling elite deems politically incorrect may be silenced.

Conclusion

On the face of it, prohibiting hate speech or acts which can harm others is characteristic of a just and tolerant society. But legislation attempting to silence hate speech proceeds from denial. If we do not talk about it or, rather, if we do not hear it, then it does not exist or it might go away. Of course, this is not the case and hate speech is not the real problem. The conditions that create a receptive audience for hate speech – ignorance, inequity, and fear – constitute the problem. To address these is much more difficult than attempting to silence the voices that remind us, by example, that problems exist. Hate speech is like a canker sore on the body politic. Legal restrictions on hate speech only suppress the symptoms; they do not treat the underlying causes of the social disease (Smith in Whillock and Slayden 1995: 260). Banning inhibits the exchange of ideas and information which is the lifeblood of democracy. Thus hate speech must be recognized as a legitimate and valuable form of symbolic expression in society – not because it is true or sound, but because it identifies discontent, injustice, inequities. To deny voices, even those voices that are vile, disgusting, and hateful, is itself an act of contempt. Hate, admitted into the open and circulated beyond the confines of its narrow constituency, faces scrutiny, provokes rebuttal, tempers its power to influence. Hate speech precludes an exchange of opinion. But once we engage in dialogue, then we have taken a step towards addressing the problems that stimulate hate speech. And, in doing so, we have compromised its power, or to extend the disease metaphor, applied an antidote and begun the healing process (Whillock and Slayden 1995: xvi).

The Constitution's hate speech clause, existing legislation, as well as the pending Prohibition of Hate Speech Bill, have set South Africa on a course which is likely to undermine freedom of expression and other civil liberties. While the authorities have a responsibility, even an obligation, to control civil strife, suppression of speech often exacerbates and intensifies the sentiments of those silenced by law. On the other hand, a convincing case can be made that fostering freedom of expression can result in greater tolerance among citizens with differing views. It is counterproductive to attempt to balance freedom of expression with the censorship of hate speech. Even a fragile democracy should not compromise freedom for the sake of political expediency and short-term advantages such as stability. In my view, then, the censorship of 'AmaNdiya' was contrary to the growth of a resilient democracy and vibrant civil society in post-apartheid South Africa.

References

Amato, Rob. 2002. 'Suppression of Ngema's controversial song unconstitutional', *Sunday Independent*, 14 July.

Bridgraj, Ajith. 2002. 'Inspiring the murder of Indians?', rediff.com, 30 August, http://www.rediff.com/news/2002/aug/30spec.htm

Boyte, Harry C. 2004. *Constructive Politics: The Contributions of the Institute for Democracy in South Africa*. Cape Town: IDASA.

Broadcasting Complaints Commission of South Africa, n.d. Constitution, http://www.bccsa.co.za/

Broadcasting Complaints Commission of South Africa. 2002. Case No: 2002/31 SABC-'Ngema Song', Human Rights Commission of South Africa (Complainant) vs. SABC (Ukhozi FM) (Respondent).

Cloonan, Martin. 1995. 'Not taking the rap: NWA get stranded on an island of realism', in W. Straw, S. Johnson, R. Sullivan and P. Friedlander (eds), *Popular Music: Style and Identity*. Centre for Research on Canadian Cultural Industries and Institutions, Montreal.

Coplan, David B. 2003. 'God Rock Africa', Thoughts on Politics in Popular Black Performance', Paper presented to The Seminar of the Center of African Studies, EHESS, Paris, 10 June.

Davenport, T.R.H. 1987. *South Africa: A Modern History*. Johannesburg: Macmillan. 3rd edition.

Drewett, Michael. 2004a. *An analysis of the censorship of popular music within the context of cultural struggle in South Africa during the 1980s*. PhD thesis, Rhodes University. Grahamstown.

Drewett, Michael. 2004b. 'Is anything undesirable these days? Changing dynamics in Popular Music Censorship in Post-Apartheid South Africa'. Paper presented to the Ten Years of Democracy Workshop, UNISA, Pretoria, August.

Duncan, Jane. 2003. 'To say or not to say: the dilemma of radio broadcasting in the light of South Africa's Constitution', paper presented to the Association for Christian Broadcasters Conference, Johannesburg, 11-12 February.

Du Preez, Max. 2002. 'AmaNdiya is just about prejudice', *Daily News*, Durban, available at http: www.3rdearmusic.com/forum/forumaug02/preezmbongemi.html.

Harris, Bronwyn. 2002. 'New song, same old tune?', *City Press*, 16 June, http://www.csvr.org.za/articles/arthar3.htm

Mail & Guardian online. 2002. 'It's an age-old song', 14 June, http://archive.mg.co.za/MGArchive/

Mail & Guardian online. 2002. 'Songs of hate', 28 June, http://archive.mg.co.za/MGArchive/

Maylam, Paul. 2001. 'The Historiography of South African Racism', paper presented to the conference on 'African Studies in the 20th Century', Moscow, September.

Media Institute of Southern Africa, 2004. 'Submission on the Draft Prohibition of Hate Speech Bill', http://www.misa.org/

Media Review Net. 2002. 'Ngema regrets public ban of "AmaNdiya"', 20 June, http://www.mediareviewnet.com/Ngema%20regrets20public%20ban.htm

Memela, Sandile. 2002. 'Memelang Memela: Ordinary folk need a voice', *City Press*, 22 June, http://www.news24.com/City_Press_Leaders/0,,186-189_1203192,00.html

Mill, John Stuart. 1975 [1859]. *On Liberty*. New York: Norton.

New York City News. 2002. 'Racism is poison, Mandela warns Serafina [sic] songwriter', 1 July, http://newarkcitynews.com/news/Article/Article.asp?News ID= 2409&sID=12

Raman, Parvathi. 2003. 'Yusuf Dadoo: Transnational Politics, South African Belonging', Paper presented to the Workshop on South Africa in the 1940s, Southern African Research Centre, Queen's University, Kingston, September. http://www.queensu.ca/sarc/Conferences/1940s/Raman.htm

Smith, Stephen A. 1995. 'There's Such a Thing as Free Speech' in Rita Kirk Whillock and David Slayden, eds *Hate Speech*. Thousand Oaks, Calif.: Sage Publications, pp. 226-266.

South African Human Rights Commission. 2000. 'Faultlines: Inquiry into Racism in the Media' August http://www.sahrc.org.za/faultlines.pdf

South African Human Rights Commission. 2002a. 'Hate Crimes and Hate Speech in South Africa', http://www.sahrc.org.za/hate_crimes_paper.pdf

South African Human Rights Commission. 2002b. 'Discussion Document: Freedom of Expression', 21 November, http://www.sahrc.rog.za/

Van Dijk, Teun A. 1995. 'Elite Discourse and the Reproduction of Racism' in Rita Kirk Whillock and David Slayden eds, *Hate Speech*. Thousand Oaks, California.: Sage, pp. 1-27.

Whillock, Rita Kirk and David Sladen. 1995. 'Introduction', to Rita Kirk Whillock and David Slayden eds, *Hate Speech*. Thousand Oaks, California: Sage Publications, pp. i-x.

Discography

Ngema, Mbongeni. 2002. *Jive Madlokovu!!!* Universal Music South Africa. CDRBL 293.

Chapter 5

ZVAKWANA! – ENOUGH! Media Control and Unofficial Censorship of Music in Zimbabwe

Diane Thram

Introduction

This chapter investigates the socio-political situation in Zimbabwe for its effects on freedom of expression for musicians with careers in the popular music industry.[1] It is my aim to illustrate how regime tactics have created an environment in which unofficial, *de facto* censorship of popular music has become the status quo throughout the country.[2] My focus is on the period following the emergence of the Movement for Democratic Change (MDC) in 1999 as a viable political party in opposition to Robert Mugabe's Zimbabwe African National Union-Patriotic Front (Zanu-PF) regime. Actions of the Mugabe regime since the MDC's significant showing in the 2000 Parliamentary elections have created and perpetuated an on-going political and economic crisis, hereafter referred to as the Crisis, the causes and ramifications of which will be discussed in greater detail below.

My research in Harare (2004) corroborates Eyre's 2001 study of music

---

[1] I wish to thank the editors for their helpful comments and acknowledge support from a Rhodes University Council Research Grant, which made possible the fieldwork necessary for this research. In some cases interviewees cited have requested anonymity due to their concern over possible repercussions from authorities. Quotes from these people will be cited as anonymous.

[2] In an attempt to determine present realities regarding the 'unofficial' *de facto* censorship of popular music in Zimbabwe, I conducted field research in Harare for three weeks (late July to mid-August 2004) and then four weeks (mid-September to mid-October, 2004), plus a week-long follow-up visit late April, 2005. Interviews with musicians, a former radio DJ, a club owner, producers of art exhibits, plays, music events, and TV shows, human rights defenders, journalists, writers, academics, Media Monitoring Project and recording industry personnel informed my research. In-print sources by legal and media organizations and historians' recent and forthcoming publications on the Crisis in Zimbabwe and its ramifications, plus articles by journalists writing for the major newspapers in Harare during the time of my fieldwork have provided additional information crucial to this research.

censorship in Zimbabwe by suggesting that the absence of 'official' (legally mandated) censorship of resistance/protest music by the Zanu-PF regime is at least in part because the country's only censorship law, Chapter 10: 04 Censorship and Entertainment Control Act (1967) of the former Rhodesian government, only addresses censorship in terms of morality.[3] The Censorship and Entertainments Control Act mandates the Zimbabwe Censorship Board (ZCB) to ban lewd and licentious literature, films and song lyrics, but does not address the issue of political content or protest against the state (Eyre 2001: 22). This chapter reveals how the Mugabe regime has, however, accomplished *de facto* censorship of music that speaks out against its policies and/or conditions of everyday life caused by the on-going Crisis.

This research has revealed that the regime's most overt vehicle to control and suppress public access to resistance/protest music has been enforcement of the Broadcasting Services Act (BSA) (2001) with its tight controls on what music receives airplay. Two less direct methods exist. The first of these is the Information Ministry's funding of musicians to compose music written to promote its propaganda. These regime-commissioned artists have been featured in propaganda videos that saturate state-owned television and radio stations as well as in the live entertainment 'galas' that were staged regularly as a propaganda tactic during Jonathan Moyo's five-year reign as Minister of Information and Publicity. The second is harassment of musicians at their nightclub shows by regime thugs.

The Broadcasting Services Act, enacted in March 2001, was the first of a series of repressive laws that impinge on civil liberties and freedom of expression authored by the former Minister of Information and Publicity, Jonathan Moyo, (appointed by Mugabe in 2000 and subsequently fired for insubordination in February 2005).[4] I argue that the Broadcasting Services Act was authored to legislate – make legal – the regime's desire for total control over access to the airwaves; and that by enacting the BSA the regime gave itself the ability to 'unofficially' censor dissent via mediation of popular music without risking the backlash of overt censorship mandated by rulings of the ZCB. Tangible examples of 'unofficial' *de facto* censorship of popular music and its effects are found in the state's BSA authorized control over radio and television programming and the impact on musicians' careers due to their loss of airplay.

---

[3] The full text of Chapter 10:04, Censorship and Entertainments Control Act (1967) is available at www.Kubatana.net.

[4] Other repressive laws passed soon thereafter are the following: POSA (Public Order and Security Act) enacted January 2002, which severely curtails freedom of assembly, movement, and expression; GLAA (General Laws Amendment Act) enacted January 2002, which disenfranchises approximately two million Zimbabweans living outside the country; and AIPPA (Access to Information and Protection of Privacy Act) enacted March 2002, which puts restrictive controls on journalists and media institutions (MMPZ 2002: 24-8).

It can also be argued that the isolation from anything beyond state-controlled radio and television experienced by the majority of Zimbabweans who do not have radios capable of tuning in short-wave, medium-wave, or foreign FM stations or the funds to purchase satellite television or access to the internet constitutes unofficial censorship. Although mediation of the regime's propagandized music is not a form of censorship *per se*, I argue with Raftopolous (2004a: 1; Interview 2004) that the onslaught of the state's propaganda through manipulation of the airwaves and state-owned newspapers is intended to cut the populous off from alternative views and as such constitutes *de facto* censorship.[5]

A synopsis of effects of the Crisis on the context for artists is followed by a brief historical accounting of the banning of music in Zimbabwe since the 1960s, with examples of state reactions to controversial hits of Zimbabwean super-stars Thomas Mapfumo and Oliver Mtukudzi. Media control tactics of the Ministry of Information and Publicity found in its authoring of the Broadcasting Services Act, its promotion of 'urban grooves' and the 'Third Chimurenga Series' and 'Pax Afro' music composed for its media campaigns, plus its sponsorship of live music 'galas' are then documented below as evidence of how *de facto* censorship of popular music was an aim the former Information Minister Jonathan Moyo accomplished during his five-year tenure as Mugabe's propaganda 'spin doctor'.

The Crisis and its effects on the context for artists

Zimbabwe has been under Robert Mugabe's Zanu-PF leadership since his election as the first president of the newly independent Zimbabwean nation in 1980, after the Second Chimurenga liberation struggle ended with the defeat of Ian Smith's independent white Rhodesian government in 1979. In the early 1980s the populace experienced an initial post-independence euphoria that witnessed both black and white citizens filled with optimism for the future of the nation. A slow and steady decline in the nation's economy and infrastructure, years of procrastination over the land reclamation issue, and widespread corruption have contributed to the

---

[5] The regime has so far done nothing to interfere with publication and distribution of books that document its human rights abuses, which include the passage of legislation that violates the freedoms guaranteed in the nation's Constitution. Weaver Press (http://www.weaverpresszimbabwe.com), a private publisher in Harare, has released an impressive series of books dealing with social issues, history and politics, and literature since 1999. In addition, two NGO publications carefully document government actions, including legislation inhibiting freedom of expression passed in the run-up to the 2002 presidential election: *Zimbabwe Human Rights Bulletin*, Issue No 5, September 2001, produced by Zimbabwe Lawyers for Human Rights ISSN 1562-5958; and *Media under Siege: Report on media coverage of the 2002 Presidential and Mayoral Elections,* produced by Media Monitoring Project Zimbabwe ISBN 0-7974-2736-8.

conditions that gave rise to the unrelenting socio-political and economic Crisis now in its sixth year (*cf* Hammar and Raftopoulos 2004: 1-47).

Rapid devaluation of the Zimbabwe dollar and sky-rocketing inflation sparked by a huge government pay-out of pensions to war veterans in 1999, defeat of the government's draft constitution in the referendum of 12-13 February 2000, government-sanctioned violent land invasions by supposed war veterans within weeks thereafter, growing strength of the opposition Movement for Democratic Change (MDC) witnessed in the violent 24-5 June 2000 Parliamentary elections (35 people died before and during the elections) in which the MDC won 61 seats, and systematic assault on the country's justice system are all contributing factors to the crisis (Raftopolous 2004b: 13-15) which has again deepened in the wake of the Parliamentary elections held on 31 March 2005. Upheaval throughout society, 80 per cent unemployment, renewed food and fuel shortages, violence against MDC supporters, and the regime's May-June 2005 assault on the 'informal' business sector and the urban poor spell the chaotic realities of life for the vast majority of Zimbabweans.

The regime's overt manipulation of day-to-day life is apparent in the state-owned and controlled newspapers (Zimpapers) and its legislated control over state-owned broadcasting media through its monopoly, ZBC. There are no privately owned television or radio stations in Zimbabwe. The airwaves and state-owned Zimpapers (*The Herald* and the *Sunday Mail* in Harare and *The Chronicle* in Bulawayo) are vehicles for dissemination of the regime's relentless propaganda themes of patriotism, sovereignty, and 'national values'.[6] Liberation struggle tactics of the Second Chimurenga (war for independence from white rule) were resurrected at the time of the regime's land reclamation exercise in 2000 to proclaim and fight the 'Third Chimurenga' against any and all opponents of the regime.

Yet, in the midst of its on-going Crisis and the regime's pervasive intolerance of any form of dissent, when this research was conducted in the latter half of 2004, Zimbabwe remained a country with an exceptionally rich output of creative expression in music, literature, theatre, fine arts and crafts. The arts were thriving in spite of, and perhaps stimulated by, the current social reality of legislated media control (BSA) and the unofficial censorship of music routinely imposed by the

---

[6] The remaining privately owned newspapers, *the Financial Gazette*, the *Standard* and the *Zimbabwe Independent*, are openly critical of the regime. The *Daily Mirror* and the *Sunday Mirror* are owned by Ibo Mandaza, a prominent Zanu-PF member. The very popular Associated Newspapers of Zimbabwe's (ANZ) the *Daily News* and the *Daily News on Sunday* was forcibly closed down in September 2003 when its offices were bombed and the courts ruled it was operating illegally under the regulations imposed by AIPPA (Access to Information and Protection of Privacy Act). The only short-lived independent television station, *Joy TV*, and the privately-owned *The Tribune* newspaper were also closed down in 2003 by enforcement of AIPPA regulations (Njini, F. Financial Gazette 24 December 2004; ZWNEWS from IRIN (UN) 1 January 2005).

Information Ministry. However, possibilities for commercial success for artists had been limited drastically by what everyone referred to as the 'economic hardship' brought on by the collapse of the currency and the economy. And musicians had suffered particularly adverse effects in the wake of the regime's legislated '100 per cent local' and its unofficial '100 per cent patriotic' policy in determining what music gets airplay on ZBC radio and television.

The ruling party's promotion of ultra-patriotism through its domination of the media and its creation of the youth militia (whose enlistees are indoctrinated in 'patriotic history' by war veterans) has produced a highly polarized society which, according to regime rhetoric, consists of revolutionaries (those who support the regime) and sell-outs (all the rest) (Ranger 2004: 11-16). Abundant evidence of the regime's use of music and dances indigenous to Shona culture as well as the music of the Second Chimurenga liberation war is found in its relentless radio and television propaganda campaigns and its release of commercial recordings to accompany them from 2000 through early 2005 when Jonathan Moyo was removed from his post as Minister of Information and Publicity. Former Information Minister Moyo used the music mentioned above as a vehicle for dissemination of 'patriotic history', the ruling party's corrected, narrowed version of the history of the liberation struggle (*cf* Ranger 2004). I argue that the regime's manipulation and use of indigenous music and dance and music of the nation's liberation struggle in its mediated propaganda is evidence of its exploitation of cultural identity and national pride, and that this tactic is the product of the anti-imperialist, openly racist and isolationist ideology of an authoritarian nationalism determined to consolidate and retain its power.

I further argue that the most glaring problem for musicians is the unofficial, *de facto* censorship of music on the airwaves that has now, in the sixth year of the Crisis, become the status quo. Adjacent problems are the self-censorship felt necessary by many musician/song-writers working to establish commercial careers in the intimidating socio-political climate and the intimidation experienced by musicians at their nightclub performances. For artists, whatever their specialty, the prevailing admonition is Be Careful! For a clandestine 'pressure group' whose graffiti graces bus stops throughout Harare, the message is *ZVAKWANA!* – ENOUGH!

The crisis deepened further when, in the midst of renewed food and fuel shortages following the 31 March 2005 parliamentary elections, Mugabe's regime deployed riot police and the youth brigade backed by bulldozers on 19 May 2005 in Operation *Murambatsvina*. Translated, 'destroy the filth', this ruthless clean-up campaign – ostensibly intended to eradicate the parallel/black market, recover foreign currency, and clean up the nation's cities – is compared in the press to the Pol Pot 'peasantification campaign' in Cambodia. News analysts are saying that the Mugabe regime's 'war on the poor' is punishing urban dwellers who voted for the opposition by driving them back to the countryside where they will be 're-educated' (www.zwnews.com).

At the time of this writing (late June 2005), with the nation's urban slums transformed into refugee camps (estimates indicate up to 1.5 million people have been left homeless), the wanton violent arrests and destruction of the homes, market stalls and belongings of untold thousands of the nation's urban poor who have resorted to informal trading as their sole means of survival continue despite an outcry from local and international human rights organizations (www.zwnews.com). This flagrant violation of human rights in Zimbabwe has exponentially added to the 'climate of fear' reigning in the country since the regime's enactment in 2001 of repressive laws legalizing media control and militaristic control of public spaces (*cf* Eyre 2001).

The ZCB and unofficial 'banning' of Mapfumo and Mtukudzi hits

The Censorship and Entertainments Control Act (Chapter 10:04, 1967, amended in 1981 and 1997), enacted during the Rhodesian era, mandates the creation of the Zimbabwe Censorship Board, spells out its responsibilities, and dictates the types of films and publications to be censored. The law addresses issues of obscenity, lewdness and personal defamation; however, it contains nothing explicit about political content. Eyre's 2001 research on censorship of music in Zimbabwe led him to assert that authorities deliberately avoid official censorship because they are aware of the dangers of it backfiring and actually elevating the popularity of the censored artist and his or her message. This type of reversal was witnessed during the 1970s with the official banning by the Rhodesian Censorship Board (RCB) of Thomas Mapfumo's political protest music which came to be known as 'Chimurenga Music'.

There is no record of official censorship by the ZCB of music by Zimbabwean artists since the creation of the independent Zimbabwean state in 1980. Eyre's (2001: 47) interviews with radio DJs indicate that written instructions banning certain music are consciously avoided for fear of repercussions from the independent press, and that unwritten directives are the method of choice by those determining the programming on Zimbabwean radio and television.

The ZCB has been largely inactive in the years since independence except to censor lewd, obscene, or sexually explicit films or literature of foreign origin. The Rhodesian regime, on the other hand, routinely used the RCB to ban records, not for political content, but because of lyrics thought to be immoral, until the banning of Mapfumo's protest music at the height of the guerrilla war of the 1970s mentioned above (Eyre 2001: 44). The only occasion of legally enforced censorship by the ZCB was in May, 2004 when it banned the re-staging of *Super Patriots and Morons*, a political satire produced for the 2004 Harare International Festival of the Arts (HIFA). The ZCB cited the 1967 Censorship and Entertainment Control Act as justification for their action and imposed a regulation that thenceforth all play scripts must be submitted to the ZCB before any theatre production can be staged (www.kubatana.net/html/archive/

artcul/04051). No such official monitoring by the ZCB of song lyrics has as yet been demanded (Interview with Maparutsa 2004).

The ZCB was not involved in the banning of controversial songs of Zimbabwean super-stars, such as Mapfumo's 'Corruption' (1988), 'Mamvemwe' (1999) and 'Disaster' (1999) and Mtukudzi's 'Wasakara' (2000). Eyre suggests that the regime, with its state-owned media and its influence on the music industry, has developed ways to restrict freedom of expression that make official proclamations of censorship unnecessary (Eyre 2001 22-3; 42). The impact of the regime's unofficial tactics is evidenced in the rumoured – never admitted or official – banning from airplay of the above-mentioned songs, and the harassment from authorities in 2000 that led to Mapfumo's decision to leave Zimbabwe and live in exile in the USA (Eyre 2001: 68-74; Zindi 2003: 67).[7]

More recent examples are found in Oliver Mtukudzi's experience surrounding live performances and airplay of his recordings. After the widely reported incident on 29 December 2000, when the lighting engineer was arrested and spent four days in jail for shining a spotlight on a portrait of the president while Mtukudzi and his band played the hit, 'Wasakara' (2000) *trans.* 'You are old and should step down' the song was no longer heard on the radio (Eyre 2001: 76-9). Another song entitled 'Murimi Mhunu' (2001), *trans.* 'A farmer is a person too', was interpreted as anti-land reclamation and consequently never received airplay (Interview with Zindi 2004). When interviewed (2004) about this kind of unofficial banning of his songs, Mtukudzi commented that he used to hear his music on the radio at least several times a week, but now he almost never does. He said, when people call in to request his songs 'they are told the CD is not available, or some such excuse.'

Eyre's interviews with Radio 3 (Power FM) DJs, quoted in his *Playing With Fire* (2001) suggest that ZBC DJs are rarely explicitly told what not to play but somehow they just know, which in turn suggests the DJs themselves are self-censoring what they play because of surveillance of their work (Eyre 2001: 48, 70, 72). A former ZBC DJ told me that directives on what music is to be played and what music is not to be played are given verbally rather than in writing (Interview with anonymous 1 2004). I was also told that the practice of never putting policy into writing is a government strategy, apparently to protect itself from recrimination. Even the land reform policy was never put into writing (Interview with Goddard 2004).

---

[7] Eyre (2001: 64-75) provides details of the circumstances surrounding the interpretation of lyrics in the Mapfumo and Mtukudzi songs and restrictions on their airplay. He also gives an account of Mapfumo's decision to move with his family to the USA in the wake of harassment in 2000 after the release of his 'Chimurenga Explosion' (1999).

Broadcasting Services Act

It is perhaps self-evident that, because broadcasting is the number one communication tool in Zimbabwe, the regime chose to accomplish unofficial, *de facto* censorship of popular music through control over programming on ZBC radio and television. The ZBC and the Rhodesian Broadcasting Corporation (RBC) it replaced enjoyed and continue to enjoy a total monopoly on radio and television broadcasting. Until the revisions enacted in March 2001 as the Broadcasting Services Act, the RBC and ZBC operated under the Broadcasting Act (1957) enacted by the government of Southern Rhodesia, which gave the government sole broadcast rights (Media Monitoring Project Zimbabwe 2002: 24).

Enactment of the BSA (2001) imposed regulations designed to make it impossible for independent (private) radio or television stations to operate in Zimbabwe. It also imposed a 75 per cent local content mandate on music permitted to receive airplay. By 2003, Information Minister Moyo had used his authority to raise the local content mandate to 100 per cent on all but one (Radio 1 airs 75 per cent local and 25 per cent international) of the four ZBC radio stations (Interview with anonymous 2 2004).

The story of an attempt to launch a privately-owned, alternative radio station in Harare is presented to inform the reader of the event that precipitated passage of the BSA as the regime's main vehicle for unofficial censorship. Capital Radio set itself up to broadcast in September 2000 after winning a Supreme Court judgment which was reported thus:

> In September, 2000 Capital Radio (Private) Limited took the Government to the Supreme Court to challenge Section 27 of the Broadcasting Act (1957), which provided for a state monopoly over all broadcasting (radio and television) in Zimbabwe. In its judgment, the Supreme Court found the Broadcasting Act to be unconstitutional. It violated the public's right to receive and impart information and the constitutional right of freedom of expression. It therefore ordered the opening up of the airwaves to other broadcasters. (Media Monitoring Project Zimbabwe 2002: 24)

With this judgment to back her project, and as the government was rushing to introduce the Broadcasting Services Bill in Parliament (designed in reaction to the Supreme Court decision with the obvious intention to block any possibility of private broadcasting) former ZBC announcer Geraldine Jackson rushed to launch Capital Radio from a temporary studio in the Monomutapa Hotel in downtown Harare. Capital Radio was illegally shut down and its equipment confiscated by government militia after only six days of broadcasting (Eyre 2001: 84-6).

In immediate response to Capital Radio's brief tenure as a private radio broadcaster the government forced new 'Broadcasting Regulations' through Parliament as a six-month temporary measure using the Presidential Powers (Temporary Measures) Act. These Broadcasting Measures and their replacement, the Broadcasting Services Act (Chapter 2:06) passed in March 2001, were authored and set before Parliament by the then Information and Publicity Minister Jonathan Moyo (Media Monitoring Project Zimbabwe 2002: 24). In terms of this legislation, the Information Minister was empowered with the sole authority to decide who is granted licence and the conditions attached, plus the authority to modify the conditions at any time. Licensing controls imposed by the BSA have served to make start-up and operation of private radio or television impossible in Zimbabwe (Goredema 2001: 106-8; Media Monitoring Project Zimbabwe 2002: 24-5).

The BSA gave the Minister of Information 'new authority to "stop, scramble, obliterate or interfere with" any broadcast to Zimbabwe from beyond our borders' (Cheater 2001: 11). It demands that all stations read the 'official' news, cover events declared by the Minister of Information to be national events, mandates 75 per cent local content (later revised to 100 per cent local content on all but one station), and prohibits any one person from holding more than a 10 per cent share in a company applying for a licence, in addition to the other restrictions listed above. Goredema (2001: 110) says, 'The passing of the Broadcasting Act demonstrates that, far from opening up the airwaves, government is committed to closing access to them, in its belief that they would open an avenue for alternative views'.

SW Radio Africa and short-wave Voice of America (VOA) Studio 7 which transmits from 7-8 p.m. daily and on its website www.voanews.com are the only sources of alternative radio available in Zimbabwe for those privileged enough to have access to a short-wave radio and/or the internet. These stations air commentary on the Crisis as well as recordings of Zimbabwean musicians whose music is not getting airtime on ZBC. Using the authority granted by the BSA to interfere with broadcasts from beyond its borders, the regime has been jamming the transmission signal of Short-wave Radio Africa (operated from London by the founders of Capital Radio) since the run-up to the parliamentary election of March 2005. ZWNEWS (1 June 2005) reported that the expense of broadcasting on multiple frequencies necessary for SW Radio Africa since the jamming has been prohibitive thus requiring the management to stop its twice daily short-wave offerings and transmit only on medium-wave 1197 kHz from 5-7 a.m. daily, and on its website www.swradioafrica.com.

The above demonstrates the regime's efforts to cut the masses off from alternative views. The result is *de facto* censorship that deprives the public of access to information from the outside world, and also of airplay of Zimbabwean popular music with lyrics that protest day-to-day realities of life in the Crisis.

Media control

Pervasive control of the airwaves and the news media through repressive legislation and the saturation of ZBC radio and television with the regime's propaganda campaigns were Information Minister Moyo's methods of choice to indoctrinate the populace. Media control and the use of music for communication of the regime's propaganda were the hallmarks of Moyo's strategy, witnessed in the release of the Information Minister's especially commissioned CD/cassette compilations of music intended to communicate the regime's political messages of a resurrected liberation struggle, ultra-patriotism, land reclamation, anti-colonialism, and pan-Africanism.

Moyo, in the BSA, legislated funds for patronage of musicians to create the music for his media campaigns by giving the Ministry of Information and Publicity permission to use the Broadcasting Fund to 'provide grants and financial assistance to Zimbabwean creative artists. He was later reportedly accused by artists of "trying to use the Broadcasting Fund to fund, control and govern artistic productions for political ends"' (Cheater 2001:11; *cf* Media Monitoring Project Zimbabwe 2002: 24-6). This accusation is documented in the many songs written by regime-sponsored artists with lyrics in support of government policies on the CD/cassette compilations commissioned by the Information Ministry, such as 'The Third Chimurenga Series' releases: 'Third Chimurenga' (2000), 'Hondo ye Minda' (2001), 'More Fire' (2002); and Moyo's self-authored 'Pax Afro' (2004) music.

Mai Palmberg (2004: 12), in discussing her research on the political use of music in Zimbabwe, concludes that 'the lyrics do not contain a personality cult of President Mugabe, but rather extol the policies, threaten the opponents and legitimize violence'. She finds that the ruling party politicizes music: first, by commissioning songs and funding performances and second, by supporting groups who do not criticize the regime by giving them airtime on radio and TV, inviting them to perform in video clips for their TV propaganda campaigns, and inviting them to play at their festivals (galas).

The then Information Minister Moyo, himself a drummer and songwriter, manipulated the airwaves for political purposes by funding the production of a series of well-produced propagandistic recordings mentioned above. Labelled as the *Third Chimurenga Series*, it began with the release of *Third Chimurenga* (2000). *Third Chimurenga* has 18 tracks of reworked liberation war era songs plus self-authored songs such as 'All Proud Zimbabweans' (2000) (Eyre 2001: 43). Another release in the series, 'Hondo Yeminda' (*trans.* War of the Land) vols 1 and 2 (2001), features Dick Chingaira, better known as 'Comrade Chinx', and the Police Band also performing reworked liberation war era music. Chinx is a singer/songwriter (famous from his airplay on Voice of Zimbabwe radio from 1974-79) who specialized in using 'liberation songs' to teach revolutionary ideology, carry messages from leaders, and boost morale among villagers and troops during the Second Chimurenga (Turino 2000: 192). This was followed by 'More Fire' (2002), produced by Zimbabwean pop singer/songwriter Andy Brown.

Moyo's mid-2004 release of entirely self-authored songs, *Pax Afro* is performed by a Bulawayo-based group he named 'Back2Black' apparently to enhance the political message of the compilation. The music on *PaxAfro* (2004), promoted as a unique 'pan-African' style, sounds like generic Western pop with some exceptions that sound reminiscent of Jit, a popular style in Zimbabwe associated with the rural areas. Song lyrics often feature propaganda regarding patriotism, sovereignty, land reform, and pan-Africanism. At the time of my field research in October 2004, selections from Moyo's self-proclaimed new 'pan-African style' on *PaxAfro* were flooding the Radio 3 (Power FM) airwaves every quarter of an hour, at least 10-15 times per day (Interview with S. Mujokoro 2004; Interview with anonymous 2 2004).

A *Sunday Mail* (Zimpapers), feature article (10 October 2004: 7) headlined 'Information Department lives up to its mandate' seeks to legitimize Information Minister Moyo's music propaganda recording projects by reviewing how they had fulfilled the President's expectations of the Department. According to the article, Moyo's mandate was to 'disseminate information, whilst at the same time bringing people together in a merry and jovial mood'. Of *Pax Afro* (2004), and the Department of Information and Publicity's mission, the unnamed 'features reporter' says:

> PaxAfro is effectively the culmination of all the projects in the catalogue into a positive African statement ... where the country is speaking to the world against a backdrop of and achievement in the form of a successful land reform programme. It is evident that the Department helped artistes do what they wanted to do and not what the Department foisted down their throats in the name of policy implementation. If the efforts of the Department were not noble, why then would seasoned artistes agree to work with them? It is obvious that they noticed nobility behind the efforts of the Department. The artistes were not given a voice but rather their existing voices were given the platform to be heard. (*Sunday Mail* 10 October 2004: 11)

The article goes on to praise urban grooves and the 'phenomenon of galas' for giving an opportunity to the youth, who were unable to participate in the revolution, a chance to "actively take part in nation building and expression of the state's policies through the 'musical Press (sic) release form'" (*Sunday Mail* 10 October 2004: 11). The patronage and promotion of 'urban grooves' and regime sponsored 'galas' is discussed below as further evidence of how media control has accomplished *de facto* censorship of broadcasting of protest/resistance music in Zimbabwe.

Urban Grooves

Airtime on Radio 3 'Power FM' – the youth oriented station – with sanction from the Information Ministry, is filled with local recordings by young, most often inexperienced musicians who are mimicking dancehall (ragga), r & b, hip-hop, and rap and calling it 'urban grooves'. Typically urban grooves recordings feature lyrics in Shona sung over sampled sounds. This music generally has shallow, insignificant lyrics and by all accounts cannot be considered distinctively

Zimbabwean or representative of the culture. Lack of musical competence has caused the quality of music heard on the radio to seriously deteriorate since imposition of the 100 per cent local mandate (Interview with anonymous 3 2004; Interview with Mtukudzi 2004; Interview with Zindi 2004). Yet, the urban grooves phenomenon has flourished due to its guarantee of airplay with the 100 per cent local mandate and its non-controversial lyrics. Another factor contributing to the rise of urban grooves was the official lifting of the formerly very high import taxes on electronic equipment. This led to the opening of many new recording studios in Harare, which in turn caused a marked increase in the production of CDs by local musicians in the urban grooves style (Interviews with anonymous 2 and 5 2004).

Oliver Mtudkudzi, despite his great popularity, has noticed that he receives very little airplay of his recent releases, presumably because his lyrics can be interpreted as critical of the regime. In discussing this problem (Interview 2004) and his responsibility, as a Shona person living true to his cultural values, to write song lyrics that are meaningful and reflect current social realities, Mtukudzi said, 'In my songs I talk about the truth, that's all'. In the same interview (2004), Mtukudzi questioned the 100 per cent local policy and the constant airplay of urban grooves on Power FM arguing, 'listeners need to know what is happening outside the country. Because there are no controls on quality, there is very little that is worth listening to'. In his opinion, urban grooves song lyrics are 'controversial to African culture'. When asked what he meant by 'controversial to African culture' he said, 'in African culture song lyrics are not acceptable if they are meaningless, and unfortunately the songs being churned out for urban grooves have nonsense lyrics that anybody can make up'. He argued further that the level of musicianship is very questionable, since in most cases the would-be musicians are 'simply cutting and pasting and not actually playing the music themselves'.

The Standard (8 August 2004), in its Sunday arts supplement, revealed Power FM's plans to re-launch its urban grooves' Top-40 show with a new requirement that only recordings backed by music videos will be considered for the chart show. R. Mberi's article, 'Power FM's Top 40 back with controversial catch' points out that the video requirement is an insurmountable obstacle for many musicians hoping to be considered. Asking why the show host, Admire Taderera would impose such a requirement, Mberi argues, 'The new proposals also expose the difficulty that Taderera faces in trying to justify a chart show of *music that basically sounds the same*' (Mberi 2004: 1, emphasis mine).

The effect is that, although some of the nation's youth jump on the urban grooves bandwagon and a select few are building recording careers as urban grooves artists, more discerning listeners simply no longer listen to Radio 3. Some report being so put off by the amount of propaganda in the programming that they no longer listen to ZBC radio at all. More seriously, local artists unwilling to abandon their cultural aesthetic with its expectation of meaningful lyrics or compromise their music to fit the standards for urban grooves set by the Information Minister receive no airplay. In the process they become victims of the unofficial/*de facto* censorship that takes place routinely on ZBC radio and television (Interviews with anonymous 1 and 3 2004).

The regime's courting of the quasi-hip, urban youth culture through promotion of urban grooves in conjunction with the 100 per cent local programming mandate is a reality replete with paradox. The lack of quality musicianship and the insipid character of urban grooves song lyrics are seen as an erosion of Shona cultural values by Oliver Mtudkudzi (Interview 2004). But, paradoxically, the recording industry has been stimulated; so much so that the major recording studios in Harare (Gramma and Shed) were constantly busy at the time of this research, despite the many new studios producing recordings for the local market. Recording studio personnel agreed that the recording industry is stronger now than before the 100 per cent local airplay policy was instituted, and this despite industry marketing personnel reports that urban grooves recordings do not sell well (Interviews with anonymous 6 and 7 2004).

Government galas

Until Jonathan Moyo's demise as Mugabe's propaganda 'spin doctor' early in 2005, the recurring regime-sponsored all-night 'galas' he orchestrated were staged in various locations throughout the country and offered a line up of well-known musical groups as entertainment. The galas also gave Zanu-PF a political platform for its candidates and/or elected officials. Walter Maparutsa (Interview 2004), theatre producer and human rights advocate offered this opinion of the regime's need for the galas by saying, 'sponsoring these music events is the only way the ruling party can draw a crowd. People will not attend if it is simply a political rally'. The social and entertainment value of galas hold an appeal, but there is also a great deal of controversy surrounding them, which is documented briefly here as further evidence of the ruling party's 'use' of some musicians to the detriment of others hoping to compete in the market for popular music in Zimbabwe.

Beyond the political agenda of galas, during the time of this research accusations of corruption, mismanagement, and affront to indigenous customs were common. Concerned citizens complained about 'use of the dead' for propaganda, as a violation of cultural values of the Shona. M.N. Mandaza, in a letter to *The Standard* (10 October 2004), suggested that Moyo's use of the recently deceased vice-Presidents of Zimbabwe, Joshua Nkomo and Simon Muzenda, as themes for galas was 'unAfrican'. 'What really is the purpose and significance of all these galas and splushes? Where in the name of sanity is all the money going?' he asks.

Moyo's most ambitious all-night gala, 'The Solidarity Bash' overtly sought to regionalize the regime's reach. It was staged in Chimoio, Mozambique on 9 October 2004. Participants were solicited via radio and television ads and transported to the event in buses supplied by the Information Ministry. The event was televised in Angola, Namibia, Mozambique and Zimbabwe and broadcast on all four ZBC radio stations at great expense to the regime. The Solidarity Bash was followed by a media blitz featuring headlines such as 'PaxAfro fever grips city' (*Sunday Mail*, 17 October 2004) and full page ads to promote Moyo's 'PaxAfro' release with a live concert at the Harare International Convention Center on 29 October 2004.

The manipulation of music for political ends is glaringly apparent in the galas, the *Third Chimurenga Series* and *PaxAfro* CD/cassette releases, and the television ads for both that were produced by the Ministry of Information under Moyo's watch. Although this use of music for propaganda does not constitute censorship *per se*, the festival-like music galas promoted the careers of the musicians who participated via exposure from radio and television adverts for the galas that saturated the airwaves, ZBC's live coverage of the events, and increased airplay of their music. Meanwhile non-participating musicians' careers were stymied because, due to their refusal to buy into the party line and participate and the Information Ministry's control over programming, their recordings received no airplay (Interview with anonymous 2 2004).

Intimidation and unofficial censorship

Unofficial censorship of music has been accomplished at live performance venues through bullying and intimidation by the militia, war veterans, and party stalwarts, who demand that certain songs not be played and threaten to use force to disrupt shows of musicians whose work has been interpreted to be critical of the regime. This has been done by threatening the bandleaders and band members before shows and during breaks. Musicians report that their bands have been told they are not welcome when they arrive to play at venues in rural areas known to be Zanu-PF strongholds. Bandleader Leonard Zhakata (Interview 2004) told me that, when this happened to him, he decided no longer to play those venues because of potential danger to his band and his fans. Oliver Mtukudzi (Interview 2004) described his experience of this type of harassment at a rural nightclub he has played for years, as 'one of the worst nights of my life'.

In another example of intimidation, a club manager reported being harassed by a group of men, apparently employed by the ruling party, who started to frequent his venue. They drank excessively while observing events at the venue and generally harassed the musicians performing there, the waiters, and the customers. They wanted to know why the manager was no longer booking Andy Brown and Tambaoga, both former critics of the regime who had since been regarded as 'sellouts' because they worked for the Information Minister. The same men came in nearly every night for several months. One night in 2003 they forced all the white customers to line up and salute them. They threatened to use their weapons on the customers if they did not do as they asked and threatened to close the place. Their presence made everyone uneasy and definitely kept customers away (Interview with anonymous 5 2004).

Career damage

Career damage has been experienced not only by musicians perceived to be anti the Mugabe regime, but also by those with previously successful local careers who have chosen to cooperate with Information Minister Moyo. It is possible that those who worked for the Minister by writing and performing songs for his media campaigns and playing at the regime-sponsored live 'galas' did so because they agree with the regime's political tactics and are truly ultra-patriotic; but there is no doubt that they did so because they need the income from playing at the galas, wanted support to make recordings, and wanted the precious airplay that cooperation with the Information Ministry afforded. However, despite securing airplay, musicians in favour with the regime often lost the respect of their fans and were labelled as 'sellouts' (Interviews with anonymous 4 and 5 2004).

The story of how the government contributed millions of Zimbabwe dollars to set up Andy Brown's Stone Studio has been widely reported (Palmberg 2004: 11). Brown in return adapted, arranged, and produced the music on 'More Fire' (2002), one of the 'Third Chimurenga Series' media campaign recordings. A manager/event promoter working in Harare attested (Interview 2004) to the career damage suffered by Brown in the aftermath and claimed the public has 'demonized' him in reaction to his decision to work for the regime. This manager, who witnessed him being booed by the crowd at a concert, reported that his record sales and opportunities for live performance have both fallen off drastically and that it is generally felt that the damage to his career is irreparable.

In contrast there is Leonard Zhakata, a singer/song-writer with great popularity throughout the country ever since he released his first record in 1988. Zhakata (Interview 2004) claims his lyrics have always spoken to the problems of daily life since long before the onset of the Crisis. However, his career (both in terms of CD sales and income from touring throughout Zimbabwe) has suffered since 2000-2001 when he lost airplay because certain song lyrics in his recent releases have been interpreted as critical of the regime. When Zhakata contacted ZBC radio to ask why his recent recordings are not receiving airplay, ZBC's legal adviser told him that his music has not been banned. Yet when he asked DJs why they no longer play his music, they replied that they were told (they did not say by whom) not to play it because it is 'politically incorrect'. Zhakata says of his music, 'I have fans from both political parties. I sing a straightforward message meant to be encouragement for everyone. My most popular songs are against exploitation of the weak. I can't abandon that'.

Despite Zhakata's intention to remain politically neutral, in April 2004 the pressure group *Zvakwana* pirated one of his songs for a compilation CD of 'resistance music' they made available for free download from the internet. When news of the CD got out, *The Standard* (18 April 2004) reported that Zhakata had been called in for questioning by the police. According to Zhakata (Interview 2004), the police did not harass him; they were only interested in what he knew about *Zvakwana*, which was nothing. Unfortunately, *Zvakwana* never approached

Zhakata for permission to use his song, and by pirating it they further politicized his music, which served to entrench his reputation as an artist who speaks out against the regime, when in fact he views his music as apolitical. Zhakata (Interview 2004) described the career damage he has suffered by losing airplay as very serious by saying, 'In our part of the world people rely on very few sources of information. Without media support your career is in trouble.'

Conclusion

The examples discussed in this chapter have been presented to support my argument that unofficial/*de facto* censorship of popular music, restriction of free expression, and career damage to pop musicians have become the status quo in Zimbabwe since passage of the Broadcasting Services Act in 2001. Although no 'official' censorship of music by the ZCB has as yet occurred, an album of protest music released by an outspoken Harare pressure group, the National Constitutional Assembly (NCA) in the aftermath of the 2005 parliamentary election may provide a test case. The NCA album was banned by the police just before its scheduled release at a public event. After the cancellation of the event due to the police ban, the NCA decided to release the album on 18 May 2005 in defiance of the police ban, arguing that the police had no authority to ban it. In response the regime sent the album to the ZCB for assessment (www.zwnews.com). The ZCB's decision in this case has not been reported to date, perhaps because news of the regime's *Murambatsvina* clean-up campaign – instigated the following day – has dominated the press ever since.

The information presented in this chapter gives a glimpse of on-the-ground realities during the time of my field research and as such speaks only for the conditions and opinions of those interviewed during that particular historical moment. From it I have drawn the following conclusion: the ruling party's resurrection of the cultural nationalism[8] of the Second Chimurenga with its *Third Chimurenga Series* media campaigns, together with the ultra-patriotic themes of the government-sponsored 'galas' has set musicians up to be used by the regime to promote its ideology through the music they are commissioned to write and perform. Musicians who prefer to be apolitical and those who refuse to work for the regime on moral grounds face the threat of no work and no airplay, plus the fear of more serious repercussions if their music is viewed as critical of ruling-party policies. The regime's isolationist rhetoric of patriotism and sovereignty that was written into the song lyrics on the Information Minister's CD/cassette releases deliberately created an enemy in the menacing Western 'other' which contributed to the climate of fear prevalent throughout the country.

---

[8] Turino defines cultural nationalism as 'the use of art and other cultural practices to develop or maintain national sentiment for political purposes' (Turino 2000: 14).

I further conclude that the impact of the Broadcasting Services Act's legislated media control and the attendant restriction of free expression actualized by the Ministry of Information under Jonathan Moyo's leadership has been felt most acutely by musicians with local careers who, as creative artists, feel a need to honestly express themselves through their music. These are the many musicians who, unlike the Zimbabwean super-stars Mapfumo and Mtukudzi, have not established global recognition and therefore rely on local airplay and live performance opportunities to establish their careers. They do not have the luxury of recording contracts and international distributors for their recordings. It quickly becomes apparent that issues of power and powerlessness are paramount in a reality that finds musicians, when they express the truth of their experience in their song lyrics, with no access to airplay. Without airplay and with very few venues for live performance beyond the ruling party sponsored 'galas', there is little chance for a musician in Zimbabwe who performs popular music to mount a successful career.

References

Cheater, A. 2001. 'Human Rights in Zimbabwe January – June 2001 A Baseline Report', *Zimbabwe Human Rights Bulletin* 5, pp. 2-100.

Eyre, B. 2001. *Playing with Fire. Fear and Self-Censorship in Zimbabwean Music.* Copenhagen: Freemuse.

Features Reporter. 2004. 'Information Department lives up to its mandate.' The Sunday Mail. (Harare) October 10. pp. 7, 11.

Goredema, C. 2001. 'Human rights legislative survey January – June 2001', *Zimbabwe Human Rights Bulletin 5*, pp. 101-14.

Hammar, A. and B. Raftopoulos. 2004. "Zimbabwe's Unfinished Business: Rethinking Land, State and Nation." in *Zimbabwe's Unfinished Business.* Harare: Weaver Press. A. Hammar, B. Raftopoulos and S. Jensen eds, pp. 1-47.

Khosa, T. 2004. 'Hosiah lashes out at Heroesplush organisers', Daily Mirror. (Harare) August 12, p. 12.

Mandaza, M.N. 2004. 'UnAfrican for ZTV to use the dead for propaganda.' The Standard. (Harare) October 10, p. 8.

Mberi, R. 2004. 'Power FM's Top-40 back with controversial catch', The Standard (Harare) August 8, p. 1.

Media Monitoring Project Zimbabwe. 2002. *Media under Siege.* Report on media coverage of the 2002 Presidential and Mayoral elections in Zimbabwe. Harare: Media Monitoring Project Zimbabwe.

Muleya, D. 2004. 'Splat goes the master of spin.' Mail and Guardian. (Johannesburg) December 10-16, p. 30.

Njini, F. 2004. 'Daily News to reopen.' Financial Gazette. (Harare) 24 December 2004, pp. unknown. (from http//www.zwnews.com)

Palmberg, M. 2004. "Music in Zimbabwe's Crisis." Unpublished paper. Nordic Africa Institute. Uppsala, Sweden. (from http// www.nai.uu.se)

Raftopoulos, B. 2004a. " 'We are really sleepwalking, corpses, zombies....We are carrying other people's world view.' Nation, Race and History in Zimbabwean Politics." Unpublished paper. Institute of Development Studies. University of Zimbabwe.

Raftopoulos, B. 2004b. "Current Politics in Zimbabwe: confronting the crisis." In *Zimbabwe The Past Is The Future.* Harare: Weaver Press. D. Harold-Barry, ed. pp.1-18.

Ranger, T. 2004. "Nationalist Historiography, Patriotic History and the History of the Nation: the struggle over the past in Zimbabwe." Unpublished paper dated May 28, 2004. available on www.kubatana.net.

Turino, T. 2000. *Nationalists, Cosmopolitans, and Popular Music in Zimbabwe.* Chicago and London: University of Chicago Press.

Zindi, F. 2003. *The Pop-Music Workbook Zimbabwe Versus The World.* Harare: Zindisc Publications.

Internet Sources

http//www.zwnews.com. 'Government accuses EU of seeking to oust it from Power.' from Zim Online (SA). 3 January 2005.

http//www.zwnews.com. 'Daily News to reopen.' from the *Financial Gazette*. 24 December 2004.

http//www.zwnews.com. 'Uncertainty over Moyo's fate.' from IRIN (UN). 1 January 2005.

http//www.zwnews.com. 'Pressure group defiantly distributes protest album' from Zim Online (SA). 19 May 2005.

http//www.zwnews.com. Rice, Xan. 'Mugabe's human rubbish dump' from *The Times* (UK). 6 June 2005.

http//www.zwnews.com. Zavis, Alexandra. 'Shades of Pol Pot' from the *Mail and Guardian* (SA). 24 June 2005.

http//www.kubatana.net.

Discography

Back2Black. 2004. *Pax Afro tapes 1&2.* Talunosiza Music.

Cde Chinx and the Police Band. 2001. *3rd Chimurenga Series. Hondo Yemindav Vols 1&2.* Shedd Studios.

Ihau Le Sizwe, Pototo, 'Sista Flame' Matenga, Tusungai Trigger. 2002. *3rd Chimurenga Series. More Fire.* Sebwe Music ROS 5.

Mapfumo, Thomas. Discography available at http://www.anonymousweb.com/thomas mapfumo.html

Mtukudzi, Oliver. 2001. *Bvuma. Tolerance.* Sheer Sound SLCD 006.

Interviews with the author

Anonymous 1. 13 August 2004. Harare.
Anonymous 2. 15 October 2004. Harare.
Anonymous 3. 10 August 2004, Harare.
Anonymous 4. 12 August 2004. Harare.
Anonymous 5. 12 August 2004. Harare.
Anonymous 6. 14 October 2004. Harare.
Anonymous 7. 15 October 2004. Harare.
Chikomo, A. 13 August 2004, Harare
Goddard, K. 9 August 2004, Harare.
Maparutsa, W. 16 August 2004, Harare.
Mtukudzi, O. 29 August 2004, Pretoria.
Mujokoro, S. 29 September 2004, Harare.
Raftopoulos, B. 15 October 2004, Harare.
Zhakata, L. 12 August 2004, Harare.
Zindi, F. 16 August 2004, Harare.

Chapter 6

And the Beat Goes On?
Message Music, Political Repression and
the Power of Hip-Hop in Nigeria

Wilson Akpan

Introduction

Conventional notions of music censorship lay emphasis on institutionalized forms of suppression. *The Hutchinson Encyclopedia* (2000) for instance defines censorship as the 'suppression by authority of material considered immoral, heretical, subversive, libelous, damaging to the state security, or otherwise offensive'. By this logic, censorship might be expected to be 'more stringent under totalitarian or strongly religious regimes and in wartime' (ibid.). Practices traditionally associated with censorship include banning and prohibition of artistic materials, arrest and detention of artists, raiding of performance concerts, refusal of music airplay (especially on public broadcast channels), and destruction of published works. They amount to 'shooting the singer' (Korpe (ed.) 2004). These practices are often traceable to specific state actors or agencies, but they may be ultimately linked to the character of the political regime. The growing interest in popular music censorship in Africa, Asia and Latin America – regions where the suppression of 'subversive' and 'immoral' artistic works often correlate with other authoritarian social tendencies – would seem largely driven by this traditional conception of censorship (Servant 2003: 79-81, Baily 2001, Eyre 2001). In an era of global human rights advocacy, the notion of censorship as 'a hallmark of dictatorships' (Global Internet Liberty Campaign [GILC] 2005) obviously has its place guaranteed.

There is concern, however, that this paradigm does not yield sufficiently intuitive insights into the ways in which the suppression of artistic creativity takes place today. Martin Cloonan (2004: 3-4) suggests, for instance, that censorship does not have to be 'systematic', nor does it have to be perpetrated 'at the behest of government or its agencies'. He argues further that a more holistic understanding of music censorship as it operates in the contemporary world might be gained through studying both the actions of the state and its agencies as well as such phenomena as 'the workings of the market'. Along similar lines, some writers have argued for the need to 'strip away the shock epithet value' attached to the conventional notions of censorship, in order to better understand how the practice manifests in the world today (GILC 2005).

Guided by this dynamic view, this chapter contributes to the discourse on the suppression of artistic creativity by focusing on the making of Nigeria's 'flourishing' pop music mainstream since the 1990s.[1] The central argument of the chapter may be understood within the context of a simple question: what has happened to the once dominant emancipatory lyrical tradition of Nigerian popular music? Why, for instance, is the lyrical idiom of much contemporary Nigerian popular music becoming intertwined with pornography?

Music as message: when suppression is not simply about 'shooting the singer'

In order to appreciate why the suppression of artistic creativity, especially as it operates in many societies today, is not simply about 'shooting the singer', it is necessary to examine the social character of Nigeria's message music genre. Music, or indeed any other art form, is essentially a form of inter-subjective communication, a dialogue between the value of the artist and that of the audience. Joost Smiers (2003: 238) has suggested that 'no work of art or entertainment is just fun, or just beautiful ... every artist takes sides within a broad range of choices' (see also Walters 2004). It is, of course, not correct to suggest, as Smiers does, that art is 'neutral' and is only 'imbued with a particular ideology' after it has been created or performed. A work of art is imbued with a particular ideology from the very beginning. Art is message, and that message aims to influence behaviour.

This perspective might be useful for understanding the emancipatory message music genre in Nigeria, and for understanding why change – and the forces compelling change – in this genre should be interrogated rather than accepted as indicative of 'normal' socio-cultural evolution (see Byerly 1996). In Nigeria, music was often about both entertainment and passing a message, as can be seen in forms such as highlife, juju, Fuji, reggae, gospel and Afrobeat, among others.

Nigeria's emancipatory message music is an important medium through which artists entertain while also conveying to their audience the 'truths' about life and 'warnings' about social existence as the singers know them. Besides 'delivery or vocal quality' the textual content of a song is valuable in itself – and this is true even for instrumental music (Blench 2004). Socio-political protest is not the defining essence of this genre; it is only one expression of it. For example the widely acclaimed highlife music as performed by Rex Lawson, Inyang Nta Henshaw, Osita Osadebe and Oriental Brothers, which utilized philosophy-of-life

---

[1] The author gratefully acknowledges the assistance of Mr. Femi Adagunodo, a Lagos-based journalist and media researcher, for providing the supporting research that led to the use of some of the examples and references in the third section of this chapter.

lyrical themes. In the past, emancipatory messages defined the musical mainstream.

It is interesting to note the reasons given by some Nigerian artists for their use of the emancipatory idiom in their lyrics. According to the Afrobeat maestro, Fela Anikulapo-Kuti (known internationally as Fela), 'there are no love songs like "Darling Kiss Me" in Africa' – an obviously untrue statement, but one that possibly reflected his conviction that a singer or songwriter should consider certain realities in the broader society as being of greater urgency for his or her vocation. 'That's why I use politics in my music' (quoted in Watrous 1989).

In a similar vein, Victor Essiet, leader of the Nigerian reggae group, Mandators, maintains that he spreads peace and understanding through his songs: 'at my shows people are uplifted. People... come with their hearts and souls' (quoted in Graves 2000). Right from their 1987 hit release, *Crisis* (which lamented the severe inflation and mass starvation in Nigeria during the mid-1980s and deplored the letter-bombing of frontline journalist Dele Giwa, among other issues), Mandators' music album sleeves have carried a bold message imploring people to focus on the song lyrics and not be carried away by the pulsating rhythms or by Essiet's fabulous voice.

Femi Kuti (Fela's son and one of Nigeria's leading Afrobeat artists) asks rhetorically, 'how can you write anything but engaged songs when you live in Nigeria?' (quoted in Servant 2003: 56). Lagbaja, another leading Afrobeat musician, maintains that the emancipatory idiom imbues his music with power. He even wears a mask as a way of shifting the audience's attention from his personality to the message in his music (Graviton 2005).

It is noteworthy that some of the artists who adopted the emancipatory lyrical idiom, such as Femi Kuti, also publicly spoke of their deeper convictions about the ideals of justice, fair play, hard work, hope, love and fellowship, and their desire to use their music to promote these values (see Servant 2003). This possibly explains why since Nigeria's political independence in 1960, much of the music in the emancipatory genre has been a form of protest against perpetrators of a 'bad' system, and in severe cases a tool of social dissidence.

It is thus important to view emancipatory message music, as used in this chapter, as a lyrical tradition rather than as a type of music. In that way we can tell when fundamental changes are occurring in the lyrical/message fabric of popular music, and can identify the kinds of pressures that (can) compel a change in this idiom. Focusing on the lyrical/message fabric also allows us to identify what one might term 'moments' and 'counter-moments' within an artist's creative career. For example, although a few of Fela's most popular songs digressed from overtly political lyrical themes, such songs are probably best regarded as 'moments' in a career that was distinguished by a lyrical theme reflecting his struggle for a 'better' Nigeria, Africa and world (Giwa 2004). The same can be said of foremost Nigerian anti-apartheid singer, Sonny Okosun (now a gospel singer), whose revolutionary album, *Fire in Soweto*, featured a raunchy track titled 'Steady and Slow'. Reference may also be made to musicians such as Salawa Abeni, Kollington

Ayinla, and Ayinde Barrister who during the mid-1990s wrote songs and/or held concerts to eulogize the 'achievements' of the notorious General Sani Abacha regime.

From the point of view of emancipatory message music, focusing popular music principally on what Eric Ture Muhammad (2002) described as 'booty shakin', thuggery and promoting the latest drugs and alcohol' – as seems to be the case in much Nigerian contemporary popular music – is probably comparable to dancing to the beat of the market. Fela once deplored this tendency as a ploy to 'use economics to destroy the culture of my people' (quoted in Watrous 1989).

It follows from the foregoing discussion that the suppression of artistic creativity will necessarily entail more than institutionalized, state-led attempts at stopping the music or eliminating the artist – as might ordinarily be expected in authoritarian societies. There are subliminal, non-state processes through which the lyrical/message fabric of popular music becomes redefined and controlled, such that even though popular music 'flourishes', its content is that which ensnares rather than emancipates. It may even be suggested, for the purposes of this chapter, that the whole essence of music censorship is for artists to censor their own creativity and produce works that they would not if they were truly free to express their creativity. This entails the ultimate creation of conditions whereby artists subvert their own creativity by propagating messages that conform to tastes and trends defined by forces other than themselves and mainstream society. Smiers (2003: 23-24) has noted in a related context that 'not so long ago, editors used to decide what books would be published', but that increasingly marketing committees play this role – committees driven not by the 'love of books' but by considerations of corporate profit.

Similar observations have been documented concerning popular music. In the United States for instance, Nelson George (1988: 173-174) notes that in the name of 'pleasing the mass market' and giving their art a measure of 'universality', black musicians have often been pressured into doing everything from 'preach[ing] sex as salvation in explicit and often clumsy terms', to 'cosmetic surgery, and the rejection of Negroid features'. However, when stripped of all the pretensions, George writes, the whole idea has been to pressure such artists to produce music videos fit for MTV. These comments re-echo those made by Simon Frith (1983), who wrote about the radical transformation of black popular music in America in the face of corporate control. 'As black music became part of the pop business', he wrote, a 'rehearsed distance' was created 'between the star and the consumer' such that important aspects of artistic creativity were effaced by the dictates of profit (Frith 1983: 19).

The subliminal suppression of creativity is such that 'recalcitrant' artists risk career hardships – as the recording studios, live performance venues, television and radio networks, and other infrastructure for exhibiting creativity are often owned or controlled by the same corporates that dictate the 'marketing criteria' for doing music. Not surprisingly famous North American hip-hop artists have been reported as packaging 'projects' that would more profoundly 'bring the two worlds of hip-hop and sex together' – projects that would differ significantly from the now pedestrian style of 'doing it for a minute [in music videos], this sex thing' (Meyer 2004a). As Meyer further notes, the view that has been imbibed by many leading hip-hop artists – as well as up and coming ones – is that 'porn is a way to reach an untapped market'. As shown later, the lyrical and cinematic convergence of popular music and pornography (as well as power and drugs) seems to be hip-hop's principal contribution to the subversion and suppression of the emancipatory music genre in Nigeria.

Looking at artistic suppression from the perspective of subliminal control has a number of implications. First, it makes it possible for researchers to look beyond police batons and the activities of formal censors' boards and 'conservative' cultural institutions, and constantly examine both 'authoritarian' and 'non-authoritarian' societies for evidence of artistic suppression. Secondly, it brings within the terrain of censorship research, the roles of transnational recording corporations, media and entertainment empires, and other 'merchants of cool' who grow rich by 'identifying', defining, inventing, controlling and trading in 'tastes' and 'trends' (see Frank 1997: 17). Thirdly, it makes it possible to interrogate the transformative impacts of the asymmetrical socio-cultural relations between, say, Nigeria and the United States of America.

Message music under political pressure in Nigeria

It is not an exaggeration to state that emancipatory message music has from time to time stoked the anger of the Nigerian political authorities. Fela Anikulapo-Kuti's strong socio-political commentaries, for example, brought on him and his family considerable physical and psychological harm. However, Fela's travails were emblematic of the challenges that emancipatory message musicians as a whole faced in Nigeria prior to the return of democracy in 1999 (although democracy has not brought a total end to such travails).

Some of the mechanisms and strategies through which the Nigerian authorities visited their wrath on defiant artists have been documented (Ogunde 2002). However, except probably for organs such as censorship boards (Servant 2003: 79), the infrastructure of artistic suppression during the prolonged season of fear in Nigeria was not separate from the totality of laws, state-controlled media, intelligence networks, police and media decrees, that were often deployed to put journalists, organized labour, civil rights activists, the student movement, sections of the diplomatic community, academics, artisans associations and ordinary Nigerians (as individuals and as collectivities) under siege.

In 1992, the National Broadcasting Commission (NBC) was established by the General Babangida regime as the broadcast industry regulator. Among other things, the Commission vets all programme content to ensure it meets the standards of objectivity, fairness and public decency. NBC's basic functions are in some ways similar to those of such bodies in other parts of the world. It allocates broadcast frequencies, sets programming standards, and is the national broadcast gatekeeper (Betiang 2004: 23), determining who gets a broadcast licence and why, as well as what the licence is valid for and where. It operates on the premise that 'social responsibility', national cultural and developmental imperatives must dictate what broadcast stations feed the public with.

One of NBC's more controversial censorial acts during the late 1990s was the banning from airplay of Femi Kuti's 'Bang, Bang, Bang', the award-winning song from the album *Shoki Shoki*. NBC's explanation was that the song contained morally offensive lyrics. Many Nigerians believed, however, that NBC's reaction to 'Bang, Bang, Bang' had very little to do with the sexual lyrical idiom, because at the time, more sexually explicit Western songs (like Salt n Pepa's 'Let's Talk about Sex') dominated the country's airwaves (see Servant 2003: 61). Even so, 'Bang, Bang, Bang' was probably just a 'counter-moment' in Femi's career – a career so far characterized by emancipatory message music. The general belief was that Fela's 'sins' were simply being visited on his son.

The operation of censorship in Nigeria prior to the return of democracy was in the form of arrests, detentions, trumped-up charges, prison terms, raiding of concert venues, forcible cancellation of performance tours, confiscation of musical instruments, destruction of musical albums, as well of banning of songs from airplay. In addition, musicians would often be accused of other 'offences', such as the handcuff incident involving Majek Fashek.[2] In Fela's case it almost always had to do with possession of marijuana. At no time, though, were the true reasons for such interrogations lost on ordinary Nigerians.

Fela was particularly confounded by the mindless obedience that characterizes the military profession. He questioned how soldiers could justify inflicting pain on other human beings by appealing to the notion that they were following orders. His hit song 'Zombie' – in which the instrumental structure reveals the behaviour of human automatons – and 'Mister Follow Follow' (literally 'Mister Can't-use-own-brains') in the same album, simply ridiculed this inexplicable professional ethic.

A most notable example of Fela's travails was the widely reported encounter with the authorities on 18 February 1977. This was when about 1,000 men dressed in military gear descended on his artistic headquarters (known as *Kalakuta Republic*) in Lagos, confiscated personal effects, flung his aged mother out of the window of a three-floor building, and burnt down the entire property. Fela would attribute the woman's 'untimely death' on 13 April 1978 to the injuries and psychological trauma resulting from that incident.

---

[2] Majek Fashek released the hit album *Prisoner of Conscience*. It featured powerful, socially conscious tracks like 'Send down the rain', 'Police brutality', 'Redemption song', 'Let righteousness cover the earth', and 'Africans keep your culture'. Shortly after the release of this album, in what looked like a self-fulfilling prophecy, Majek was arrested by the police, interrogated, briefly detained and then released. The official explanation of the police at the time was that they wanted to ascertain how the musician obtained the handcuffs he wore to pose for the album's cover photograph!

In 1997 the Nigerian Drug Law Enforcement Agency (NDLEA) detained Fela along with 35 members of his band. He was released after only six days in detention. NDLEA's official explanation was that the musician's ill health prevented them from keeping him longer than they did. On August 2 that year Fela died from AIDS-related health complications.

Among the songs through which Fela criticized military rule, government corruption and the collusion of the political and business elite in the suppression of the citizens were 'Unknown Soldier', 'Coffin for Head of State', and 'ITT – International Thief Thief' (literally 'international rogue').

As noted earlier, for some artists, emancipatory song lyrics are often a reflection of a deeper ideological and philosophical commitment. Femi Kuti typifies this. Widely seen as continuing in his father's legacy, he frames his musical career within the broad emancipatory grassroots struggles in Nigeria. His association, the Movement Against Second Slavery (MASS), serves as 'a loudspeaker for the new civil society'. This commitment has only exposed him to various acts of 'victimization' by the Nigerian authorities (Servant 2003: 58-61).

One of Nigeria's best-known pop artists, Charles Oputa (popularly known as Charly Boy), has suggested that artist 'victimization' impacts negatively on the growth of emancipatory message music in the country. It is against the looming possibility of victimization, he says, that 'some of my colleagues don't want to rock the boat' (quoted in Servant 2003: 61).

While musicians like Fela, Femi Kuti, Mandators, Lanrewaju Adepoju, and Gbenga Adewusi have been known to criticize corrupt and repressive governance using straightforward song lyrics, many message musicians during the military era capitalized on the power of veiled protest. Among them was Ras Kimono, whose song 'We no want – Dis shitstem (literally 'we don't want – this smelly system), subliminally attacked the Babangida regime and was listed as 'Not to be Broadcast' (NTTB) by all government-owned radio stations, at both the federal and state levels. There were no private broadcast stations in Nigeria at the time.

Another popular reggae artist, Orits Wiliki, deployed Biblical verses for his song lyrics and spoke to the Nigerian malaise using the fiery metaphors of Old Testaments prophets. His approach obviously helped him to evade the censorship trap – and detention cells. But he did not evade the authorities altogether, as he was on several occasions questioned by the State Security Service (SSS).

Message music – pressures of western cultural globalism

Crucial as the foregoing politics-related factors are in understanding the travails of emancipatory message music in Nigeria, they offer only a partial picture. Servant (2003) has suggested a number of other factors that have contributed to putting popular music under pressure in Nigeria – factors that incidentally synchronize with popular images of Nigeria, especially in Western eyes. They include Sharia

Law (commonly associated with 'political Islam' in many northern Nigerian states), and corruption (as exemplified by payola).

The travails of message music can also be understood from the point of view of the self-censorship pressures induced by the avalanche of Western music styles into the country – especially since the 1990s – and the prominence enjoyed by such styles as hip-hop and ragga in the country's electronic media.

While the actual mechanisms and exact degrees of influence of Western hip-hop, rap and ragga on the contemporary Nigerian pop music scene would be difficult to determine, the very prominence given to these music forms by FM radio stations and satellite and terrestrial television networks over the years has helped to make them the defining signatures of commercially viable music styles in the country. However, what is at issue, as indicated earlier, is not necessarily the beat of the music but the lyrical/message fabric.

The influence probably began to be noticeable during the early 1980s, with the rise of FM radio stations in the country, all of which devoted huge portions of their programming to American popular music. Of interest is that until the early 1990s when Raymond Dokpesi's company, Daar Communications, launched Ray Power 100 FM (and a UHF television station, Africa Independent Television, AIT) in Lagos, all FM and television stations in the country were government-owned. While none of the stations had a 24-hour programming schedule (24-hour broadcasting in Nigeria was pioneered by Ray Power 100 FM and AIT), Western popular music became so dominant on the new FM stations, especially in southern Nigeria, that by the mid-1980s, people were wondering aloud at drinking joints whether the whole idea of FM stations was not a deliberate ploy by the CIA to flood Nigeria with American popular culture and cultural commodities! By the end of the 1990s, FM broadcasting in Nigeria had become almost synonymous with giving free rein to Western pop music broadcast. There were over 20 private FM radio stations in the country in 2004, and probably twice as many government-owned ones. With the exception of Brilla FM (a sports station), Spectrum FM (a news station) and Rhythm 93.7 (which promotes itself as offering 'more music, less talk') there is no market specialization in the Nigerian radio broadcast industry. Hence, there are no exclusively jazz, classical, R & B or highlife stations. Most of them offer 'more music, less talk'.

Also during the 1980s state government-owned UHF television stations emerged as the media on which to watch what was 'hip' and 'cool' – namely, large doses of Western movies, sitcoms, soaps and pop music videos. Judged from their programming, these channels seemed poised to antiquate the federal government-owned Nigerian Television Authority (NTA), established in 1977. The 1979 constitution stripped NTA of its monopolistic position and provided the legal basis for the establishment of both private and state government-owned UHF television channels. There were over 30 state government-owned television stations in the country in 2004. However, some stations (such as Zamfara State Television Service, Bauchi State Television Corporation, Katsina State Television, Sokoto State Television), which are owned by Nigeria's northern 'Sharia states' might be expected to adhere to a 'shariaphrenic' (Servant 2003: 69) programming ethic and thus influence their audiences differently from stations in, say, Cross River, Akwa Ibom, Edo, Delta, and Rivers states in the predominantly Christian south.

In 1994, South Africa's Multichoice pioneered (analogue) pay television in Nigeria. When digital satellite retransmission became possible some years later, South Africa's DStv bouquet – which included the music channels MTV, VH1 and Channel O – became widely available in Nigeria. These music channels would become the top choice in subscribers' homes, and at hotel lobbies and rooms, pubs, bank lounges, shops, restaurants and fast-food joints. They would, at least in theory, offer many youthful patrons of these outlets a window into the products of Western 'merchants of cool', or what Thomas Frank (1997: 17) calls the 'power of marketing over the ingenuous revolutionary potential of the young'. By 2004, NBC had granted 14 satellite retransmission and 33 'wireless cable' licences (NBC 2005), and many had commenced operation. These services are concentrated in southern Nigeria.

The question now arises: what is the 'cool' condiment that has become infused into the lyrical/message fabric of Nigerian popular music, and to what extent has the emancipatory lyrical/message tradition become disfigured as a result? We examine this question by examining the lyrical fabric of Nigerian popular music mainstream in the 1990s.

Besides the political crisis of the time, Nigeria entered the 1990s on the waves of a new sexually indulgent pop music orthodoxy, notably hip-hop, rap and ragga. Like the big artists whose music had been the staple of Nigerian FM stations during the 1980s, most of the foreign artists that dominated the local airwaves in the 1990s were on music labels owned by the cartel that defines and controls global entertainment tastes and trends. It includes corporations like AOL/Time Warner, Viacom, Vivendi Universal, Sony and Bertelesmann. These five own and/or have interests in such labels as Warner Brothers, Elektra, Atlantic Records, Island Records, Columbia, Epic, BMG and RCA – and in MTV and VH1 (Miller 2002). Clearly dominating the Nigerian pop music scene were artists like Maxi Priest ('Close to You'), Salt 'n Pepa ('Let's Talk About Sex'), Shabba Ranks ('House Call' – duet with Maxi Priest; and 'Mr. Loverman'), Chakademus and Pliers ('Tease Me') and Patra ('Romantic Call' and 'Worker Man').

The question of whether the marketing strategies of the entertainment giants could inhibit artistic creativity and freedom in Nigeria cannot be separated from the broader debate on the impact of an emerging global entertainment oligopoly on global artistic diversity (see Horwitz 2004: 5-6, Smiers 2003, Miller 2002). I shall reflect more on this in the last section. For now it is important to highlight some interesting issues that I consider pertinent to the concern of this chapter. One is the observation by critics of media concentration and cultural globalization that 'when audiences appear to prefer locally made fare, the global media corporations, rather than flee in despair, globalize production' (McChesney 2001). This process of cultural penetration and infiltration, McChesney writes, is 'even more visible in the music industry' – an industry he regards as the 'most open to experimentation and new ideas'. It would reasonably be expected that in places where audiences might 'prefer locally made fare', the pressure on artists and audience – at least in the immediate – may not necessarily be on the 'form' of music, but on the lyrical/message fabric.

Writing about the dominance and influence of hip-hop in parts of Africa, Gesthuizen and Haas (2003) have suggested that Western hip-hop has caught on despite the fact that the 'language barrier makes it near to impossible for most of the ... audience to understand what rappers are talking about'. They further argue that although hip-hop is now the creative currency in the region, local artists find it difficult to produce 'texts in English with a similar richness of metaphor and slang expression as that of the American rappers'. This is a simplistic picture of how the lyrical theme of Western hip-hop influences and takes root in the African artistic arena, and, in the case of Nigeria, how it contributes to the suppression of emancipatory lyrical idioms. These writers ignore the role of music videos in driving home the often sexually provocative and violence-jaded lyrics. For instance, it is no secret that music videos meant for pay television channels such as MTV and VH1 (both owned wholly or in part by Viacom Inc) are produced to 'aesthetic standards' set by these channels, and that besides lip-synching, the artists have little control over their performances in the videos: every action is scripted and directed by 'specialists'. It is also probably common knowledge that to achieve utmost impact through their music videos – or, as Frank Meyer (2004a, 2004b) puts it, to further consolidate 'the porn industry's move to mainstream' – Western hip-hop artists (and/or those who pay for the making of their videos) now commonly employ the services of specialist hardcore pornography production teams.

Following the overgenerous airplay in Nigeria of sexually indulgent Western songs, it did not take long before many local artists devoted their energies to sexual lyrical themes. By the 1990s when hip-hop had already become intertwined with the pornography industry in the West (Meyer 2003), it had grown in Nigeria to the point where emancipatory lyrical theme became stigmatized as 'old school'. Sex had left the bedroom and hip-hop was turning Nigerians into voyeurs.

By the close of the 1990s, only a few artists, like Lagbaja and Femi Kuti (in addition to the hundreds of gospel artists – many of whom saw in gospel a fast way of earning a living at a time when Pentecostalism was experiencing explosive growth in Nigeria), still used their music to directly inspire hope and speak to the Nigerian condition. Faced with an unfavourable political climate, an inexorable avalanche of Western hip-hop, and the drastic reduction (not total black-out) in emancipatory music airplay in the country's electronic media, a critical segment of the creative community found themselves confined to non-emancipatory lyrical themes. Emancipatory music maestros like Majek Fashek, Mandators and Ras Kimono simply left the country. A new generation of mainly hip-hop artists took over, singing and rapping about sex, power and violence, with some of the artists demonstrating remarkable creativity in 'rapping' around these themes in their mother tongues. Nigerian pop music lovers will probably remember that during the

1990s these artists merely provided brief interludes to the undisputed dominance of foreign hip-hop on the local airwaves, and that when emancipatory artists had their moments on the airwaves, it was often their 'harmless' songs that enjoyed the most airplay.

By the mid-1990s, Nigeria's volatile political climate had taken such a heavy toll on economic activities that most foreign businesses, including most major music labels, withdrew from the country (Servant 2003: 33). However, Nigerian streets were inundated with pirated copies (both audio and video) of Western hip-hop. Given the free flow of 'sex' and 'love' on the airwaves and live performance venues (especially in southern Nigeria) on the one hand, and widespread political repression and economic hardship on the other, the time seemed ripe for many local artists who wanted to make a living from traditional musical forms, like *Fuji*, to literally reinvent them by adopting a 'new' lyrical/message theme. For example, Obesere – among several other *Fuji* artists – during this period seemed poised to raise x-rated lyrical content and stage performances to heights never before witnessed in Nigeria. One commentator defines 1990s *Fuji* as 'rough', 'sexy', 'armed robbery', and 'hip-hop in the original sense' (cited in Servant, 2003: 36). However, says the same commentator, 'we haven't theorized fuji enough to understand the potential of it'.

The difficulty in 'theorizing' *Fuji* may very well be as a result of its 1990s lyrical reinvention:

> When [in 2002] Abass Akande Obesere did his latest music video, *Apple Juice*, with [a known] semi-porno actress ... he shocked his numerous fans then by becoming the only fuji crooner whose best selling point is sex. Even before now ... Obesere's name [has been associated with] lewd fuji music. With phrases like *Tosibe* [literally: 'urinate in there!'] ... Abass Akande's lyrics [smack] of raw sexual gestures ... Somehow, Abass' [pornographic style] has caught the attention of [his musical] siblings. (*Nigerianewsnow* 2003)

To be sure, *Fuji* is an Islamic music style, sometimes called *Were* or *Ajisari*. It was the sound of percussions and chants with which Muslims woke the community to their *sari* (early morning meal) in preparation for the dawn-to-dusk fast during the month of Ramadan. Sikiru Ayinde Barrister, Kollington Ayinla, Dauda Epo Akara and others transformed *Fuji* into popular music during the mid-1970s. At the time *Fuji* was widely seen as a challenge to the dominance of *Juju*, one of the most popular music genres in (south western) Nigeria. Barrister, Kollington and Epo Akara initially retained the (mainly eulogy) message and percussion tradition. Over time, King Wasiu Ayinde Marshal (KWAM I), Adewale Ayuba, Obesere and others introduced further innovations, experimenting with saxophone and strings, and doing collaborations with rap artists. These efforts further popularized *Fuji*. By the early 1990s, *Fuji* was introduced to the lyrical idiom of the moment: sex. As Obesere says in one of his songs, 'Asakasa', when he asked God for inspiration to continue singing about the virtues of hard work, beauty and love, God told him there was nothing left of those themes – and that he was free to pick the only remaining theme, 'Asakasa' ('strange/vulgar talk' – see also Davies 2005). Equally interesting, in *Mr. Teacher*, Obesere sings of how Nigerians avoided his records when he dwelt on 'clean' lyrical themes, but how he shot to stardom the moment he switched to 'vulgar' lyrics. What should be noted, as one source has highlighted, is that 'Obesere has not always been a raw singing artist...[In] his earlier music, his style was very much like that of the legendary Alhaji Sikiru Ayinde Barrister' (*Nigerianewsnow 2003*). A recent interview has also revealed that his creative transition is increasingly giving him 'unhealthy' inner tension (Daramola 2005).

The return of democracy in 1999 did not mean a sudden end to Nigeria's socio-economic and political woes. The country is still plagued by poverty, unemployment, HIV/AIDS, brain drain, debt burden, corruption, fraud, an escalating cost of living, political instability, a serious international image problem and widespread social despair – themes for emancipatory song lyrics. With the exception of the gospel artists and a few 'secular' musicians, today's artists would consider such lyrical themes 'old school'. Gospel remains the most noticeable, surviving form of emancipatory message music in Nigeria, but even this genre is increasingly being redefined, not by hip-hop as such, but by survivalism and what Cloonan (2004: 4) calls 'the workings of the market' (see also Bukwa 2004).

Recent indications are that a section of Nigeria's creative community, represented by the Performing Musicians Association of Nigeria (PMAN), is disturbed by the impact of Western cultural globalism on the country's creative culture. PMAN is advocating the imposition of quotas on foreign music broadcasts and wants 80 per cent of radio music programming reserved for local music. It is also seeking a licence to establish a radio station that will play only Nigerian music. In addition it wants to help the regulators to monitor local music for lyrical content, quality and originality (Bunshak 2004: 8). The frightening thing, however, is that Nigerians may someday be asked to name their preferred form of censorship.

Conclusion

One of the major criticisms that proponents of cultural imperialism have faced, especially since the 1980s, has been that despite fears to the contrary, 'world musical homogenization is not occurring' (Robinson *et al*, quoted in Shuker 2001: 71). What is occurring, according to Timothy Taylor (1997: 197), is the emergence of 'new ethno/mediascapes' characterized by 'new musics' – and Nigeria's 1990s *Fuji* and so-called 'Nigerian hip-hop' might typify this. This supports the argument that cultural 'imperialism' is 'a historical artefact' that should be jettisoned (McChesney 2001). In its place the term 'cultural globalization' has been promoted – a term that emphasizes cultural 'networking' (see Shuker 2001: 71). Some even portray globalization as an escape route from the forces of suppression at the local level and as a process through which human creativity has entered a 'new Golden Age' (see McChesney 2001). Interestingly, however, even those who hold this benign view of globalization acknowledge that many so-called 'new musics' 'sound increasingly North American' (Taylor 1997: 197).

My use of 'cultural globalism' in this chapter has not been to endorse naïve notions of 'networking', but to emphasize the obvious asymmetry in the relationship between contemporary North American 'sound' and 'sounds' from, say, Nigeria. The point has been to show that certain aspects of the social character of American hip-hop is 'globalizing' (into Nigeria) with damaging intensity. There is little consolation in the argument that 'Anglo-American popular culture has become established as the international preferred culture of the young since the 1950s' (Shuker 2001: 71). As shown in this chapter, some of the mechanisms and strategies by which such 'preferred culture of the young' is manufactured, disseminated and imposed are no longer a mystery.

It is clear from the transformations taking place in the emancipatory message music genre in Nigeria, that popular music in the country is increasingly taking on a 'new' social character, and that this transformation is attributable to factors other than the censorial activities of the state and of conservative cultural institutions. While homogenization might not be occurring in the sound of the drum or the twang of the guitar, it might be occurring in the lyrical/message fabric – especially in the 'mainstreaming of pornography' through hip-hop (Meyer 2004a, 2004b). This, in fact, is why Nigeria's 1990s *Fuji* may be described as 'rough', 'sexy', 'armed robbery' and 'hip-hop in the original sense' (see Servant 2003: 36).

Like most other spheres of contemporary Nigerian society, popular culture is hobbled by both endogenous factors and by forces from afar, and analyses of the travails of local popular culture should not focus exclusively on one set of factors (cf: Wallis and Malm 1984: 60-119). In the case of the emancipatory message music genre, suppression has occurred through intolerant political regimes (among other local forces), and through an asymmetric pattern of global relations in which local cultural production and consumption, rather than reflect local socio-political and cultural realities, are twisted out of character by external impositions. For socially conscious popular music in Nigeria, it is a case of being caught, as the cliché says, between a rock and a hard place.

References

Baily, J. 2001. *'Can You Stop the Birds Singing?' The Censorship of Music in Afghanistan.* Copenhagen: Freemuse.

Betiang, L. 2004. 'Public Broadcasting in National Development'. *NBC News.* Vol. 6 No. 4. October-December. 18-25.

Blench, R. 2004. 'Federal Republic of Nigeria'. In L. Macy (ed.), *Grove Music Online.* http://www.grovemusic.com. [Accessed January 5, 2005].

Bukwa, V.O. 2004. 'The attempt to steal my hit number – Ifeanyichukwu Oru, gospeller'. *Daily Sun* (Lagos, Nigeria). May 7.

Bunshak, T. 2004. 'More Local Music on Air, Please'. *NBC News.* Vol. 6 No. 4. October-December. Page 8.

Byerly, I.B. 1996. *The Music Indaba: Music as Mirror, Mediator, and Prophet in the South African Transition from Apartheid to Democracy.* Ann Arbor, Mich.: UMI Dissertation Services, 1996.

Cloonan, M. 2004. 'What is Music Censorship? Towards a Better Understanding of the Term'. In M. Korpe (ed.), *Shoot the Singer: Music Censorship Today.* London: Zed Books. pp. 3-5.

Daramola, D. 2005. 'I'm crazy about women – Obesere'. *Daily Sun.* April 16.

Davies, B. 2005. 'Life as a Fuji Star – Obesere'. *NigeriaNewsNow.* March 13, 2005.

Eyre, B. 2001. *Playing with Fire: Fear and Self-Censorship in Zimbabwean Music.* Copenhagen: Freemuse.

Frank, T. 1997. *The Conquest of Cool.* Chicago: The University of Chicago Press.

Frith, S. 1983. *Sound Effects: Youth, Leisure, and the Politics of Rock 'n' Roll.* London: Constable.

George, N. 1988. *The Death of Rhythm and Blues.* London: Penguin.

Gesthuizen, T. and Haas, P. 2003. 'Ndani ya Bongo – Kiswahili Rap: Keeping it Real'. http://www.africanhiphop.com/core/index.php?module=ubjects&func= viewpage&pageid=157 [Accessed 5 January, 2005].

Giwa, T. 2004. 'Felasophy Through the Years: Fond Recollections of Fela Kuti'. *Chimurenga.* December. http://www.chimurenga.co.za/modules.php? name=News&file=article&sid=72. [Accessed January 12, 2005].

Global Internet Liberty Campaign (GILC). 2005. 'What is Censorship?' http://www.gilc.org/speech/osistudy/censorship/. [Accessed April 20, 2005].

Graves, A. 2000. October 28, 2000. 'Reggae Performer Spreading His Gospel Through Music'. *The Morning News.*

Graviton (African Arts Network). 2005. 'Lagbaja: Biography'. http://www.graviton.net/index2.php?option=com_content&do_pdf=1&id=15. [Accessed 20 May 2005].

Horwitz, R.B. 2005. 'On Media Concentration and the Diversity Question'. *The Information Society.* 21 (3).

The Hutchinson Encyclopedia. 2000. 'Censorship'. Sheffield: Helicon Publishing.

M. Korpe (ed.), 2004. *Shoot the Singer: Music Censorship Today.* London: Zed Books.

McChesney, R.W. 2001. 'Global Media, Neoliberalism, and Imperialism'. Monthly Review. Volume 52, Number 10. March. http://www.monthlyreview.org/301rtm.htm [Accessed May 25, 2005]

Meyer, F. 2003. 'Damage Control'. *The Porning Report.* December 15. http://weblogs.variety.com/the_porning_report/2003/12/damage_control_.html. [Accessed 23 April 2005].

Meyer, F. 2004a. 'Hip Hop Peep Show'. *The Porning Report*. February 10. http://weblogs.variety.com/the_porning_report/music/index.html [Accessed 23 April 2005].

Meyer, F. 2004b. 'Music Biz Allows What Film Biz Eschews'. *The Porning Report.* 13 February. http://weblogs.variety.com/the_porning_report/music/index.html [Accessed 23 April 2005].

Miller, M.C. 2002. 'What's Wrong With This Picture?' *The Nation.* January 7. Muhammad, E.T. 'Social commentary and Black rap'. http://www.finalcall.com/perspectives/eminem_chuck10-08-2002.htm [Accessed 4 January 2005].

National Broadcasting Commission (NBC, Nigeria). 2005. 'Satellite Retransmission Stations/Cable Stations (Using MDDS Channels)'. http://www.nbc-nig.org/Cable_stations.asp. [Accessed 23 April 2005].

Negus, K. 1996. *Popular Music in Theory: An Introduction.* London: Wesleyan University Press.

Nigerianewsnow. 2003. 'How Obesere Brothers Introduced Sex to Fuji'. September 8. http://nigerianewsnow.com/News/September03/080903_ Obeseresex.htm. [Accessed 17 January 2005].

Ogunde, O. 2002. 'The revolutionary essence of Fela Kuti's music'. *African Communist.* Fourth Quarter. http://www.sacp.org.za/ac/ac162l.html. [Accessed 15 January 2005].

Olukotun, A. 2004. *Repressive State and Resurgent Media Under Nigeria's Military Dictatorship1988-1998.* Uppsala: Nordiska Afrikainstitutet.

Servant, J. 2003. *'Which Way Nigeria?' Music Under Threat – A Question of Money, Morality, Self-Censorship and the Sharia.* Copenhagen: Freemuse.

Shuker, R. 2001. *Understanding Popular Music.* Second Edition. London: Routledge.

Smiers, J. 2003. *Arts Under Pressure: Promoting Cultural Diversity in the Age of Globalization.* The Hague: Hivos.

Taylor, T.D. 1997. *Global Pop: World Music, World Markets.* London: Routledge.

Wallis, R. and Malm, Krister. 1984. *Big Sounds from Small Peoples: The Music Industry in Small Countries.* London: Constable.

Walters, P. 2004. 'Citation of Award of the Degree of Doctor of Music *Honoris Causa* on Zenzi Miriam Makeba'. February 20. Grahamstown, South Africa: Rhodes University.

Watrous, P. 1989. 'Fela Offers a Mosaic of Music and Politics'. *New York Times.* 28 July.

Discography

Chakademus and Pliers. *Tease Me.* Island, 1993.
Fela Anikulapo-Kuti. *Coffin for Head of State.* Kalakuta, 1981.

Fela Anikulapo-Kuti. *ITT.* Arista, 1981.
Fela Anikulapo-Kuti. *Unknown Soldier.* Phonodisk/Skylark, 1979.
Fela Anikulapo-Kuti. *Mister Follow Follow.* Creole, 1976.
Fela Anikulapo-Kuti. *Zombie.* Creole, 1976.
Femi Kuti. *Bang, Bang, Bang.* Barclay/Polygram, 1999.
Femi Kuti. *Shoki Shoki.* Barclay/Polygram, 1999.
Mandators. *Crisis.* Polygram, 1987.
Maxi Priest. *Close To You.* Atlantic, 1990.
Obesere (Abass Akande). *Mr. Teacher.* Sony 1997.
Obesere (Abass Akande). *Asakasa.* Sony, 1993.
Patra. *Romantic Call.* Sony, 1994.
Patra. *Worker Man.* Sony, 1994.
Ras Kimono. *Under Pressure.* Polygram, 1988.
Ras Kimono. *We no Want – Dis Shitstem.* Polygram, 1988.
Salt 'n Pepa. *Let's Talk About Sex.* Next Plateau, 1991.
Shabba Ranks. *Mr. Loverman.* EPIC, 1992.
Shabba Ranks (with Maxi Priest). *House Call.* EPIC, 1991.
Sonny Okosun. *Fire In Soweto.* EMI, 1978.
Sonny Okosun. *Steady and Slow.* EMI 1978.

PART 2
Case Studies

Chapter 7

Traditional and Popular Music, Hegemonic Power and Censorship in Malawi: 1964-1994

Reuben M. Chirambo

Introduction

Dr H.K. Banda, popularly known as *Kamuzu* or *Ngwazi*, led Malawi to independence from British colonial rule in 1964 and ruled the country via a single-party dictatorship of the Malawi Congress Party (MCP) up to 1994. Malawi under his leadership was described as a land 'where silence ruled' (Africa Watch 1990: 1) 'a land of pervasive fear' (Zeleza 1995: 33). It was also referred to as a land of 'death and darkness' (Chirambo 2001: 217), because of, among other things, harsh censorship laws and practices. It was a country intolerant of criticism and opposition. In terms of censorship, hundreds of popular songs, books, newspapers, and other publications were severely censored and/or banned under the censorship law (see below). Many opponents and critics of Banda were detained without charge, tortured, and/or killed. Some of them found refuge in exile for the entire reign of Banda.[1]

However, beyond conventional censorship methods, Banda's regime, as a hegemonic dictatorship, used traditional and popular music in Malawi as instruments for censorship. First, songs as popular voices legitimized and popularized Banda's dictatorship and thereby undermined the possibilities of a critical consciousness against Banda. Second, songs not only vilified and castigated Banda's critics and opponents, but incited hatred and violence against critics and opponents of Banda. In other words, traditional and popular songs promoted an atmosphere where dissent was difficult to articulate (Chirambo 2004: 1).

Some musicians, despite the tough censorship laws and practices, resisted and tried to elude censorship to subvert Banda's political establishment. These musicians interrogated and derogated Banda's dictatorship with varying degrees of success. Some of the criticism was decoded and the songs banned.

---

[1] For details of how Banda used detention without trial and torture to silence criticism and opposition see Amnesty International (1989) and Africa Watch (1990).

In this chapter, I firstly examine Banda's censorship machinery in which he used familiar and conventional methods such as detention without trial, torture, and the law. Secondly, I examine how traditional and popular songs, once appropriated for hegemonic politics, censored dissent in Malawi. I suggest that censorship by hegemony was one of Banda's most effective censorship methods because it involved ordinary people with their everyday cultural activities such as songs and dances.

Banda's censorship machinery: censorship law and practice

The Censorship Act of 1968 in Malawi was meant to make censorship, if anything, arbitrary. Arbitrariness was coded in the deliberately ambiguous law that claimed to aim at 'undesirable publications', by proscribing materials that were 'contrary to the interests of public safety or public order' (Malawi 1968: 1), among other things. What was meant by 'undesirable' or what constituted 'public safety or order' was open to any interpretation. The Censorship Board established under the act, regulated and controlled, for example, the circulation of all materials for public and private consumption published inside or outside Malawi. The list of banned books, magazines, songs, cinematography, and other publications was extensive and difficult to explain or justify, suggesting what Gibbs (1982: 76) refers to as 'confusion and ignorance' among censors about what standards to follow. In less than ten years, the board banned over eight hundred books, a hundred periodicals and sixteen films, mostly on the basis of political motives (Malawi 1975).[2]

While the Censorship Board periodically listed banned materials in the government gazette, in some instances books, songs and similar materials were simply withdrawn from public places by way of memos or verbal instructions. Mapanje (1989: 8), for example, quotes a memo from the Ministry of Education to schools and colleges, which says: 'I would like to inform you that *Of Chameleons and Gods*, [sic] a collection of poems by Dr Jack Mapanje has been declared unsuitable for schools and colleges in the country. Any copies of the collection should be withdrawn from use in our schools and colleges without delay'.[3] Such decisions were more often than not the result of political pressure. After all, the board was not under obligation to give exact reasons for banning or withdrawing any material given that the law never provided such an obligation. There was

---

[2] James Gibbs (1982: 69-83), who taught English and drama in the English Department of the University of Malawi in the 1970s, gives details of correspondence with the Censorship Board on plays he submitted for review. The correspondence shows just how difficult it was to determine how the board arrived at its decisions. He also shows how playwrights and producers outwitted the board.
[3] In the same memo the Ministry of Education withdrew Felix Mnthali's *When Sunset Comes to Sapitwa*. Such withdrawals were not published in the gazette. See also note 20 below.

therefore a lot of secrecy surrounding the banning of materials that were not announced in the gazette as banned. The decisions of the board could not be challenged or reviewed in courts or anywhere in Malawi. The decisions were final without the possibility of arbitration.

In practice, therefore, vague terms and provisions in the censorship act made it subject to abuse, leading to the silencing of even legitimate voices of complaint or dissent in the country. For example, the censorship act encouraged any member of the public to report to or submit by way of complaint or materials to the board anything they considered offensive or in breach of the censorship code (Malawi 1968: 3). Such individuals could remain anonymous. This provision was taken advantage of by party militias, which included the Malawi Young Pioneers (MYP), MCP Youth Leaguers, party functionaries or activists, and the Police, especially the secret service. These groups carried out an unimaginably brutal form of censorship in that they could persecute, detain, and torture individuals for holding or spreading dissenting views to Banda's, or authoring materials they considered not acceptable. In doing this, in addition to the censorship law, the authorities invoked the Preservation of Public Security Act of 1966 under which individuals could be held in indefinite detention and even be tortured for threatening public security.

Efforts to determine who made such decisions that were clearly not provided for in the law often led to nowhere or to no one in particular because everyone was supposedly acting on instruction from someone above them. Mapanje (1997: 73-4) observes that these higher authorities were never clearly spelt out and often turned out to be 'an indiscriminate confusion of police chiefs, army generals, principals of colleges, company managers, drivers, messengers, market vendors and other ordinary mortals'. Any party zealot could censor in the name of a higher authority that was no higher and nowhere. Zeleza (1995: 34) makes a similar observation when he says that even friends, spouses or partners were recruited in the service of spying for Banda, and therefore became part of the censorship machinery. This situation diffused responsibility and obliterated culpability of anyone in Banda's censorship scheme. No one could trust anyone. In other words, as Mapanje (1997: 72) suggests, Banda and his censors 'subtly left no traces by which the perpetrators could be pinned down in future'. Their actions, however, induced fear and suffocated speech in Malawi. Hence, Mapanje (1997: 73) argues that:

> Perhaps the most outrageous legacy of censorship that our dictator and his sycophants invented for us is one where they censored without actually censoring; where they banned without invoking the banning order; where they censored us or our creativity by implication, by nuance, by suggestion; where they effectively let you ban yourself. Self-censorship is not an adequate concept to describe this kind of censure which was too subtle and too brutal for description.

Censorship in Malawi was cruel as it was insidious for it threw the onus of censorship on the individual authors and not on the censor. For those censured,

Mapanje says, 'you [were] meant to discover what it is you are supposed to have written to deserve the ban. You [were] supposed to feel guilty for having done whatever they claimed was subversive' (ibid.). Similarly, Zeleza (1995: 33) argues that Banda's censorship '[begot] self-censorship, a numbing collective fear of meaningful social conversations, of public discourse, of openly questioning the way things are and imagining what they ought to be'. Censorship was an iron veil hiding what Zeleza calls 'the lies, deformities and fantasies of a ruthless, unproductive power [of Banda]' (ibid.). Traditional songs and popular music under these circumstances were routinely and heavily censored. Composers had to work carefully to avoid antagonizing the board. They therefore censored themselves. Whenever they sang about politics, most musicians often chose praises for Banda instead of criticism. Otherwise, apolitical subjects such as love and infidelity were considered safe.

Censorship through the hegemonic discourse of Kamuzuism

Over and above the familiar and obvious forms of censorship above, which are consistent with what Ilan Peleg (1993: 110-133) describes as a Third World phenomenon of censorship by repressive regimes, Banda also censored by hegemony. By this I mean that the hegemonic discourse, while promoting Banda, also undermined and stifled critical and dissenting voices in Malawi. Antonio Gramsci (1971: 12) defines hegemony as 'spontaneous consent given by the great masses of the population to the general direction imposed on social life by the dominant fundamental group'. Gramsci gives central place to ideas, values and beliefs as the means by which a hegemonic class governs the subordinate groups. In other words, hegemony is 'a relation [between rulers and the ruled] of consent by means of political and ideological leadership' (Simon 1982: 21). Femia (1981: 39) suggests that when Gramsci speaks of consent, 'he refers to a *psychological*[4] state, involving some kind of acceptance…of the socio-political order or of certain vital aspects of that order'. He argues that consent may 'flow from a profound sense of obligation, from wholesale internalization of dominant values and definitions; or their partial assimilation' (ibid.).

Gramsci (1971: 199) calls values, ideas, beliefs, and so on, shared between the ruling class and the subordinate groups 'common sense'. Boggs (1984: 161) explains that 'when the ruling ideas are internalized by the majority of the people and become a defining motif of everyday life, they appear as common sense'. Under a hegemonic situation, Boggs observes, the ruling class 'always seeks to justify their power, wealth, status ideologically, with the aim of securing popular acceptance of their dominant position as something "natural", part of an eternal social order, and thus unchallengeable' (ibid.). The masses regard the hegemonic social order as the only viable form of society. The masses may go beyond

---

[4] Emphasis in original.

acceptance of the social order to be actively engaged in protecting the status quo. That is, they may challenge and fight against forces and voices that seem to threaten the status quo, or fight individuals or groups that may be refusing to conform to the demands of the hegemonic social order. Achille Mbembe (2001: 133) call this an inversion when 'in their desire for certain majesty, the masses join in the madness and clothe themselves in cheap imitations of power to reproduce its epistemology'.

Banda's dictatorship was hegemonic in that Banda mobilized consensus of a large section of the people of Malawi to subscribe to his ideology and political leadership, presented as Kamuzuism. The regime appropriated and manipulated the popular voices of traditional songs and popular music, besides other avenues, as instruments to propagate and disseminate the ideology of Kamuzuism. The political discourse in songs legitimized and popularized Banda's leadership. The songs explicitly suggested that Banda was a God-given Messiah, therefore, president for life. This also meant that his authority could not be challenged let alone be criticized. Banda devised four cornerstones that became linchpins of Kamuzuism: Unity, Loyalty, Obedience, and Discipline. He argued that the party (MCP) and the government of Malawi were founded on these principles. To question, criticize, or even to complain against Banda was considered disobedience, as it was indiscipline. To challenge Banda was a threat to national unity and disloyalty to the party, government, and Banda. Because Malawi was a single-party dictatorship, there was no separation between the party, government, and Banda. The majority of the people of Malawi internalized these ideas of Kamuzuism, which became the basis of their everyday lives.

Songs and dances were key elements of all public functions in which Banda participated in Malawi. Almost all traditional songs and popular music articulated ideas of Kamuzuism that affirmed Banda's leadership as unchallengeable, rejected any alternative leadership to Banda and any form of dissent. Chirwa (2001: 14-15) suggests that the 'perception and treatment of the opposition', for example, was one of the key discourses in political songs in Banda's Malawi. The songs denigrated the opposition, created fear and hatred for criticism and the opposition. They even suggested and rejoiced in the use of violence to silence dissent. As such, the discourse of Kamuzuism became a weapon for censorship. It de-legitimized opposition.

The following songs are examples of both traditional and popular songs that effectively stifled criticism and opposition, becoming instruments for censorship. Saleta Phiri and AB Sounds, for example, composed and performed the following song that enunciates Kamuzuism, 'Ife Ndife Ana a Malawi' (1988) (We are Children of Malawi):

We're the children of Malawi
And we're supposed to follow Malawian customs.

These customs are:

Unity, Loyalty, Obedience and Discipline.
Give reverence to elders
Respect them
Let us not forget, please, let us not forget.[5] (By permission)

AB Sounds rightly suggested that everyone in Malawi was expected to behave according to the four cornerstones. Everyone's conduct or behaviour was judged on whether or not they complied with these principles. AB Sounds here enunciated principles that stifled dissent, because the principles made criticism a threat to the social political order, an order that Zeleza (1995: 33) calls 'a dull uniformity that criminalized difference, ambiguity, and creativity'.

Most political songs were more forthright in their rejection of criticism and opposition. The following chorus was sung at the annual MCP conventions and other party functions in the country suggesting that there could be no other Chief, Lion or Leader, greater than or equal to Banda. Banda was called Messiah/Saviour, Chief, Lion, Life President, among other titles. These titles could only be used for Banda in Malawi (Malawi Congress Party 1965: 11)

There's no other King
Greater than Kamuzu
He has fought the war with words only
There's no Lion greater than Kamuzu
There's no Leader greater than Kamuzu.[6]

The war that Banda fought with words alone is the independence struggle. Banda led Malawi to independence without the use of arms or soldiers. Hence, he was called Lion, Fire, besides King and *Ngwazi*. *Ngwazi* means Conqueror.

---

[5] *Ife ndife ana a dziko lino, la Malawi*
Ndipo tiyenera kusunga mwambo wa chiMalawi
Miyambo yache ndi iyi:
Pali Umodzi, Kumvera, Kukhulupilika, ndi Kusunga mwambo.
Kuopa achikulire
Kuwapatsa ulemu
Anzanga tisayiwale, chonde tisayiwale.

[6] This song and others following, unless otherwise stated, were recorded by the Department of Information and Malawi Broadcasting Corporation (MBC) at former President Banda's public functions between 1958 and 1994. Source: National Archives, Zomba, Malawi. As oral materials, these songs circulate in the public domain in Malawi as non-copyrighted oral materials.

Palibe Mfumu yina
Yoposa Kamuzu
Wamenya nkhondo ndi mawu okha
Palibe Mkango wina, woposa Kamuzu
Palibe Mtsogoleri wina, woposa Kamuzu.

The following song says that the people in Malawi do not want any other leader apart from Banda, who is life president.

> Whom do we want today?
> *Ngwazi* alone
> No one else, no one else
> But Ngwazi alone
> *Ngwazi* is for life.[7]

Banda became life president of the MCP in 1961 and of the government in 1971. The two songs above rule out the possibility of an alternative leadership to challenge Banda in Malawi. Hence, Banda and his supporters through government banned opposition parties in the country, making it a one party dictatorship in 1966 (Malawi Congress Party 1985: 12).

The song below was performed by *Ingoma* dancers from the Mzimba district. It says that everyone must keep quiet before Banda. Because Banda is a winner, is *Ngwazi*, all must show respect to him by keeping quiet. Banda was supposed to be obeyed and revered in silence without criticism or complaint.

> Keep quiet before Kamuzu
> *Ngwazi* today is a winner
> Before Kamuzu, keep quiet
> We have seen London
> He has won, Kamuzu is a winner.
> In Zomba he has spoken.
> Keep quiet before Kamuzu, be quiet.[8]

Silence before elders (especially when a leader is included) is a virtue in traditional Malawian society. It is disrespectful for anyone to challenge or criticize leaders in public. One is expected to listen to them. When such ideas are brought to apply to national issues of the state, of the president and his leadership, they serve to silence

---

[7] *Ife tifuna yani lero?*
Ngwazi yekha
Winanso yayi, winanso yayi
Ngwazi yekha
Yawo Wamuyaya.
[8] *Khalani chete kwa Kamuzu*
Lero Ngwazi yawina
Kwa Kamuzu tikhale chete
Tawona ku London
Wawina, Kamuzu wawina
Ku Zomba wayowoya,
Khalani chete kwa Kamuzu
Wawina Ngwazi Banda
Kwa Kamuzu tikhale chete, chete, chete.

not just criticism but even legitimate complaints. Since the regime was totalitarian, this song tells people to suffer in silence.[9]

In the song below by Women's League of Mangochi district, the message is that everyone who refuses to buy the MCP membership card must be arrested or sent out of the country into exile. Given that Malawi was a single party dictatorship, membership of the party was mandatory for every Malawian. One form of resistance to this coercive membership was by delaying or even completely avoiding the purchase of the card. The party in turn forced membership by requiring everyone to show the card in order to enter the market, board public transport, receive treatment at the hospital, and so on. Some of the major victims of this were members of the Jehovah's Witnesses. They refused to join any political or civic organization or to participate in political activities (Watchtower 1968: 72). The movement was banned in Malawi in 1967.[10] The song below proposes that everyone without the membership card be arrested.

> Anyone without the card must be arrested
> Those without the card are crying
> Those without the card are not sleeping
> Everyone without the card must be arrested.
>
> Everyone without the card must leave Malawi
> Anyone without card the Malawians do not want them
> Anyone without the card must be arrested.[11]

In the third line the song says that those without the card are crying and not sleeping. This refers to the fact that they were being persecuted and tortured. The hegemonic influence of Kamuzuism meant that the majority of the people in

---

[9] The Malawi Congress Party Rules and Regulation (1969), in reference to Banda, state: 'The Life President, as the Supreme Leader and Symbol of the Supremacy of the Party, must be respected, honoured and revered by every member of the Party, high or low, and Party members, high or low, are expected to conduct themselves in a courteous and respectful manner in his presence' (cited in Short 1974: 168).

[10] The September 1967 MCP annual convention recommended that Jehovah's Witnesses be banned in Malawi because, it claimed, 'the attitudes of its adherents is not only inimical to the progress of this country but also so negative in every way that it endangers the stability of peace and calm' (Malawi Congress Party 1985: 5). A special Government Gazette Supplement Notice 235 of October 1967 officially banned the sect.

[11] *Wangali kadi muwakamule ni muwatawe*
Wangali kadi kulira akulira wele
Wangali kadi kugona ngakugona wele
Wangali kadi welewo muwakamule ni muwatawe

Wangali kadi atoche ku Malawi
Wangali kadi a Malawi akukana
Wangali kadi welewo muwakamule ni muwatawe

Malawi felt that everyone must conform to their form of society envisaged under Banda. Those who refused to conform must be sent into exile. No one was allowed to be different, even if they wanted to keep out of politics or stay neutral. Everyone had to be a member of the MCP to live in Malawi.

In the song below, Nyerere and his group from Mulanje threaten that if they see anyone confusing the people, Banda will hear about him/her when it is all over. In other words, people would deal with the individual before telling Banda. The people, like Banda, had become the law.

> If we see anyone confusing people, you'll hear the story when it is over
> Such a person, if he/she is lucky to be apprehended alive
> We will tear him/her piece by piece until all of us get a share
> Because you, Ngwazi, you have brought us sweet things in Malawi.[12]

Causing confusion here included criticizing or complaining about the president, party, or government, and other acts of rebellion. Banda and his supporters labelled individuals that disagreed with them 'dissidents', 'rebels', 'traitors', and similar names. The song promises that the people will torture and even kill whomever they caught causing confusion among the people. The song justifies mob violence as a weapon against political dissidents. This was never an empty threat. The experience of the Jehovah's Witnesses is one example. They were persecuted, tortured, raped, and killed while members of the party and ordinary people looted their property (Watchtower 1968: 71-89; Klaus Fiedler 1996: 149-176). This was besides what Banda and the government did, locking up hundreds of them in indefinite detention without trial (Africa Watch 1990: 63-67).

The following song is about Banda's so-called Enemy No. 1, Kanyama Chiume, one of the 1964 cabinet rebels.[13] It was sung by women of Karonga district.

> We, in Malawi, in this district

---

[12] *Tikamuwona munthu wosokoneza muzamva zokuthaitha*
Munthu amaneyo akangokhala ndi mwayi ndikugwidwa
Ife tizamusina pang'ono pang'ono tonse tikwanire
Chifukwa inu a Ngwazi mwaza ndi zokoma kuno ku Malawi.

When Muwalo was arrested for plotting to overthrow Banda in 1976, Nyerere and his group sang: *Boma la Malawi lili ndi chifundo/Koma zoona kumtenga Muwalo/Koma kumuyimika mkhoti kumzenga milando.*[The government of Malawi is very kind/Is it true that they caught Muwalo/And put him in court for trial?]. The song says people wished Muwalo was given to them for punishment.
[13] Kanyama Chiume and five other cabinet ministers rebelled against Banda in September 1964 immediately following independence because, among other things, they claimed Banda was a dictator. For details see, Colin Baker 2001. *Revolt of the Ministers: The Malawi Cabinet Crisis, 1964-1965.* London: I.B. Tauris Publishers.

Reject Kanyama
We tell you in this country of Malawi
We reject Kanyama.[14]

Other rebels were similarly rejected and ridiculed. The message was clear; the people of Malawi would not tolerate rebellion, opposition, or criticism of Banda or their society.

In these songs, everyone in Malawi was expected to adhere to the four cornerstones of Unity, Loyalty, Obedience and Discipline. It was a country where Banda, as life president, was supposed to lead without challenge, criticism or complaint. Banda was to be revered and even worshipped. As the songs show, Malawi was an extremely intolerant society, where fear and hatred of criticism was deep rooted. Therefore, the political discourse in the songs while affirming Banda's hegemony undermined and stifled dissent.

Counter-hegemonic discourses in traditional and popular music

Hegemony is always a contested situation, always under threat from contending forces trying to establish their own hegemonies. Thus a hegemonic class must always work against counter-hegemonic forces. Despite a harsh censorship regime, appropriation, and monopolization of political songs for Banda in Malawi, possibilities of criticism of Banda or dissent within this set up still existed and were sometimes exploited. Mapanje (1997: 76) observes that 'because almost everybody suffered some form of censorship or self-censorship in Banda's Malawi we were forced to find alternative strategies for survival; alternative metaphors for the expression of our feelings and ideas'. These alternative strategies and metaphors included thematic and linguistic adaptations of the oral materials to criticize Banda. Some musicians, like poets, for example, adopted ambiguity to criticize Banda. They hoped to avoid detection and detention in that way. The use of ambiguity and innuendo shows how difficult it was to compose songs in Malawi that were overtly critical of Banda (See Drewett 2003, for a discussion of similar strategies in apartheid South Africa).

Some of the criticism in songs came about because of the changing political circumstances rather than by deliberate design by composers or performers. Examples are songs for Honala. Honala is a dance performed by members of Paka Town Band of Chintheche in Nkhata-Bay district since the 1940s. It is called Honala because they use an accordion. John Banda (no relation of President Banda) and late Vein Nkhata were amongst song composers and performers of

---

[14] *Muno m'Malawi m'boma ili*
Tikukana cha Kanyama
Tikumuphalirani m'charu cha Malawi
Tikukana cha Knayama.

Honala. The song, 'Wamzenga ku Mapiri' (You're going to Live in the Hills) below, was originally performed as an anti-federation[15] nationalist song in the 1950s (Interview, 2002). The song warns people supporting the federation that they would be chased to the dry hills away from the lakeshore once federation is defeated. Anyone who supported federation was considered a traitor and called Capricorn.[16] The song says,

> You're going to live in the hills, woman
> You're going to live in the hills, man
> Money that you've received
> Has brought you trouble, woman
> Has brought you trouble, man
> Because of money you're going to live in the hills.[17]

People of Chintheche in Nkhata-Bay, like most people living along Lake Malawi, rely on fishing for their survival. To be sent away from the lakeshore onto the dry hills is being cut off from sources of livelihood. It is, therefore, a severe punishment. The song claims the Federal government gave money to people to support the federation, hence the warning of punishment. After independence, the song was sung in praise of Banda as a nationalist leader. Banda led Malawi to secede from federation in 1963 when the country became self-governing and then to independence in 1964.

Until 1970, Banda seems to have had no problem with the song. However, in the 1970s the people in Chintheche area were moved from the lakeshore by Banda's government to make room for a paper factory and related development that Banda proposed and promised. People that were moved to the hills were given money as compensation. However, the factory did not materialize neither did the other development projects. Once this became apparent in late 1980s, people wanted to return to the lakeshore areas but the government rejected their wish. When the song was played for Banda this time the new connotations became implicit, suggesting that Banda has deceived people into giving up their life near the lake for dry unproductive hills in exchange for money. It should be mentioned

---

[15] The British colonial government declared Northern Rhodesia (now Zambia), Southern Rhodesia (now Zimbabwe) and Nyasaland (now Malawi) a federation in 1953. The majority of the people of Nyasaland resisted the federation but some supported it.

[16] The Capricorn Society was made up of liberal whites who, while not condoning colonial exploitation and oppression, did not encourage radical solutions such as the end of colonialism or the break up of the federation in this case. See Bizek J. Phiri (1991).

[17] *Mwamzenga ku Mapiri, ama,*
Mwamzenga ku Mapiri, ada
Ndalama mwalondazo
Zamtayanimo, ama
Zamtayanimo, ada
Mwamzenga nazo ku Mapiri.

that the wording of the song did not change at all. It was the meaning derived from the new circumstances that made the song protest instead of praise. The song became an expression of the people's disenchantment with Banda's politics. Vein Nkhata and John Banda claimed that once the new meaning became obvious the national radio station MBC and John Tembo queried them (Interview 2002). The group feigned ignorance of any other meaning than the nationalist cause. However, Paka Town Band stopped singing the song out of fear for reprisals.

Another song for Honala, 'Wateremuka *Ngwazi*' (*Ngwazi* has Escaped), again dates to the anti-federation days. The full title of the song reads, 'Wateremuka *Ngwazi* ku Chisazga' (*Ngwazi* has Escaped from Federation) meaning that Banda has outwitted the white man and slipped out of the federation. However, after 1973 the song took on a new meaning. At the 1973 MCP annual convention in Mzuzu, Banda introduced a request by Manoah Chirwa, Matthews Phiri, and Charles Matinga to return home from exile. These had sided with white led pro-federation parties during the struggle for independence, hence were called Capricorns. After independence, they found life untenable in Malawi when they were persecuted as white man's stooges. They escaped into exile. Banda asked delegates to deliberate and decide what to do with the request. Apart from party activists and functionaries, traditional chiefs were among the delegates. Taking him on trust, many delegates accepted what they thought were Banda's intentions to pardon Manoah and others. However, by the close of the convention Banda was furious with those who supported their return, accusing them of sympathizing with rebels (*Daily Times* 5, 6, 10, 11 September 1973). Several chiefs who supported the motion from Nkhata-Bay, Manoah's home district, and other delegates were beaten up, arrested and tortured, and/or killed in detention.[18] The song, 'Wateremuka *Ngwazi*', gained the meaning, '*Ngwazi* is a trickster'. It suggested, implicitly, that Banda tricked delegates into thinking he wanted to pardon Manoah and his colleagues while in fact he simply wanted to accuse them of supporting rebels. Instead of federal authorities, it was the delegates to the convention that Banda had outwitted. Therefore, what had all along been praise became a protest song against Banda with the changing circumstances. Despite this new meaning, the song was never queried or banned. It successfully eluded censorship.

Probably one of the most prominent and accomplished popular musicians who dared to challenge Banda is Wambali Mkandawire, a gospel musician whose career dates back to the 1970s. While primarily performing gospel music, some of his songs make social-political comments on events in Malawi. In his songs, sung at a time of extreme repression and censorship, he relies more on innuendo than overt criticism.

'Kayuni Njuwi' (1988) and 'Ulanda Wera' (1991) in *Timtamande* and *Kavuluvulu* respectively, use innuendo to protest Banda's politics of violent

---

[18] Amongst those beaten up and deposed included the following chiefs: Malengamzoma, Kabunduli, M'bwana of Nkhata-Bay district, Chikumbu of Mulanje district, and Mwase of Kasungu district. Chief Mwase later died in detention and his chieftainship was abolished.

suppression of dissent and misappropriation of history and tradition for purposes of his politics. 'Kayuni Njuwi' narrates the killing of three cabinet ministers (Dick Matenje, Aaron Gadama, and Twaibu Sangala) and a Member of Parliament (David Chiwanga) in Mwanza in May 1983 for what were political reasons (Nation 1993: 1; Malawi 1994).[19] The song employs oral traditional materials and deliberate ambiguity to contest the government's story (Daily Times 1983: 1) that the four politicians died as a result of a road accident. Wambali uses a folk narrative about greed, murder, cover up, and lies to insinuate the government's attempted cover-up of the murders (Chirambo 2001: 211-217).

> Go away, bird!
> Why did you deny?
> Saying you have not killed him?
> What about the bird?
> What is it saying?
>
> You have spilled, you have spilled
> The blood of an innocent person.[20] (Mkandawire 1988. By permission)

The bird here represents witnesses to and evidence of the murders. 'Go away, bird' refers to the efforts to get rid of the witnesses and evidence of the murders and other similar mysterious disappearances of Banda's critics and opponents in Malawi. Such commentary, even by innuendo was extremely dangerous given the fact that it was only five years after the incident, and therefore poked at a raw wound. But despite his efforts to camouflage his criticism, authorities still decoded the message and withdrew 'Kayuni Njuwi' from the public radio, MBC, though the song continued to circulate in the country.[21]

In 'Ulanda Wera', Wambali reclaims tradition and history to complain against Banda's abuse of power. He expresses disillusionment with Banda's shattering of the dreams and aspirations of independence by lamenting the detention and killings

---

[19] Wambali's song, which was released six years before a government inquiry into the alleged accident of 1994, fed on rumours and speculation.

[20] *Fya mbalame!*
Bwanji m'nkakana?
Kuti tsimnaphe?
Nanga mbalame?
Kachenjerekete Kachenjerekete Ka
Ikuliranji?

Mwakhetsa, mwakhetsa!
Mwazi wa munthu wosalakwa.

[21] Wambali was informed by a sympathizer/fan at the radio station that verbal instructions had been issued not to play the song (Interview, 1998).

of political opponents such as Orton Chirwa and Dunduzu Chisiza, for whom, Wambali says the nation of Malawi mourns.

> When Chirwa protested, he was arrested,
> Leg irons hurt on my way to jail.
>
> We're crying
> We children of Malawi today
> We're crying for Chilembwe
> We're crying for Dunduzu.[22] (Mkandawire 1991. By permission)

After the 1964 cabinet rebellion, Orton Chirwa formed and led an opposition party called Malawi Freedom Movement (MAFREMO) in exile. In 1981, secret service agents posing as underground members of his party inside Malawi lured him to the border between Malawi and Zambia. He was arrested and taken into Malawi, tried and sentenced to death for treason. His sentence was commuted to life and he died in prison in 1991. Wambali, in the song above, refers to Chirwa as he was dragged in leg irons between prison and court during the trial. Dunduzu Chisiza was amongst the nationalists that invited Banda to lead the independence movement in 1957. He died in a car accident at Thondwe Bridge in Zomba in September 1962, a year before self-rule and two years before independence. His death is suspected to have been a result of foul play by agents of Banda (Power 1998: 369-396; Chirambo 2001: 220-201). British colonial forces killed John Chilembwe in 1915 when he led the first rebellion against colonial administration. He is therefore regarded as the first Malawian martyr. His name, evoked here, suggests that Banda has shattered the dreams and aspirations of independence for which Chilembwe fought.

In both 'Kayuni Njuwi' and 'Ulanda Wera', Wambali deliberately used ambiguity and insinuation to express the frustration of many Malawians over Banda's abuse of power that included detention without trial, torture, and killings of opponents and critics.

---

[22] *WaChirwa wayowoyeko, simbi mmawoko zalira*
Unyolo mmalundi kuwawa, ulendo waku Mbwani uwo.

Tikulira
Tawana waku Malawi lero
Tikulira a Chilembwe
Tikulira a Dunduzu.

Conclusion

The influence of hegemonic power on the masses can be enormous, and where the hegemony is a totalitarian regime, the consequences on fundamental human rights such as free speech and freedom of association, among others, can be catastrophic. First, because as Jeffrey Taffet (1997: 92) argues:

> In manufacturing consent, cultural hegemony eliminate[s] the masses' ability to conceive of the conceptual tools to challenge the structure of the system. Hegemony [keeps] alternatives from public's consciousness; revolution, or reaction against the system, as beyond the range of the mass ideology and thus impossible...not within the masses' range of consciousness.

Banda's hegemonic dictatorship in Malawi meant that the dominant political consciousness was of Banda. As Zeleza (1995: 33-34) notes, 'a whole people were homogenized, infantilized and demeaned, their tongues burdened with voicing and singing only praises and support for Banda'. In other words, the people hardly heard or articulated an alternative ideology to Banda's Kamuzuism. This denied them the conceptual tools to develop a critical awareness of Banda.

Second, Kamuzuism as the dominant ideology in political national discourse stifled dissent and undermined opposition. Hegemony entails active consent and not passive submission, and in this case activism involved suppressing dissenting voices. Songs, for example, rejected all forms of criticism and opposition to Banda. Therefore, in a subtle yet pervasive way, the hegemonic discourse was an instrument for censorship.

In the end, Banda's hegemony and the censorship law and practice created a world of Foucauldian panopticism in Malawi where everyone felt they were being watched or listened to in the manner of Big Brother-is-watching-you that George Orwell describes in *1984*. The saying that 'walls have ears' gained urgency in Banda's Malawi where even a whisper in the dark was dangerous. Zeleza (1995: 33) aptly sums up the nature of censorship in Malawi in this description when he says:

> [Malawi] was land of pervasive fear where words were constantly monitored, manipulated, and mutilated, a country stalked by silence and suspicion it censored memories, stories, and words that contested and mocked its singular authority....Banda's regime waged an endless war against plurality, against voices that told different stories or sang different songs, stories or songs that did not glorify the everlasting king's infinite wisdom....What they wrote, sang, read, thought and dreamt had to be placed under constant surveillance.

And as Mapanje (1997: 74) concludes, Banda's world 'choked with institutions, notions, images, symbols and the language of control and censure', much of which was expressed in traditional songs and popular music. Therefore, while accepting the perniciousness of Banda's conventional censorship in Malawi, this chapter suggests that the Banda and the MCP's hegemony, though subtle, was yet a more pervasive and insidious form of censorship because it operated at the level of ideology. Banda and the MCP turned vibrant Malawian cultures and traditions of entertainment into instruments for censorship. They employed traditional and popular songs as vehicles of the hegemonic ideology of Kamuzuism that insisted on the four cornerstones, which as ideology and practice undermined and stifled dissent, becoming a form of censorship.

References

Africa Watch. 1990. *Where Silence Rules: The Suppression of Dissent in Malawi.* New York: Human Rights Watch.

Baker, C. 2001. 'Revolt of the Ministers: The Malawi Cabinet Crisis, 1964-1965', London: I.N. Tauris.

Boggs, Carl. 1984. *The Two Revolutions: Antonio Gramsci and the Dilemmas of Western Marxism.* Boston: South End Press.

Chirambo, Reuben. 2001. 'Protesting Politics of "Death and Darkness" in Malawi', *Journal of Folklore Research* 38.3, pp. 205-227.

Chirambo, Reuben. 2004. 'Political Songs, Violence, and the Making of a Political Tradition in Banda's Malawi, 1964-94', paper presented at AIGES Conference, 'From Conflict to Civil Society', Nordic Africa Institute, Sweden.

Chirwa, Wiseman Chijere. 2001. 'Dancing Towards Dictatorship: Political Songs and Popular Culture in Malawi', *Nordic Journal of African Studies* 10.1, pp. 1-27.

Daily Times (Malawi). 1973. 'MCP Annual Convention', September 5, 6, 10, and 11.

Daily Times (Malawi). 1983. 'Move to Dispel Rumours, Unsubstantiated Speculation', May 21, p. 1.

Drewett, M. 2003. 'Music in the struggle to end apartheid: South Africa', in M. Cloonan and R. Garofalo (eds), *Policing Pop*. Philadelphia: Temple University Press, pp. 153-165.

Femia, Joseph V. 1981. *Gramsci's Political Thought: Hegemony, Consciousness, and the Revolutionary Process.* Oxford: Clarendon Press.

Fiedler, Klaus. 1996. 'Power At the Receiving End: the Jehovah's Witnesses' Experience in One Party Malawi' in *God, People and Power in Malawi*, ed. Kenneth Ross. Blantyre, Malawi: CLAIM, pp. 145-176.

Gibbs, James. 1982. 'Of Kamuzuism and Chameleons: The Experiences of Censorship in Malawi', *The Literary Half-Yearly* 23.2, pp. 69-83.

Gramsci, Antonio. 1971. *Selections from Prison Notebooks of Antonio Gramsci.* Ed. and trans. Q. Hoare and G.N. Smith. New York: International Publishers.

Malawi Congress Party. 1965. *Constitution of the Malawi Congress Party and Rules and Regulations.* Limbe: National Committee.

Malawi Congress Party. 1985. *Malawi Congress Party Annual Convention Resolutions, 1965-85.* Lilongwe: National Committee.

Malawi. 1968. *Censorship and Control of Entertainment Act.* Zomba: Government Printer.

Malawi. 1975. *Catalogue of Banned Publications, Cinematograph Pictures and Records from 1968 to 1st October 1975.* Zomba: Government Printer.

Malawi. Commission of Inquiry. 1994. *Mwanza Road Accident: Verbatim Report of Proceedings.* Limbe: Civic Offices.

Malawi Congress Party. 1985. *MCP Annual Convention Resolutions, 1965-85.* Lilongwe: National Committee.

Mapanje, Jack. 1989. 'Censoring the African Poem', *Index on Censorship* 9, pp. 7-9, 11.

Mapanje, Jack. 1997. 'Leaving No Traces of Censure', *Index on Censorship* 5, pp. 71-81.

Mbembe, Achille. 2001. *On the Postcolony.* Berkeley: University of California Press.

The Nation (Malawi). 1993. 'Report on the Mwanza Murders', August 23, p. 1.

Peleg, Ilan. 1993. 'Freedom of Expression in the Third World: The Human Rights of Writers in Developing Countries' in *Patterns of Censorship around the World*, ed. Ilan Peleg. Boulder: Westview Press, pp. 110-133.

Phiri, B.J. 1991. 'The Capricorn Africa Society Revisited: The Impact of Liberalism in Zambia's Colonial History, 1949-1963. *International Journal of African Historical Studies*, Vol 24, no 1, pp. 65-83.

Power, Joey. 1998. 'Remembering Du: An Episode in the Development of Malawi's Political Culture', *African Affairs* 97.388, pp. 369-396.

Short, Philip. 1974. *Banda.* London: Routledge and Kegan Paul.

Simon, Roger. 1982. *Gramsci's Political Thought: An Introduction.* London: Lawrence and Wishart.

Taffet, Jeffrey. 1997. '"My Guitar is Not for the Rich": The New Chilean Song Movement and the Politics of Culture', *Journal of American Culture* 20.2, pp. 91-103.

Watchtower. 1968. 'Shocking Religious Persecution in Malawi', January 2, pp. 71-89.

Zeleza, Paul Tiyambe. 1995. 'Totalitarian Power and Censorship in Malawi', *Southern Africa Political and Economic Monthly* 8.11, pp. 33-37.

Discography

Mkandawire, Wambali. 1988. 'Kayuni Njuwi', *Timtamande.* Cape Town: Krakatoa Music Works.

Mkandawite, Wambali. 1991. 'Ulanda Wera', *Kavuluvulu.* Glasgow: Jump Productions.

Phiri, Saleta and AB Sounds. 1988. *Malawi.* No record label details.

Interviews with the author

Banda, J.B. and Vein Nkhata. Chintheche, Nkhata-Bay, 14 July 2002.
Mkandawire, Wambali. Blantyre, 28 February 1998.

Chapter 8

Why Don't You Sing about the Leaves and the Dreams? Reflecting on Music Censorship in Apartheid South Africa

Johnny Clegg and Michael Drewett

Introduction

Probably the most systematic and formalized attempt at censoring popular music on the African continent took place in South Africa during the apartheid era. The Nationalist government rose to power in 1948 and instituted a plethora of repressive apartheid laws aimed at promoting the interests of the white population at the expense of other designated race groups, and attempting a system of racial and ethnic purity by keeping different groups apart. However, it was only in the 1960s that the government specifically turned its attention to the control of publications in general, including music. Through the control of music on the airwaves, control of publications by means of a central government censorship board and police surveillance and harassment of musicians, South African popular music was routinely monitored and censored as part of the state's attempt to maintain apartheid hegemony.

This hegemony was maintained, in part because of state censorship and control of the broadcast sector, for the next three decades. However, by the late 1980s resistance to the state became increasingly widespread and ultimately led to the demise of apartheid in the early 1990s.

This chapter provides a general overview of popular music censorship during the apartheid era with a particular focus on the experience of two groups formed by musician Johnny Clegg: Juluka, who released their first seven-inch single in 1976 and broke up in 1985, and Savuka, who were formed in 1987 and continued into the 1990s. The chapter not only considers the censorship of music but also the way in which musicians attempted to overcome obstacles to being heard by as wide an audience as possible.[1]

---

[1] This chapter comprises a short contribution from Johnny Clegg which has been critically elaborated by Michael Drewett, based on his own research and information from an in-depth interview conducted with Johnny Clegg in April 1998.

State control and censorship at the level of broadcast

The apartheid government set about applying its apartheid polices to the broadcast
sector when it passed the Broadcasting Amendment Act (Number 49) of 1960.
According to the Act a whites only Bantu Programme Control Board was
established (in 1960) to oversee radio programming for black South Africans on
the state-owned and controlled South Africa Broadcasting Corporation (SABC).
This saw the establishment of separate radio stations for each of the major black
languages of the South African homelands. The idea was to bring 'home to the
Bantu population that separate development is, in the first place, self-development
through the medium of their own language and that, by this means, there will be
progress in all spheres of life' (SABC Annual Report of 1967, cited in Hamm
1995: 194). The SABC was divided into numerous stations which each catered for
particular language groups. For example there was an English service, an
Afrikaans service and seven Radio Bantu stations, each catering for an 'indigenous
bantu' language. The official policy was that on these stations languages were not
to be mixed. On the Radio Bantu stations African languages were separated from
each other. For example, listeners did not hear Sotho on a Zulu station.

In addition to administering structural control through the establishment of a
multitude of radio stations, during the 1960s and 1970s the South African state
developed a set of censorship regulations which were divided into four broad areas:
political, sexual, religious and cultural. The airwaves were at this time completely
owned by the state with no independent radio or TV. As a musician operating in
this context it was a given that one's work would be screened by the SABC's
censorship board. During this period record companies were obliged to submit
written lyrics of all songs or singles seeking airplay. If the lyrics were too sexually
explicit, had any political content questioning the government's actions, offended
the Calvinistic interpretation of the Bible or used Jesus' name in vain and finally if
the song broke any interpretation of the laws of cultural segregation, the song
would not be playlisted. If the record company felt that the song was strong they
would have to build in extra adspend and promote the song in record bars and other
outlets, finding ways to bring the song to the attention of the public. A number of
examples will give an indication of how the system operated.

In 1976, a Juluka song called 'Woza Friday' was refused airplay in terms of the
cultural segregation laws. The song was a folk pop melody and included a mix of
English and Zulu in the lyrics. It was essentially American-European in its musical
structure, with the Zulu lyric introduced and the song built around it. The chorus
included the lines 'Woza, woza, Friday my darling,' 'Woza, Woza, Friday my
sweetie' (Come to me Friday my darling, Come to me Friday my sweetie). The
head of Radio Zulu (a white man) said 'look, you know, these are adopted, you
could have used a Zulu word for this, and this is an insult to the Zulu people'. They
said that they could not play the song because it would insult the Zulus. The head
of the station explained that the laws of cultural segregation were particularly
strong against language mixing. This was presented as the government 'protecting'
the integrity of indigenous African languages against Anglicization and 'linguistic
dilution' by western culture. The fact that there already existed a cross over

'Tsotsi' patois and that Zulu spoken in the street bore little resemblance to the classical forms and mannerisms being protected by the state apparatus, was seen as an aberration. In a clear example of Franz Fanon's notion of the 'mummification' (1970: 44) of African culture, these African languages and cultures were 'frozen' into a timeless representation that the government required in order to maintain an impression of independent tribal worlds which apartheid was trying to maintain.

As stated above, apart from censorship for cultural reasons, the SABC also refused airplay to songs for religious, sexual and political reasons. For example, when the Beatles proclaimed that they were more famous than Jesus, their music was pulled off the air on the SABC until they had apologized. In the 1980s Hot Chocolate's 'You Sexy Thing' and Carrie McDowell's 'Casual Sex' were censored because they were sexually suggestive while in the same decade many more songs were censored for political reasons, including Latin Quarter's 'No rope as long as time', Savuka's 'Asimbonanga', and Sipho Mabuse's 'Chant'.

The SABC's stringent approach to censorship ensured that a narrow lyrical variety was heard on South African airwaves, and as previously mentioned, musicians whose music was not played had to seek alternative forms of publicity if they wanted their music to be heard.

Central government censorship

A further mechanism for controlling music was introduced by means of the Publications and Entertainment Act (Number 2) of 1963. It was the first attempt by the nationalist government to implement an apartheid censorship system at central government level (Stewart 1990). Accordingly, a state censorship mechanism was established to inspect publications submitted to the Publications Control Board by the members of the public, customs officials and the police. Publications could be banned on two levels. First, a publication could be banned for distribution, which meant that it could not be sold in retail outlets or imported. However, people already in possession of a copy could keep it without legal ramifications. Secondly, publications regarded as particularly subversive could be banned for possession. This meant that in addition to the conditions of the aforementioned type of banning, it was also illegal to possess such material.

The system especially focused on films and books. University libraries had to keep banned books under a special section. The books had to be read in the library and had to be prescribed in the coursework of department in which the student was registered. Readers' names were also recorded in a library register. As indicated, possession of certain highly banned books and records carried jail sentences. People could also be banned in the sense that they could not be quoted or have their photographs published in South Africa. Correspondence from them was also illegal.

Although the Act was primarily intended to deal with film and printed publications, it was also used to censor vinyl recordings, including a variety of popular music recordings, such as Pete Seeger's 'We Shall Overcome' and Blue Mink's 'Melting Pot', both of which were subject to distribution bans. The former was banned because of its political message while the latter was banned because it promoted inter-racial sex and the breaking down of racial barriers. By the time the Film and Publications Act (Number 42) of 1974 replaced the 1963 Act, music regularly featured in the new Directorate of Publications' government gazette lists of banned music.[2] During the student protest marches in 1980, Pink Floyd's song 'Another brick in the wall' with the line 'We don't need no education' was subject to a distribution ban because school children sang it as they marched. Other songs to be banned from distribution included Peter Gabriel's 'Biko', the Special AKA's '(Free) Nelson Mandela' and George Michael's 'I want your sex'. The ultimate ban, whereby it was illegal to own a copy of a record, was placed on Roger Lucey's *The Road is Much Longer* album, because of its political content.

Police harassment and apartheid laws

Apart from legislative censorship practised by the SABC and centralized government censorship boards, the police regularly monitored musicians' activities and periodically harassed those who stepped outside of what the police believed to be permissible activity. Juluka's experience bears this out. Their situation was made more difficult because there were both black and white musicians in the group. In the 1970s and 1980s white performers were supposed to apply for a permit to go into townships. The police would ask the group for a permit – which they had not applied for on principle. When the group could not produce a permit the promoter would get into trouble and the police would close the show down, sometimes using dogs and tear gas. In one particularly intimidating incident in Daduza Township in Nigel in the early 1980s the group was playing on the stage in full cry when three policemen with shotguns went onto the stage in camouflaged uniforms. One of them grabbed the microphone and said 'that's it, the show's over'. The group members were really angry because it was a provocative and scary moment for everybody.

As with many groups (especially those with black and white members), Juluka would also experience problems at police roadblocks when travelling to gigs. This was particularly the case in the conservative Orange Free State province where, during the same period, the police would stop them to search their vehicle. On realizing who they were, the police would order the group to offload all their equipment from their three and a half ton truck. The delays would make them late for gigs.

Apart from direct harassment from the police, throughout the 1970s and 1980s Juluka and Savuka were also subject to ongoing police surveillance. Apartheid security branch policeman, Paul Erasmus, revealed that the police had indeed monitored both groups' activities:

---

[2] The main feature of the Film and Publications Act (Number 42) of 1974 was that it consolidated the power of the central state censor.

Johnny Clegg had a file. I personally made entries in that file. Just updating them a bit. I can't remember which LP or which work they'd done at the time. But we never detained those people because their profile was too high. Can you imagine? I mean Savuka – when they so popular in France? Est Zulu blanc, I remember. That would have caused a huge stink. I think then the security establishment were ... being more sort of circumspect, you know, rather leave these okes. (Interview with Michael Drewett 2001)

The police's attitude allowed Juluka and Savuka the space to tour South Africa knowing that they were unlikely to be arrested and thrown into jail. Nevertheless, as the preceding discussion suggests, they needed to tread cautiously, so as not to provoke the police who at the best of times could be unpredictable.

Apart from the police, musicians also had problems with local authorities who could place obstacles in the way of performance. A fairly bizarre example of this occurred in the late 1970s when the Pietersburg town council banned Juluka. They said that the group was engaged in bastardizing western culture by mixing it with African culture, and the two cultures should not be promoted in that way. Although culture was put forward as the reason for the banning, the underlying reason was political. For the conservative members of the council, Juluka were involved in a political act against cultural segregation, against the whole idea of separate cultures. As a result they were shut out, just as they had been when the SABC refused to play 'Woza Friday'.

Musical resistance to apartheid

Despite the various government strategies used to silence musicians, musicians with a resistant message nevertheless sought ways to be heard by their potential audience. For example, when Juluka's 'Woza Friday' was refused airplay on SABC (as discussed above) Johnny Clegg realized that there were small little cultural spaces that existed in South Africa at that time, where musicians could go out and play. They were all behind the scenes, but could be found if musicians were prepared to go and perform. In fact some police were prepared to turn a blind eye as long as musicians were not causing trouble and making fiery speeches.

Juluka's approach from the outset was to seek out spaces where performance was possible despite apartheid strictures. They initially sought private venues such as university and church halls because the officials could not close these down as easily as public venues such as town halls. Ironically Juluka also began to perform in the homelands because the internal laws of the homelands contradicted apartheid laws, and the internal police forces of the homelands were not concerned about the politics which Juluka represented. As a result Juluka used the homelands as a platform from which to play their music and take forward their message. They consequently became popular in places such as Mafikeng and Mbabatu in Bophutatswana.

To begin with Juluka was a vehicle through which Clegg explored the issue of being a white African and finding a place for European culture in a base of African music. Yet it was also a platform whereby traditional music could be appreciated from another angle. Juluka created a context in their live performances in which white audiences became far more open to traditional music with the incorporation of African languages than what they would otherwise have been. In this sense Juluka made white audiences (in particular) more aware of Zulu culture and promoted racial and ethnic mixing as a way of life. Musician David Kramer bears testimony to this:

> If I think of Johnny Clegg, what he really achieved initially was phenomenal. When I first went to a concert of his in Cape Town – it was the first time I'd ever seen Johnny Clegg – it took all our breath away. And I remember everyone was on the edge of their seats. It felt like a Beatles' concert. And here we saw these whites and blacks performing in this band together, this new kind of South African Zulu music, and it was just that whole thing was so exciting because it was a living example of what South Africa could be. So that – the image of that – and the excitement was really where the power lay in what Johnny was doing. Regardless of what he was singing. (Interview with Michael Drewett 1998)

Importantly, Kramer emphasizes the value of performance as a means of resistance/protest. Although Juluka's lyrics often expressed important political sentiments, for Kramer the importance of their music lay in the image of racial collaboration and non-racism revealed to the audience through Juluka's performance. This was particularly important within the context of apartheid. White youth were especially drawn to the image presented by Juluka, precisely because the images they saw contrasted with apartheid ideology and the racist respectability of their parents' generation. Lipsitz (1994: 54) argues that in such circumstances white audiences can 'identify with transgression while at the same time distancing themselves from it by connecting the violation of cultural norms with the ostensibly "natural" and biologically-driven urges of a despised (racial and ethnic) group'. In providing the audience with a window into Zulu culture, Juluka tapped into a forbidden curiosity which allowed the audience to safely consider an alternative at a distance. However, the analytic categories of 'other' 'cultural' and 'natural' should not be stretched too far. Nhlanhla Ngcobo (1982: 6) points to the wide acceptance and popularity amongst black South Africans as Juluka's successful intervention on a socio-cultural level in dissolving racial stereotypes and prejudice. In Juluka's music and performance: 'The common error of equating "traditional" with "primitive" and "Western" with "civilised" is challenged and replaced by attitudes of compatibility and equality' (Ngcobo 1982: 6).

As a result of the South African context within which Juluka performed, their cultural exploration took on important political significance. While their message was not a confrontational political one, it was a coded mesh of culture and politics. The coded message lay in the way they dressed (the mixing of African and western cultures), the way they moved, (wearing skins and other Zulu dress and doing Zulu war dancing) the mixture of English and Zulu language and the exploration of Zulu culture musically and in the lyrics of their songs. For the band members Juluka was an experiment which did not always work, but which nevertheless constituted a genuine adventure, of trying to find a way through a society characterized by cultural ignorance and separateness.

Juluka's exploration of Zulu culture in the South African context, where for a long time it was illegal to share basic amenities such as toilets, park benches and buses, communicated a vision of a different South Africa to the audience. In this way music was used to prepare Juluka audiences (through the image of inter-racial collaboration and freedom of association) for a post-apartheid future. The imagery of Juluka acted as a means of publicly challenging apartheid notions of racial and ethnic separateness. The very justification and legitimacy of representations of apartheid inequality were threatened by Juluka's demonstration of an alternative which challenged apartheid's values by demonstrating a freedom more alluring than apartheid separation.

This theme was also portrayed on the group's album covers. Juluka albums' covers typically included photographs of Johnny Clegg and Sipho Mchunu together wearing traditional Zulu dress. The images were always of equality and strength. The cover of the *Universal Men* (1979) album is a photograph of Johnny and Sipho posing defiantly on a mine dump. A cryptic message lay in the representation of the group's name, positioned in the sky. Richard Pithouse (1999:40) elaborated on the image:

> The name of the band appeared as an engraving on a gold bar. Its shimmering glitz clashed, pointedly, with the more organic colours of the sky, the rocks, the men and their clothes. Juluka means sweat in Zulu and the message couldn't have been clearer: Johannesburg's wealth and glamour is built not just on gold but also on the sweat of the men, the migrant labourers, who mined that gold.

On Juluka's follow-up album, *African Litany* (1981), Johnny and Sipho are shown in a smiling, friendly pose, Sipho helping to put a bangle on Johnny's arm. The back cover comprises a collage of drawings and photographs placed against a wagon wheel, suggesting that all the images depicted are connected to the turning of the wheel. There are images of Zulu warriors, settler soldiers and a boer on a horse, black mineworkers, a black refuse collector, images of urban areas and a white woman lying on a deckchair in the sun. There is also a photograph of a surfer on the Durban beachfront. As with the *Universal men* imagery, the implication was that the prosperous side of South African life was built on the backs of forced black labour. Yet amongst the divergent images there are also pictures of Zulu dancing and music, a reminder that leisure and cultural celebration continue despite apartheid.

Lyrically the group began with an exploration of Zulu culture and history, but increasingly addressed political issues, although Juluka were never apolitical. On the group's first album, released in 1979, subversive political messages were disguised in symbolism. For example, the battle against apartheid was encrypted through the use of a Zulu proverb about two fighting bulls. One bull is large with strong horns while the other is small with tiny horns. But when they fight the little one wins because of superior fighting knowledge. In 1983 the far more politically overt song 'Mdantsane' about the Mdantsane bus boycott was released. In the song someone asks the singer why he does not sing about the leaves and the dreams, and in reply the singer explains that it is because he has seen 'mud-coloured dusty blood on the road to Mdantsane'. In other words, the singer has a responsibility to sing about political issues, and not remain apolitical. When Clegg's long-time musical partner, Sipho Mchunu, left Juluka in 1985, the group disbanded and were followed thereafter by Savuka, a far more politically overt band. Savuka addressed pertinent political issues of the day, such as political assassinations and the continued incarceration of Nelson Mandela.

Unionization as a form of taking forward musicians' interests

Apart from opposing the apartheid state through their music and related activities, progressive musicians decided to form a musicians' union in the late 1980s. The idea was to support musicians' rights in general, which included both their economic and political interests (which in any case were often interrelated). As a result the South African Musicians' Alliance (SAMA) was formed with Mara Louw as the President and Johnny Clegg as the Vice President. In order to overcome differences between musicians who advocated divergent political positions, the alliance did not affiliate to any particular political organization, but did put forward its own political position based on the political needs of musicians within apartheid South Africa. After much discussion SAMA was developed around three freedoms: freedom of association, freedom of expression and freedom of movement. Those three freedoms were crucial for the daily livelihood of musicians because they had to move around, they had to be able to sing about what they wanted to sing, and they had to be able to associate with people of other races and other ethnic groups to do their work. This political position was debated and accepted by the umbrella anti-apartheid United Democratic Front (UDF), thus giving SAMA important political clout within the anti-apartheid movement. In exchange, musicians who became a member of the alliance, had to subscribe to SAMA's political position.

For progressive musicians, one of the advantages of joining SAMA turned out to be its ability to assist them in navigating their way around the obstacles created by the cultural boycott. As indicated in Chapter 2, Clegg's argument was that there is a difference between the culture of the oppressed masses and the culture of the ruling elite. It was important that there be some kind of a mechanism whereby the organizers of the boycott could see that. Yet before the launch of the UDF there was not an internal structure which could monitor the situation and inform the organizers of the boycott that particular bands were not part of a government- or state-funded group and were not promoting the division of South Africa into homelands: that they were just musicians. When SAMA was formed in 1988 it assisted the UDF in taking a position on the boycott. The argument from progressive musicians was that they were the ones who were being boycotted, being censored, banned and having their shows stopped. As result they wanted to have a say in how the boycott operated. After negotiations and discussions with overseas anti-apartheid groups it was agreed that members of the alliance were considered as acceptable for overseas performances. However, as revealed in Chapter 2, disputes over who could perform where and when nevertheless abounded. Regardless of the difficulties, SAMA was undoubtedly an important initiative taken by musicians wanting more security and control over their own lives in a severely repressive context. This was especially the case when musicians supported UDF causes by performing at political rallies for organizations such as the End Conscription Campaign and the Congress of South African Trade Unions.

Conclusion

Although South African musicians were confronted with a myriad of censorial mechanisms overseen by the apartheid state, those who wanted to were able to find spaces within which to get their message heard. The examples of Juluka and Savuka provide valuable insight into the ways in which apartheid censorship operated, yet we are also able to learn important lessons about the need to explore the terrain in search of platforms from which musicians can nevertheless communicate with and be heard by their potential audiences. Those South African musicians who achieved this formed part of an important soundscape of resistance which beat against the walls of apartheid. Through their effort they indeed helped to tear down the wall.

References

Drewett, M. 2004. 'Aesopian Strategies of Textual Resistance in the Struggle to Overcome the Censorship of Popular Music in Apartheid South Africa', in Beate Müller (ed.), *Censorship and Cultural Regulation in the Modern Age*. Amsterdam: Rodopi. pp.189-207.

Fanon, F. 1970. *Toward the African Revolution*. Harmondsworth: Penguin.

Gramsci, A. 1971. *Selections from Prison Notebooks of Antonio Gramsci*. New York: International Publishers.

Hamm, C. 1995. *Putting Popular Music in its Place*. Cambridge: Cambridge University Press.

Lipsitz, G. 1994. *Dangerous Crossroads: Popular Music, Postmodernism and the Poetics of Place*. London: Verso.

Ngcobo, N. 1982. 'Glimpses into South Africa – A Perspective Through Juluka Music'. *Reality* Volume 14 Number 1, January.

Pithouse, R. 2000. 'A National Treasure Turns 21'. *Mail and Guardian* October 20 to 26.

Stewart, P. 1990. 'Beyond the Mythology of Censorship in South Africa'. *Reality* Volume 22 No 4.

Discography

Blue Mink. 1969. 'Melting Pot'. Philips.
Gabriel, Peter. 1980. *Peter Gabriel* (3rd album). Charisma Records.
Hot Chocolate. 1987. 'You Sexy Thing'. EMI.
Juluka. 1976. 'Woza Friday'. Released on *Ubuhle Bemvelo*. 1982. Minc.
Juluka. 1979. *Universal Men*. CBS.
Juluka. 1981. African Litany. Minc.
Juluka. 1983. *Work for All*. Minc.
Latin Quarter. 1986. *Modern Times*. Rockin' Horse Records.
Lucey, Roger. 1979. *The Road is Much Longer*. 3rd Ear Music.
Mabuse, Sipho. 1989. *Chant of the Marching*. Gallo.
McDowell, Carrie. 1987. 'Casual Sex'. Motown.
Michael, George. 1987. 'I Want Your Sex'. Sony.
Pink Floyd. 1979. *The Wall*. CBS.
Savuka. 1987. *Third World Child*. EMI.
Seeger, Pete. 1963. 'We Shall Overcome'. CBS.
Special AKA. 1984. 'Free Nelson Mandela'. 2 Tone Records.

Interviews with Michael Drewett

Johnny Clegg	Johannesburg, April 1998.
Erasmus, Paul	George, August 2001.
Kramer, David	Cape Town, July 1998.

Chapter 9

Popular Music Censorship in Tanzania

Kelly M. Askew and John Francis Kitime

Introduction

Music censorship – be it direct censorship by an institutional body or self-censorship by duty-bound or politicized musicians – bears a long history in the East African nation-state of Tanzania. To trace its roots, one needs to begin in the colonial era when legislation was first introduced to constrain the political potentials and perceived moral threats of popular *ngoma* (traditional dance) and newly introduced Western films. The motives and methods of music censorship over subsequent decades would, however, change in tandem with the significant political/economic shifts this nation would undergo. These include: the nationalist period (1954-1966), during which independence was achieved; the socialist period (1967-1985); and the current period of economic and political liberalization (1985-present).

Any study of music censorship in Tanzania is further complicated by the fact that this is a nation composed of two formerly independent entities: the Republic of Tanganyika (independent in 1961) and the People's Democratic Republic of Zanzibar (composed of the islands of Zanzibar and Pemba; independent in 1963). Even after the formation of the United Republic of Tanzania in 1964, each unit maintained, and continues to maintain, its own Ministry of Culture and its own censorship board, with varying approaches to and motivations for censorship. This chapter will survey the history of music censorship in Tanzania across the different periods outlined and explore ways in which censorship has and has not influenced the production and performance of popular music.

Colonial censorship: 1910s-1954

The territory now known as Tanzania was, at various times in its history, colonized by Portugal, Oman, Germany, and Great Britain. Little is known of Portuguese and Omani attitudes toward local musical performance, but German colonial authorities (who claimed Deutsch-Ostafrika as a colony in 1885) did restrict the performance of some ngoma (musical events encompassing music, dance, song, characteristic instrumentation, and a characteristic rhythm) and prohibited at least one called

Ubena.[1] This ngoma, possibly the same as another named Beni, featured Waruguru dancers carrying sticks and singing martial songs. It was apparently last danced in Kilosa District sometime around 'the 1914/18 war and was banned at that time owing to a serious fight which took place as a result of it'.[2] Yet predating this, German authorities in Mwanza region (western Tanzania) looked with suspicion on the activities of Gumha Misinzo, leader of a dance/medicinal/magical society in Sukumaland. Gumha's followers would ultimately form the Bagaalu branch of the Wigashe society, fierce rivals of the Bagiika branch – a competitive dualism that took root after World War I and that remains a key feature of Sukuma communities today (Gunderson 2000). Oral tradition, however, tells of how German soldiers were sent to threaten Gumha with arrest on account of songs he sang flaunting German authority, such as:

> I stand above other singers, Gumha son of Misinzo
> Samike son of Nkanga begot a fierce fire
> You white man, sending your soldiers to fetch me!
> I am coming myself; I do not send others.[3]

Gumha would prove to be the first in a long line of Sukuma singers to run afoul of government authorities. After Germany's defeat in World War I, Tanganyika was designated a British 'Mandated Territory'. In 1930 another Sukuma named Kalungwa Kudahwa was arrested for insulting the local administrative officer and proclaiming resistance to British rule through song.

> The Administrative officer
> At the District Headquarters
> It is the guns of your fathers
> Which make you arrogant
> Your words are many and meaningless
> We'll jump into the graves
> To escape from you -
> You have something hidden in your head
> Just carry on -
> Since you have chosen
> To persecute the helpless
> Just carry on -
> The German gave us up to hyenas
> They ran away, for good![4]

---

[1] Ubena is a genre of ngoma.

[2] Provincial commissioner, Eastern Province, to senior commissioner, Zanzibar, 18 December 1948, ref. no. 792/101, Zanzibar National Archives (henceforth ZNA), AK 14/10, 'Ngomas, 1936-69', Provincial Administration. See also Ranger 1975: 91.

[3] Gumha Misinzo, 1900, 'Nene Nabakilila Balingi' (I Am Above Other Singers), in Songoyi 1988: 225-226.

Terence Ranger's rich history of the Beni ngoma, which spread far and wide throughout Tanganyika in the early 1900s, reveals the high level of concern shared by colonial officials over the popularity of this musical form. In the same year it took over Tanganyika (1919), Great Britain instituted an office of censorship that, among other things, kept close tabs on Beni performances for fear that they constituted outlets of Germanophile sentiment and resistance to British rule. Given that Beni dancers imitated German military drills and formations, and that their leaders bore titles such as 'Kaiser', 'Konig', and 'Bismarck', this was not a wholly unfounded fear. But the far greater threat to British power lay in Beni's ability to mobilize and unite people from various ethnic groups across vast distances, 'a degree of co-ordination which the Europeans had certainly not intended or expected them to be able to achieve' (Ranger 1975: 44). Indeed, the Censor's General Report of September/October 1919 states:

> the fact that most of these societies appear to be organized by educated natives, who held posts of some little importance under the Germans, coupled with an adherence to the German system of organization and discipline, would render them a valuable aid to any person who might be entrusted with the work of anti-British propaganda among native tribes.[5]

In addition to the Censor, political officers in Lindi and Dar es Salaam also warned of the potential political importance of Beni, which by this time could be found in all principal coastal and upcountry centres.[6]

British administrators attempted to thwart the inherent potential for political organization in Beni by initiating a policy of discouragement, first by means of snubbing it and alarming African elites, and second, by creating a new apparatus of control over all publicly held dances, consisting of mandatory fees and licences introduced in Tanganyika in 1920 (Ranger 1975:91).[7] In at least one locale, this led to a significant decrease in Beni performance; but elsewhere, the ngoma thrived and is credited by Ranger with the successful spread of nationalist sentiment throughout the territory.

The Ngoma Regulation Decree of 1934, composed and implemented by British authorities in Zanzibar, a British protectorate since 1890, decreed that ngoma and *maulidi* (Islamic religious recitations accompanied by tambourines and drums) were not to be held without acquisition of a permit and payment of a fee. Given that in the early 1930s, colonial record-keepers documented the performance of 2,450 ngoma in urban Zanzibar (roughly seven different ngoma per night), as well as some 800 maulid annually (Fair 2001: 23, 181), this constituted a lucrative

---

[4] Kalungwa Kudahwa, 1930, 'Wanashauli wa Ha Bomani' (The Administrative Officer), in Songoyi 1988: 226.
[5] Quoted in Ranger 1975: 59.
[6] See Ranger 1975: 44, note 3; also, 61-62.
[7] Also Askew 2002: 162-169.

source of revenue. A list of five prohibited ngoma, which were not to be allowed under any circumstances, accompanied the ruling. Although no explanation was provided for why those particular ngoma were prohibited, correspondence between various colonial officials reveal negotiations over the addition of other ngoma to the 'prohibited' list and expansion of the definition of 'ngoma' so as to widen the net of government control. A subsequent amendment to the decree went so far as to redefine 'ngoma' as 'any Arab, African, Indian or other oriental entertainment or dance whether accompanied or not by music, drumming or singing'.[8]

Concerns voiced in discussions over the banning of ngoma during this period were almost exclusively moral ones. In 1938, the District Commissioner of Zanzibar attempted to ban an unidentified ngoma at Uzi 'on account of the lavish and wasteful expenditure that was intended to be incurred'.[9] The earliest accounts of ngoma performance describe a widespread pattern of competitive dualism wherein one ngoma society would attempt to out-perform a rival group by attracting the largest audience – an East African predilection already exemplified in the Beni and Sukuma Bagiika-Bugaalu traditions. As a nineteenth-century Swahili commentator noted, 'In their dance competitions they danced all night for six or seven nights of continuous dancing. They spent a great deal of money, because if one society killed two goats, the other would kill four' (Bakari 1981 [1903]: 84). More frequently, authorities attacked ngoma that contained 'obscene' behaviour and/or foul language, or collected 'unsavoury' audiences. A Comorian ngoma performed in Zanzibar known as Shambe, featured men dressed as women and was considered objectionable due to 'this effaminancy [*sic*] in the open by immoral men which is abhorred or resented by the public. Their congregation is the attraction of many evils although in fact the evils are there in their hearts before'.[10]

From a colonial censor's perspective, ngoma were not the only source of immoral ideas and representations. Cinema arrived in East Africa in the 1920s amidst great concern over its potentially enlightening and potentially dangerous effects. The first film house in Tanganyika, called 'New Cinema', opened in 1925, with a second, 'Empire Cinema', opening in 1929. They served primarily European and (South) Asian audiences. In 1930, discussions began about establishing a cinema house for 'natives', the goal being 'to bring the native races into touch with modern civilization, to show what Great Britain has done for the Empire, and to stimulate trade by the repeated exhibition of British industrial and commercial activity'.[11] The company overseeing the project stated its commitment 'to co-

---

[8] *The Laws of Zanzibar*, n.d., chapter 178, 'Ngoma Regulation', 2.

[9] District commissioner, Zanzibar, to provincial commissioner, 28 April 1938, ZNA AK 14/10.

[10] District commissioner, Zanzibar (Urban), to senior commissioner, 16 February 1956, ZNA AK 14/10.

[11] 'Proposals for a Scheme of Adult Education and Entertainment by Means of the Cinematograph among the Native Races of British Colonies, Protectorates and Mandated Territories of the Empire', c.1930, Tanzania National Archives (henceforth TNA), 20496.

operate with Colonial Censorship Authorities' and 'eliminate from the films it distributes anything which, either in picture, dialogue or story, might be derogatory to British prestige or prejudicial to the dignity of Europeans in the eyes of native populations'.[12] Over the following decades, more elaborate and detailed film censorship guidelines were developed (see Ivaska 2003: 50-63), many of which paralleled those in the censorship of popular music. In particular, these two domains of censorship shared concerns with promoting morality and 'decency', silencing perceived challenges to British political and economic power, and preventing any questioning of the colonial order.

The nationalist period: 1954-1966

In the years leading up to independence, a number of artists lent their voices and talents to the cause of liberation. In Tanganyika, nationalist discourse took active shape in the Tanganyika African National Union (TANU), established in 1954. TANU was an outgrowth of the Tanganyika African Association (TAA), established in 1929, that in turn had grown out of the Tanganyika Territory African Civil Service Association (TTACSA), established in 1922. Ironically, the nationalist movement owes a debt of gratitude to colonial censorship policies. As described above, British authorities worried greatly about the political dangers posed by ngoma associations, especially the Beni societies. They countered the threat by prohibiting membership of African civil servants in ngoma associations (Ranger 1975:92). This incited civil servants to create their own association, namely, the TTACSA, which served partly as a welfare association and partly as a trade union. Within a decade, the TTACSA association expanded into the territory-wide TAA (Iliffe 1979: 406-408), and although it would face a series of difficult decades and threat of extinction, the TAA eventually reformulated itself as the Tanganyika African National Union (TANU) with the dynamic, well-educated, and impassioned nationalist Julius Nyerere as its president. Not surprisingly, given this history, a strong core of TANU leaders and activists consisted of musicians, poets, and dancers (Askew 2002: 95-96).

A key theme that emerged in nationalist discourse was that of unity. 'Unity is strength' was a TANU slogan, and this theme held repercussions for musicians in that ngoma rivalries were reevaluated by TANU activists as perpetuating colonial divide-and-rule strategies (Ranger 1975: 95). In a letter addressed to ngoma leaders in Tanga sent six months before Tanganyikan independence, the TANU district secretary wrote,

---

[12] M. Miller Kearney, general manager and secretary, British United Film Producers Co., to the chief secretary, Tanganyika Territory, 20 January 1932, TNA 20496.

Since many of you are members of TANU, you therefore agree with the TANU policy of UNITY. It is therefore a matter of great regret to see that our members are divided on account of ngoma.

This party issues its position that this custom must cease, in particular the behavior of one society insulting another or one member ridiculing another member. If we cannot leave such traditions behind, I believe our efforts are spent on destruction rather than on construction.

A copy of this letter is being sent to the town Akida[13] requiring him to deny any ngoma society permission to hold an ngoma until this TANU office has reviewed the request first. This is to prevent the continuation of divisive behavior.[14]

As if to prove the TANU suspicions correct, the British provincial commissioner responded immediately to say that TANU had no authority to issue or deny ngoma permits and, moreover, that to his mind ngoma were not a source of trouble in Tanga.[15] Although not wholly successful in this case, we see here the emergence of censorship concerns within the nationalist movement, albeit with a quite different rationale than that guiding colonial censors.

In this period, then, musical performance, even that performed purely for entertainment, took on political overtones. Musicians faced two sources of censorship and ran the risk of being cast as colonial pawns or targets for colonial repression. Mzee Mwinamila, a famous Nyamwezi singer and friend of Nyerere, rallied people to the TANU cause by singing songs such as 'Amka Msilale' (Wake Up, Don't Sleep), even as the British banned TANU chapters in parts of the territory.

> Wake up, don't sleep
> Don't be fools, people of Tanganyika
> This is our property
> Independence is coming this year
> The flag of Africa is about to rise
> Let us have the cards
> With all our hearts
> To be ruled by a foreign nation
> How shameful it is!
> The people of Ghana have stirred up
> They have cut the ropes

---

[13] 'Akida' was the title of a local government official appointed by the colonial authority, the equivalent of today's 'Mayor'. The German administration was the first to introduce the position as a solution to the absence of chiefs in the coastal districts. See Iliffe (1989 [1979]: 209).

[14] S.D. Hemed, TANU district secretary, to all ngoma leaders in Tanga, 19 June 1961, Tanga Regional Archives (hereafter TRA), accession 5, box 6, file C1/12, 'Ceremonial, 1948-71'; translation ours, emphasis in the original.

[15] C.C. Harris, provincial commissioner, to district commissioner, 28 June 1961, TRA C1/12.

Tanganyika is our property
We shall get it back
If we claim it back
The Honourable [Nyerere] has been given
A cup by God
Greetings to you, Chief.[16]

Mwinamila managed to escape colonial punishment and, significantly, chose Kiswahili, the language of the nationalist movement (which would later become the national language) as his medium.

After independence, the new nationalist government became the sole source of censorship. Having inherited a tradition of government censorship, including an elaborate apparatus of established fees and licences for public performances, the Tanzanian government chose to continue it (Askew 2002: 157-195). Elias Songoyi documented the legacy and impact of Mzee Mwinamila and compared it to that of another singer, Kalikali, a Sukuma artist in the tradition of Gumha and Kalungwa. Both singers started out serving the nationalist cause, before and immediately after independence. Yet while Mwinamila continued singing TANU politics and encouraging support for the new nation well into the socialist period, Kalikali grew disillusioned with the slow pace of change and his songs started to take a critical tone two years after independence. He pointed out that the fruits of independence were being doled out to a select few and denied to those peasants whose support brought TANU to power.

We have really got independence
The people of Tanganyika
Truly we are independent
They are giving thanks to independence
The ones with big jobs
The ones who earn hundreds
Month after month
But the growers of cotton
Have nothing to gain
Slavery has not ended.[17]

Despite receiving warnings from government officials to cease singing anti-government songs, he continued his musical attacks and was subsequently arrested and jailed for two months in 1965 for singing about political corruption:

Division secretaries your buttocks are getting fat
Area commissioners your buttocks are getting fat

---

[16] Salehe Ramadhani Mwinamila, 'Amka Msilale' (Wake Up, Don't Sleep), c.1954, in Songoyi 1988: 129-130.
[17] Kalikali, 'Litingaga I Libusese' (Slavery Has Not Ended), 1964, in Songoyi 1988: 77-78.

You are growing fat because of the money you steal
All the time you tell people to contribute whole-heartedly
You eat some of the money.[18]

Although Mwinamila would also take a very critical stance vis-à-vis the state, Songoyi concludes that the timing of Mwinamila's disillusionment in the late 1960s occurred when the new state was more secure as a state than it had been in 1964-65 when Kalikali initiated his critiques. Despite equally harsh denunciations of government policy and government officials, Mwinamila never experienced the punitive capabilities of the state.

In Zanzibar, although the African nationalist Afro-Shirazi Party (ASP, which had strong ties to TANU) won the popular vote, the British granted independence to a Sultan-headed Arab minority government in December 1963. One month later, a violent revolution put the ASP in power and four months after that, Julius Nyerere and Abeid Karume (ASP leader, and president of post-revolution Zanzibar) merged their respective countries into the United Republic of Tanzania. Each half maintains its own internal government, thus censorship is pursued independently in Zanzibar from that on the mainland. Zanzibari government censors, due to the unique history of the islands, operated with a quite different rationale in the nationalist period. Because Omani sultans used Zanzibar as their base for controlling nineteenth-century East African and Indian Ocean trade networks, and because much African slave labour was imported to work the islands' clove plantations, racial/ethnic dynamics in Zanzibar developed along much more politicized lines than in Tanganyika.

Music here again assumed political connotations and roles.[19] Particularly popular in the islands is a form of sung Kiswahili poetry called *taarab*. Taarab started out as court music performed exclusively in the Sultan's palace, yet early in its history it was localized by musicians who sang in Kiswahili rather than Arabic, and who, in violation of the Sultan's orders, performed taarab outside the palace walls (Fair 2001: 313, n.6). After independence, but before the revolution, the Sultan's government required all music aired on the radio to be Arabic music, thus fuelling fears that Zanzibar was being turned into an Arab, rather than an African, state. After the revolution, President Karume responded by banning the performance and broadcast of taarab for a while 'due to what he perceived as its affinity with Arab domination. During this time, the government also destroyed many of the early taarab recordings made and stored at the radio station (Graebner 2004: 181). However, Karume was quickly convinced by taarab fans, island musicians, and supporters within his own Ministry of Culture to 'change his tune' (Fair 2001: 314, n.12) and embrace, or at least tolerate, taarab music, viewed by many as the quintessential Zanzibari music. Censorship in Zanzibar during the

---

[18] Kalikali, untitled, c.1965, in Songoyi 1988: 82-83.

[19] Askew has argued elsewhere that in East Africa music and politics are rarely, if ever, divorced from each other (Askew 2003).

nationalist period was thus more a matter of limiting access to forms of music defined along ethnic/racial lines as part of the wider contest over how and by whom the Zanzibari 'nation' would be defined.

The socialist period: 1967-1985

In 1967, Julius Nyerere issued the Arusha declaration formalizing Tanzania's commitment to African socialism. The previous year, during preparations for the party congress in Arusha, Nyerere remarked that freedom of opinion should be subordinated to more important political goals (Sturmer 1998: 120, 166), thus paving the way for more active government involvement in censorship as well as stronger societal pressures toward self-censorship. Music and all the arts were placed squarely in the centre of these debates.

> Theatre cannot be purely seen as a means to an end. It should be exploited to reach higher ideals and indeed a means of educating the masses. So we will sing about socialism as a means to ending poverty. We will dramatize about a man who is ill and does not go to hospital so that our people should see the importance of going to hospital when they are ill. (Ministry of Culture and Youth n.d.: 13)

Drawing on the writings of socialist philosophers such as Ernst Fischer and Bertolt Brecht, Tanzanian intellectuals saw art as justified only insofar as it promoted the socialist cause. Art as pure entertainment was dangerous in distracting citizens from their duties to help build the new nation, as well as in being a source of bourgeois capitalist relations.

> Under bourgeois democracy the individual is said to be free and he is entitled to freedom of expression. However, under capitalism, freedom and equality are the rights of the propertied classes. The wage labourer, including the intellectual labourer, such as the artist, is never free except in the sense of being free to be exploited by whoever owns the means of production. This explains why the living condition of the artists – singers, writers, musicians, dancers and actors – is in no way better than that of other labourers in the capitalist and neo-colonialist societies. Most of the artists live and die miserably. The owners of the means of production – publishing houses, music and film companies – exploit them until they die. (Songoyi 1988: 12-13)

Thus, through extensive government-directed efforts, including party enrollment campaigns, schooling (primary level through adult education), and government-owned media, Tanzanians were conscientized to be good socialist citizens. According to Songoyi, many Tanzanian artists were transformed into 'faithful ideological instruments of the state' who 'propagated and interpreted the Party and Government policies and philosophy to the masses' (Songoyi 1988: 14).

Government monopoly over mass media, in particular radio and television, greatly enhanced the power of the censors. On the mainland, the only radio station in existence until 1994 was the government-run Radio Tanzania Dar es Salaam (RTD); in the islands, it was Sauti ya Tanzania Zanzibar (STZ). In all of Tanzania, the only television station, again until 1994, was Television Zanzibar (TVZ), which only broadcast for a few hours daily. Both STZ and TVZ were/are owned and operated by the Zanzibari government. Censorship on the mainland was pursued by an RTD-based committee that reviewed all song lyrics before they could be approved for recording or for broadcast. Songs could be rejected on many counts, the most common being depiction of immoral behaviour or disloyalty to party or state – virtually the same issues colonial censors found objectionable. The committee searched for songs with 'mafunzo' (lessons or teachings) to improve society. For example, if a love song was under review, a determining factor for its approval would be whether or not it spoke of marriage as the ultimate goal. Songs missing the reference to marriage would be interpreted as advancing promiscuity and banned from broadcast.

John Kitime has performed on guitar and vocals with a number of Tanzanian *dansi* (urban jazz) bands starting in the mid-1970s and continuing into the present. He was a member of the Orchestra Mambo Bado in 1983 when the band made its first professional recording at the RTD studio (Kitime 2003: 1). At that time, the only recording facilities in the country were RTD or the Tanzania Film Company (TFC). Since both facilities were government owned and operated, censorship was part of the process determining what would be recorded. Bands that had the means to do so would often travel to neighbouring Kenya to record rather than submit their songs to the censorship process. The committee, Kitime discovered, could be very capricious. One of the songs they wanted to record included the following verse:

Mpenzi wangu wa moyo mama
Nakupenda kutoka uvunguni mwa moyo wangu
Kama ni usumbufu mama
Nimsumbue nani kama siyo wewe.

Love of my heart
I love you from the bottom of my heart
Even if it is a nuisance, dear
Whom else shall I bother if not you?

The RTD committee took issue with the word 'uvunguni' (the bottom) and asked the band to change it to 'ndani' (inside). No explanation was given. In another case, Mlimani Park Orchestre-Gama was censored when trying to record a song that said:

Tafadhali ungeniambia mapema ohh Gama
Nililazwa hospitalini miezi mitatu
Miezi sita gerezani kote hukunijali
Kote hukunijali wee Gama.

If only you would have told me earlier, oh Gama
I was hospitalized for three months
Jailed for six months
You did not care, you Gama.

The committee required that the song be altered to say, 'I was hospitalized for three months, in school for six. You did not care'. Here it would appear that the committee objected to a criminal being portrayed as the subject of a love song. Were a song rejected, musicians had at least two options: they could either pay a bribe (which may have been the committee's motivation in rejecting a song in the first place) or, more commonly, wait until the committee's membership changed and resubmit the song.[20]

The RTD committee also rarely approved songs in languages other than the national language of Kiswahili (in Tanzania, there are over 120 languages) for fear that they communicated subversive messages that might be missed by the committee. Take, for example, the case of a song arranged by John Kitime and performed by the Tancut Almasi Orchestra called 'Wifi' (Sister-in-Law). This is a traditional Kibena marriage song, welcoming the new sister-in-law to her husband's house. Kibena shares a lot of vocabulary with Kiswahili, so the band performed the song in the mid-1980s with its original lyrics:

Wifi twende tuwuyage
Wifi yetu wa gharama wa gharama.

Sister-in-law, let's go, let's go
Our high-class sister-in-law.

The only word from this song that is not also shared in Kiswahili is the word 'tuwuyage'. On account of the one non-Kiswahili word, the song was nearly rejected for recording by the RTD committee, and only approved on the condition that it be altered to feature exclusively Kiswahili lyrics:

Wifi twende nyumbani
Wifi yetu karibu mama karibu sana.

Sister-in-law, let's go home
Welcome, our sister-in-law, warm welcome.

The most severe form of censorship in Tanzania occurs when a song (or film or other public form of expression) is publicized in the newspapers as banned by the

---

[20] As far as the authors are aware, the committee membership is not published anywhere. Musicians simply wait a while, assume the committee will one day change, and try their luck again.

government (*kupigwa marufuku*). This is a rare act. One of the more famous bans was that issued against soul music on 12 November 1969 by the Coast Regional Commissioner, Mr. Songambele (whose authority extended over the capital of Dar es Salaam).[21] At a meeting with primary school teachers who complained of students' bad manners that they attributed to the influence of soul music, Commissioner Songambele spontaneously issued an announcement, published the following day in *The Standard*, that soul music was 'banned from being played in Dar es Salaam', effective immediately (quoted in Ivaska 2003: 139). Hardly a planned government policy move, the ban was nevertheless backed by the Director of Information Services, A.A. Riyami, one week later in a letter to the editor of *The Standard* after a torrent of some 30 letters to the editor protesting the ban (ibid.). Yet, as would happen with other bans, little effort was made to enforce it since the government lacked the means to control and monitor all music venues throughout the country. One exception was a ban issued on 27 December 1975 against the broadcast of foreign music on RTD (a not-unrelated follow-up to the soul music ban) – part of an effort to promote local culture and impede Western cultural (and capitalist) imperialism (Sturmer 1998: 130). Because the government owned the radio station, this was easy to enforce and remained in effect for years to come.

Another case is that of the ban issued in 1983 against an Orchestra Mambo Bado song entitled 'Bomoa Tutajenga Kesho' (Demolish – We Will (Re)build Tomorrow). Inspiration for the song came from the cracked walls of one of the clubs wherein Orchestra Mambo Bado performed. A band member told the club owner that he ought to repair the cracks lest the walls fall down the day of their performance. The owner's response was simply 'Bomoa tutajenga kesho'.

Bomoa bomoa bomoa mama
Tutajenga kesho himaa
Tutajenga kesho imaa.

Demolish, demolish, demolish, Mama
We will (re)build tomorrow quickly
We will (re)build tomorrow, let it be.

Although no rationale was ever released as to why this song was banned, it is significant that in this case the ban was issued by the youth wing of Chama cha Mapinduzi (Revolutionary Party, CCM), the ruling party formed from the merger of TANU and ASP. The youth league was well established in practices of policing culture as evidenced by the campaign called 'Operation Vijana' (Operation Youth). On 3 October 1968, the youth wing issued a ban, announced in front-page newspaper headlines, on 'mini-skirts, wigs, women's bleaches, and tight male trousers' (quoted in Ivaska 2003: 130). Born of the same fervent nationalist and anti-foreigner sentiment that underlay the subsequent ban on soul music, Operation

---

[21] The Standard (Tanzania). 1969. 'Songambele Bans "Soul" Music', November 13.

Vijana pursued active enforcement of the ban, which distinguished it from the ban on soul music. Street patrols by youth league cadres targeted for punishment those deemed 'indecently dressed'. Typically it took the form of violent attacks on women. Pronounced a successful operation in January 1969, the campaign was nevertheless resurrected one year later in response to a resurgence of mini-skirt-clad women, this time, however, through police enforcement. During 1970 and 1971, anywhere between 25 and 100 women were typically arrested in evening raids that occurred twice weekly (Ivaska 2002, 2003).

During the socialist period, music censorship proceeded apace across the channel in Zanzibar. In 1983, a National Censor Board was legislated under Section 22 of Act No. 6 (Sturmer 1998: 301) whose primary purpose was to censor foreign films according to criteria that have been described as: 'No sex and the hero must win' (Lederbogen 1992, quoted in Sturmer 1998: 301). Yet the board also reviewed song lyrics and found fault with many for similar reasons as on the mainland. Socialism was pursued no less actively in Zanzibar than on the mainland, especially during the Karume presidency. Zealous party functionaries sometimes took censorship into their own hands by destroying taarab recordings as 'purveyor of bourgeois mentality' (Graebner 2004: 187), and by ordering radio announcers to stop playing select records. Those who refused to comply were dismissed or hit with a cane (Sturmer 1998: 301).[22]

The socialist period thus introduced a new measure of 'appropriateness' to the censorship process, namely, the idea of art as serving didactic, socialist ends. Yet at the same time, we see here the reemergence of colonial-era concerns with policing morality and protecting the political order. It appears that colonial censors left behind an enduring legacy, one that continues, if altered, into the present.

The period of liberalization: 1985-present

In 1985, after a period of profound economic hardship blamed by many on his socialist policies, Julius Nyerere voluntarily stepped down from the presidency and welcomed an advocate of liberalization, Ali Hassan Mwinyi, to lead the country. Known on the streets as 'Mzee Ruksa' (Mr. Permissiveness) for the sudden openness of the economy to foreign capital and the lifting of many previous restrictions on local investment, Mwinyi began instituting structural adjustment programmes and in 1992 oversaw constitutional reform to allow for multiparty politics. Liberalization of the media followed in 1993 with the passing of the Broadcasting Services Act, which enabled the creation of private radio and television stations (Perullo 2003: 178).

Examination of the relationship between the censorship committees and taarab bands provides a musical point of entry into the liberalization process. Taarab

---

[22] We did not find any evidence, anecdotal or otherwise, for similar treatment of radio announcers on the mainland.

poetry revels in double entendre and metaphoric meanings; indeed, this is one of its defining characteristics. Like songs in local languages, then, taarab songs could contain potentially subversive elements. But if a song's meaning was well hidden, it could pass censorial review without much trouble. And so taarab songs about a welcoming mat on which many guests rest (a promiscuous spouse), a rifle devoid of bullets (an impotent man), and a tasty curry spoiled by lime juice (an attractive woman spoiled by a certain man) passed in the 1970s and 1980s and are still aired today. In fact, according to some estimates, more taarab songs than dansi songs have passed the committee's review (Kitime 2003).

Yet success was not guaranteed for taarab songs. The song 'Mkomesheni' (Make Him Stop) by Babloom Modern Taarab was rejected in 1992 for RTD broadcast but approved two years later with no changes made to the song whatsoever. Different sensitivities due to a different political environment may have had a lot to do with the decision, as well a change in the committee membership. The song says,

> I want to send you to go tell him
> I won't leave him to complain. Better he know the truth
> Tell him to stop harassing me, to shed his love for me
> Make him stop harassing me. He should forget about me
> Why should I give my reasons for the world to know?
> Let him look for someone else who can suffer his behavior
> Even though I erred to make him mine
> I have already corrected my mistake. Better I be far away from him
> He doesn't understand love. Let him boast all he wants
> I will never explain my reasons – he knows them all
> I do not wish to publicly shame him for failing to stay true
> He should forget about me. I have vomited his love.[23]

It may well be that use of the term 'vomit' incurred censorial ire for crudeness, or that the verb – *koma* – ('stop, cease, desist') was considered an impolite way of asking someone to do something, but given that the president had recently announced the introduction of multiparty politics, it alternatively might have been interpreted as a rejection of that president and his government.[24]

With the introduction of multiparty politics, the Tanzanian government found itself in need of a new image and created a cultural troupe called Tanzania One Theatre (TOT) to tour throughout the country rallying support for CCM. TOT composed and performed taarab songs that contravened all previously-established bounds of decency, songs like 'Nyama ya Bata' (Duck Meat), 'TX Mpenzi' (Expatriate Lover), and 'Mtwangio' (Pestle):

---

[23] 'Mkomesheni', poetry by Khalid Akida and music by Seif Kisauji, Babloom Modern Taarab, Tanga. For the original Kiswahili lyrics, please refer to Askew (2002: 321).
[24] This interpretation was proffered by a former employee of the Ministry of Culture.

I praise this pestle with which I pound
For pounding, it is number one. I give it praise
I will never try to use another
I do not desire someone else's. I am accustomed to this one
I tell you the truth, it is no joke, my relatives,
When it enters the mortar, this pestle of mine,
It pounds perfectly in my mortar.
Pestle, pound and do not tire, oh pestle
Pound without worries, you my pestle
The mortar accepts you.

More astonishing, however, is that these songs were aired on RTD until popular protest, in the form of letters to newspaper editors, decrying the apparent double censorship standards for TOT as opposed to those applied to other bands, forced the station to stop playing them.

The mid-1990s saw the emergence of a number of bans relating to music and HIV/AIDS. Around the time the government issued its 'Tanzanian National Policy on HIV/AIDS/STD' (1995), the popular dansi star Remmy Ongala, an internationally renowned artist on the Real World label, composed his song 'Mambo kwa soksi' (Matters for Socks):

We 'bad ones' strut proudly these days
Thinking we don't have AIDS
Sister, watch out, don't die of AIDS
Your whole family can die
You can infect us
If a man seduces you, first ask him whether he has 'socks'
If not, buy them for him
'Where do you get them'?
'In any hospital'
'It would be better if they were sold in bars and guesthouses'
'No, they should not be sold at all: when you buy
A bottle of beer, you get one free as a present
When you sleep in a guesthouse, you get a towel, soap and spare socks.'[25]

Although the national policy on HIV/AIDS/STDs targeted prevention and 'safer sex' as key concerns (Tibandegabe et al. 1998), some officials felt the song promoted promiscuity, and the government thus issued a ban prohibiting the song from both radio play and live performances (www.chezasalama.com). Pressure from public health agencies led to a subsequent repeal of the ban, and the song today still holds significance for local and national discourse on the epidemic, which people on the streets and in the statehouse sometimes refer to as 'mambo kwa soksi'. In related attempts to thwart the continued spread of the disease, the

---

[25] Translation, slightly modified, from Thubauville 2004: 3.

government issued in 2000 a ban on live dance music during the week (Perullo 2003: 361) imitated by local officials in particularly hard-hit villages (Phillips 2001), and in 2002, it banned a song called 'Segere' by Young Stars Modern Taarab purporting that it encouraged people to get AIDS. The song includes the line:

Nipe UKIMWI nihangaike nao.
Give me AIDS that I may suffer with it.

which authorities, such as Mr. Shogholo Chali, executive secretary of Tanzania's National Arts Council, interpreted as undermining efforts to curb the spread of the disease (BBC News 2002). Defenders, on the other hand, argued that the song criticized the continuing practice of forced marriages, which often occur between young women and older HIV-infected men who believe that sex with a virgin is a cure for AIDS. At first, the song was banned from radio or television play and from live performance, but then alternative lyrics were produced for the controversial line:

UKIMWI ni hatari.
AIDS is dangerous.

The change enabled the song to be performed and re-recorded for broadcast. Eventually, however, the ban was lifted altogether.

Censorship thus continues in Tanzania today. Bands on the mainland and in Zanzibar must still obtain licences and permits to perform in public, and this allows for indirect censorship in that authorities can deny permit requests from bands whose music they consider detrimental to national interests. However, major changes have taken place due in large part to liberalization of the media. By 2003, 20 private radio stations had emerged on the mainland (Perullo 2003: 188), none of which have censorship committees. This means that there is little incentive anymore for musicians to go through the censorship process at RTD since they can air their songs elsewhere.

In Zanzibar, the censor board deals almost exclusively with foreign films. Although it actively reviewed song lyrics into the 1990s, it does not do so anymore because musicians no longer turn in their lyrics for review (Graebner 2004: 187). Periodic government complaints about this mass refusal to submit to the board can be heard, such as those voiced in a September 2004 newspaper article by Joseph Castico, Director of the Department of Culture. He was quoted as insisting that taarab clubs submit their lyrics to the board for approval before recording any new songs and threatened dire consequences if they continue to evade this requirement. Castico claims that it is because musicians have stopped submitting their lyrics that so many vulgar recordings are flooding the market, and that these in turn encourage bad behaviour among the youth (Mgeni 2004).

Further instances of recent efforts to curb the supposed ill effects of music on youth are the short-lived ban on rap music in Zanzibar instituted in 1999 and lifted in 2000 (Strong 2004), as well as mainland bans on *mchiriku* (a musical precursor to Swahili rap especially popular among urban underclass youth) in the 1970s and again in the 1990s for 'its lewd lyrics and erotic dance style' (Graham 1994: 256; Graebner 1999: 687; also Perullo 2003: 50). Yet, because of the relatively recent emergence of hip hop music, locally known as 'Bongo Flava', there is a new generation of artists who have never been subjected to the strict censorship period of the RTD. More than 20 privately-owned recording studios now operate in Dar es Salaam alone, none of which take censorial interest in the lyrics of the songs they produce. But concerns about the production of songs containing 'lewd' lyrics has very recently prompted the National Arts Council (BASATA) to form a committee to cross check the lyrics of Bongo Flava songs.

Conclusion

Censorship of Tanzanian popular music is not a new phenomenon either in form or content. State institutions pursue it and, despite changing political contexts, remain true to colonial-era goals of limiting challenges to moral and political authority and controlling (or at least monitoring) artistic expression. Sensitivities have varied according to place (mainland Tanganyika versus island Zanzibar) and time (colonial versus nationalist versus socialist versus liberalization periods). Yet as Werner Graebner (1997: 113) notes, 'Difficulties between the musicians and policy-makers exist, there are accusations of censorship leveled by the musicians, nevertheless one is surprised to hear so many songs on the radio that openly criticize social conditions; in fact, critical songs are a common characteristic of Tanzanian dance music'. Askew has argued elsewhere that the same holds true for ngoma and taarab (Askew 2002, 2003), and we posit that it proves no less true of other Tanzanian musical genres such as Swahili rap, Swahili reggae, mchiriku, and Bongo Flava. Thus, despite state designs to subordinate musical expression to imperial or national interests, musicians have, throughout Tanzania's history, found ways to evade this aspect of the state and remain true to their long-standing responsibility to provoke reflection on the state of society, as well as on the state of the state. From non-compliance to camouflage, Tanzanian musicians continue to come up with creative solutions to the restraints censors would place upon them.

References

Allen, James de Vere. 1984. 'Appendix III. *Ngoma*: Music and Dance', in *Desturi za Waswahili*, by Mtoro bin Mwinyi Bakari, et al. (eds), and trans. J.W.T. Allen. Berkeley: University of California Press, pp. 233-246.

Askew, Kelly M. 2002. *Performing the Nation: Swahili Music and Cultural Politics in Tanzania*. Chicago: University of Chicago Press.

Askew, Kelly M. 2003. 'As Plato Duly Warned: Music, Politics, and Social Change in East Africa,' *Anthropological Quarterly*, 76:4, pp. 609-637.

Bakari, Mtoro bin Mwinyi. 1984 [1903]. *Desturi za Waswahili*. ed. and trans. J.W.T. Allen. Berkeley: University of California Press.

BBC News. 2002. 'Tanzania Bans Song "Promoting AIDS"', July 24. http://news.bbc.co.uk/1/hi/world/africa/2149686.stm.

Fair, Laura. 2001. *Pastimes and Politics: Culture, Community, and Identity in Post-Abolition Urban Zanzibar, 1890-1945*. Athens, OH and Oxford: Ohio University Press with James Currey.

Graebner, Werner. 1997. 'Whose Music? The Songs of Remmy Ongala and Orchestra Super Matimila' in *Readings in African Popular Culture*, Karin Barber (ed.) Bloomington, In and Oxford: Indiana University Press/James Currey, pp. 110-117.

Graebner, Werner. 1999. 'Tanzania/Kenya-Taarab: The Swahili Coastal Sound', in *World Music: The Rough Guide. Vol. 1: Africa, Europe, and the Middle East*, Simon Broughton, et al. (eds). London: The Rough Guide/Penguin, pp. 690-697.

Graebner, Werner. 2004. 'Between Mainland and Sea: The *Taarab* Music of Zanzibar' in *Island Musics*, ed. Kevin N. Dawe. Oxford: Berg Publishers, pp.171-197.

Graham, Ronnie. 1994. 'Tanzanian New Wave'. In *World Music: The Rough Guide*, Simon Broughton et al. (eds). London: The Rough Guide, p. 356.

Gunderson, Frank. 2000. 'Witchcraft, Witcraft and Musical Warfare: The Rise of the Bagiika-Bagaalu Music Competitions in Sukumaland, Tanzania' in *Mashindano! Competitive Music Performance in East Africa*, Frank Gunderson and Gregory Barz (eds) Dar es Salaam: Mkuki wa Nyota Publishers, pp. 407-419.

Iliffe, John. 1989 [1979]. *A Modern History of Tanganyika*. African Studies Series 25. Cambridge: Cambridge University Press.

Ivaska, Andrew M. 2002. '"Anti-Mini Militants Meet Modern Misses": Urban Style, Gender and the Politics of "National Culture" in 1960s Dar es Salaam, Tanzania', *Gender and History* 14:3, pp.584-607.

Ivaska, Andrew M. 2003. 'Negotiating "Culture" in a Cosmopolitan Capital: Urban Style and the Tanzanian State in Colonial and Postcolonial Dar es Salaam.' Ph.D. dissertation. University of Michigan.

Kitime, John F. 2003. 'Music Censorship in Tanzania: My Experience.' Paper presented at the 2003 Zanzibar International Film Festival workshop entitled, 'Music and Freedom Of Expression'. July 7, Zanzibar, Tanzania.

Mgeni, Zuhura. 2004, 'Vikundi vinavyokwepa Bodi ya Sensa kukiona', Zanzibar Leo (Tanzania), September 2, p.12.

Ministry of Culture and Youth. n.d. Cultural Revolution in Tanzania. Dar es Salaam: Government Printer.

Perullo, Alex. 2003. '"The Life that I Live": Popular Music, Agency, and Urban Society in Dar es Salaam, Tanzania'. Ph.D. dissertation, Indiana University.

Phillips, Michael M. 2001. 'New Taboos: To Help Fight AIDS, Tanzanian Villages Ban Risky Traditions – Bawdy Dances, Night Trysts, Even Flirting Outlawed; A Model for Prevention? – "It's Survival of the Smartest"', Wall Street Journal, January 12, p.A1.

Ranger, Terence O. 1975. *Dance and Society in Eastern Africa 1890-1970: The Beni Ngoma*. Berkeley and Los Angeles: University of California Press.

Songoyi, Elias Manandi. 1988. 'The Artist and the State in Tanzania. A Study of Two Singers: Kalikali and Mwinamila,' Ph.D. dissertation, University of Dar es Salaam.

Strong, Nolan. 2004. 'Congolese Government Bans Rap and Foreign Music,' June 28, http://www.allhiphop.com/hiphopnews/index.asp?ID=3282.

Sturmer, Martin. 1998. The Media History of Tanzania. Salzburg: Afro-Asiatiches Institut.

Thubauville, Sophia. 2004. 'Remmy Ongala'. http://ntama.uni-mainz.de/content/view/27/29/1/2/.

Tibandebage, Paula, et al. 1998. 'Expenditures on HIV/AIDS in Tanzania' in *Confronting AIDS: Evidence from the Developing World*, Martha Ainsworth, Lieve Fransen (eds), Mead Over. Brussels and Washington, DC: European Commission/World Bank, pp.289-296.

www.chezasalama.com./article.php?id=351. 'Muziki, Dansi na Maigizo: Mambo kwa Soksi, Mambo kwa Kondomu'.

Discography

Culture Musical Club. 1989. *Music of Zanzibar: Taarab 4*. London: Ace Records/Globestyle CDORBD 041.

Culture Musical Club. 2003. *Waridi: Scents of Zanzibar/Parfums de Zanzibar*, Paris: Jahazi Media/Virgin JAHMCD 510.

Ikwani Safaa Musical Club. 1988. *Music of Zanzibar: Taarab 2*. London: Ace Records/GlobeStyle CDORB 033.

Kidumbak Kalcha. 1997. *Ng'ambo: The Other Side of Zanzibar*. Todtnauberg: Dizim Records 4501-2.

Mbaraka Mwinshehe and the Morogoro Jazz Band. 2000. *Masimango*. Dizim Asili Series, Vol. 2. Todtnauberg, Germany: Dizim Records.

Music from Tanzania and Zanzibar, 1, 2, and 3. 1997. Stockholm: Caprice Records CAP 21554, 21573, and 21577.

Orchestra Maquis Original, et al. 1995. *Muziki wa Dansi*. Detroit: Africassette AC 9403.

Remmy Ongala and Orchestre Super Matimila. 1989. *Songs for the Poor Man*. Corsham, UK: Real World/Virgin CAROL 2305-2.

Remmy Ongala and Orchestre Super Matimila. 1992. *Mambo*. Corsham, UK: Real World CAROL 2320-22.

Remmy Ongala and Orchestre Super Matimila. 1995. *Sema*. Corsham, UK: Real World WSCD 002.

Salum Abdallah and Cuban Marimba. 2000. *Ngoma Iko Huko*. Dizim Asili Series, Vol. 1. Todtnauberg, Germany: Dizim Records.

Tanzania – Music of the Farmer Composers of Sukumaland: We Never Sleep, We Dream of Farming. 1997. Barre, VT: Multicultural Media MCM 3013.

Zanzibar: Soul & Rhythm (De l'âme à la danse). 2003. Moerlenbach, Germany: Jahazi Media/Virgin JAHM 511-512.

Various Artists. 2001. *Spirit of Africa*. Corsham, UK: RealWorld 11110. [Includes the Remmy Ongala song, 'Mambo kwa Soksi'.]

Chapter 10

Silencing Musical Expression in Colonial and Post-Colonial Kenya

Peter Muhoro Mwangi

Introduction

In December 1963 Kenya emerged as a nation-state from British colonial rule. The powerful colonial administration with its purported mission to 'develop' Africa had created a bitter conflict with the indigenous communities. The Gikuyu of Central Kenya vigorously opposed the imperialist system through political activism. Their resistance was given voice by the song-narrative[1] genre. The Gikuyu, who today stand at a population of over four million, felt especially wronged when foreigners from the west occupied their land. In the pre-colonial days, the Gikuyu used to have infrequent and limited intertribal cattle raids/wars with the neighbouring Maasai and Akamba communities. The colonial powers encouraged these rivalries to divide and rule.

The process of ruling local communities was in part achieved through censorship. This chapter begins with a consideration of how the colonialists and their supporters censored popular music during the colonial era. In turn the focus will shift to post-colonial censorship, with its origins in colonial era censorship processes. In particular, the Government Censorship Board (GCB) curtails the freedom to access material which it deems unfit for public consumption. There does not appear to be a coherent law regarding censorship, but rather the government uses the GCB in an *ad hoc* manner to control the media whenever it produces material deemed to promote antisocial behaviour, violence and breaching of the peace in the nation.

Despite such censorship throughout the twentieth century, music criticizing government excesses has nevertheless emerged and continues to do so. This chapter now turns to an exploration of various songs censored in the colonial and postcolonial era in Kenya, contextualizing such censorship within a broader political framework.

---

[1] 'Song-narrative' is a term used in folklore studies to denote the aspect of performance of songs whereby a given artist sings verses and alternates with speaking: performance intertwined with narration of events in a story form.

The Colonial Era: the 1920s to the early 1960s

With the onset of European imperialism, traditional African styles of music were undermined by the imposition of European music on African society. While the Europeans (particularly missionaries) were initially disdainful of traditional African music, ongoing cultural struggle gradually gave rise to a process of acculturation. In Kenya, the earliest recorded instance of a form of musical censorship occurred at the beginning of the nineteenth century when European missionaries in a settlement near Mombasa forbade drums because these were regarded as pagan (Stapleton and May 1987: 9).

However, it was only in the 1920s that the popular song format began to reflect broader contests between colonial authorities and Kenyans. By the 1920s gramophone records were beginning to be sold to a steadily growing 'group of urbanized and marginally educated indigenous people working in Nairobi' (Gecau 1995: 562). This development, together with the establishment of first nationalist associations and their newspapers, led to the growth of popular songs during this decade. Kimani Gecau (1995: 562) reveals that these developments led to 'the acceleration of the creation of popular songs in addition to those which had already been composed about the conquest, building the railway, conscription into the First World War, the migration of people to new cities and commercial farms and various other themes arising from new experiences under colonialism.

A clear example of the link between music and broader social contest in the 1920s involved the political Muthirigu[2] song and dance form. This form of dance evolved from the Sengenya dance of the coastal Mijikenda communities of Kenya but spread into the central parts of Kenya in the late 1920s. Importantly, the spread of Muthirigua was promoted by the nationalist Kikuyu Central Association and the 'Muigwithania' (the 'Unifier' or 'Reconciler') newspaper (Gecau 1995: 562). The significance of the Muthirigua lay in the way it used allegory to foster an understanding of the socio-political issues of the day. Kyle (1999: 32) notes that the form was revamped by drawing from Gikuyu traditional folk songs: 'Among the Gikuyu men and women there developed a passion for the Muthirigu dance-song, whose body movements were from the coastal Swahilis but words were freshly improvised'.

The woman's place was and is still very central in sexual reproduction for she is a symbol of the continuation of life. Failure to circumcise women, as advocated by African Christians and colonial power barons, was regarded as a threat to traditional cultural practices. To the Gikuyu this exacerbated tensions that began with land dispossession under colonialism, an act that made squatters of legitimate landowners. The Muthirigu dance represented the struggle to maintain of Gikuyu cultural practices, and by extension, African values more generally and

---

[2] Muthirigu is a traditional Gikuyu dance that was very popular in 1920s. The singers espoused traditional values like female circumcision. However, the dance was largely politically oriented.

repossession of their land. In the folksong, 'You Will be Loved', the anti-colonial mood of the 1920s was clearly captured:

> The colonial despots posed a question:
> 'Who and who' sang *Muthirigu?*
> I Kiremanditi[3] son of Mwihoti raised my hand.

Kanogo (1987: 79) explains the tension which surrounded the colonial authorities' attempts to undermine local traditions:

> The Karinga School Movement and the Kikuyu Independent Schools Associations (KISA) grew up as a reaction against mission control over formal education in general, but especially against the missionaries' onslaught on Kikuyu traditions. The centre of controversy was over the issue of female circumcision which the missionaries condemned and which they forbade their adherents, both church members and pupils, to undergo.

It is against that backdrop that the performance of *Muthirigu* was deemed as anti-Christian and a rebellion against modern civilization's mission advanced through colonialism. During the 1920s skilful bards used the song-genre to reflect tensions caused by colonial rule. Allegory and symbolism were used to scoff at foreign cultural practices. The majority of the members of the Gikuyu community responded by singing and dancing the art form more vigorously than ever before in their homes, river valleys, churches as well as in the Kenya African Union (KAU) political meetings in Gikuyu land and its diaspora. One folksong ridiculed colonial opposition to female genital mutilation:

> I cannot marry an uncircumcised woman
> She is naughty – she climbs castor oil trees
> She urinates in bed and claims it is water.

Through reference to female genital mutilation the song voiced objection to colonial rule, suggesting that 'enough was enough'. For the performers colonialism was as ugly as an uncircumcised person.

In response to the popularity of the *Muthirigu*, in the early 1930s, the colonial administrators used the 'Public Order Act' to ban the singing and dancing of *Muthirigu*. However, the singers and dancers defied the banning and continued to perform it. Those who were caught were arrested and tortured. Despite the colonists' attempt to frame *Muthirigu* in a religious framework it was clear that it was a forum for social cultural and political activism. The eviction of the Gikuyu to pave the way for the creation of the White Highlands for the settlers from the West generated conflicts over land and lack of freedom in the heart of the British East Africa colony. Throughout this period songwriters created awareness and

---

[3] Kiremanditi is a corruption for the English word claimant.

sensitized the colonial subjects to the evils of imperialism despite attempts to ban the *Muthirigu*. Performers expressed angry opposition, pitting the colonial administration and especially the Presbyterian Church of East Africa church on one side and the *Muthirigu* adherents on the other.

The antagonism between the pro-*Muthirigu* forces and the supporters of colonial hegemony intensified, leading to a colonial administration crackdown on performers who were arrested and detained. Anybody who was deemed to be pro-*Muthirigu* or a sympathizer was criminalized. The antagonism between the two forces eventually led to violence and the consequent armed struggle of the 1950s. In spite of the banning of *Muthirigu* in the early 1930s, it is clear that the cutting down of a tree does not end the germination of seedlings so long as there is soil with nutrients.

The emergence of Gikuyu Mwomboko[4] song-narratives

African Service Corps returning from participation in the First and Second World Wars, were influenced by Western culture. Veterans introduced new musical instruments, including the accordion. As a result, Gikuyu traditional folk songs and those of other communities interacted with Scottish dance resulting in the emergence of the famous and fabulous *Mwomboko* dance. The singers modelled *Mwomboko* as a traditional-cum-modern dance which acted as an ethnopoetic weapon for social and political protest song sub genre in Gikuyu land. The contents in the *Mwomboko* sub genre hinged on allegorical oral poetic discourse spiced with love matters. No sooner did the colonial establishment realize that these were anti-establishment and pro-pan African songs than it started hunting the singers, players and dancers. For instance, in the song, The Battle of *Ndaka*-ini, recorded by popular artist Joseph Kamaru, the singer proclaims:

> The heroes we have sent to Naivasha,
> Are Kimathi and the valiant Mbaria
> They assailed the enemy with vigour and fortitude
> Till the guerilla leaders were overjoyed.

The resolve of these heroes/heroines inspired the youth and the elderly to rally behind the stoic freedom fighters. The words of the song spread like bushfire as Kimathi emerged as a living legendary figure, the ultimate undisputed Field Marshall of the Mau Mau guerilla army. As I have previously noted (Mwangi 2002: 65):

---

[4] Mwomboko is a popular Gikuyu traditional-come-modern dance. It emerged in 1940s among the Gikuyu community who interacted with other communities in Kenya. It also borrows elements of the Scottish dance style. Like *Muthirigu* it was an allegory of Kenya's political climate during the colonial era.

On discovering that *Mwomboko* poetry was an ethnopoetic weapon against their very existence, the government banned the performance of the art form. Anybody who acted to the contrary was thrown into prison or detention camp as *Mwomboko* poetry was associated with Mau Mau-ism and the general aspect of rebellion against the colonial administration.

The colonial administration was shaken by and uncomfortable with the new found spirit that engulfed the heart of Kenya. Between the late 1940s and 1950s the singing of *Mwomboko* songs was outlawed and the accordion musical instrument condemned as a catalyst of disloyalty. The Agikuyu continued singing and performing *Mwomboko* in the bush and along river valleys where they could evade the colonizer. The government claimed that the dance was luring young people, especially girls, away from school. The colonial chiefs and their captains were deployed to the bush and river valleys where the so-called clandestine *Mwomboko* was being performed. The dancers fought with the colonial administrators till one side had to give up. *Mwomboko* was banned on 17th March 1950 through the Public Order Act.

The first struggle for liberation[5] and the emergence of Mau Mau song-narratives

In the late 1940s political activists intensified their campaign and propaganda against colonialism. Since the colonizers advocated the singing of Christian hymns the schemers composed anti-establishment songs using pseudo-Christian hymns of the day. According to Kinuthia Mugia, a popular cultural musicologist among the Gikuyu, this scheme went on unabated as the colonizers thought that the subjects had turned into loyal god-fearing people. L.S.B Leakey (1954: 56) notes that Mau Mau hymns were solid and appropriate tools for spreading political and war propaganda for 'they were a quick and effective way to reach the hearts of the people' during Kenya's struggle for emancipation. Finnegan (1970: 285) agreed with Leakey, suggesting that: 'One of the best examples of the use of songs for secret propaganda is the hymns used by Mau Mau movement in Kenya in the early 1950s'. The composers of Mau Mau songs also incorporated Gikuyu traditional tunes to fit with the new thematic concerns of the struggle for Kenya's First Liberation. Some of the traditional tunes were from *Mugoiyo, Gitiiro, Nduumo, Muthunguci,* and *Mwomboko* sub genres.

The pseudo-Christian songs augured well with the mobilization of the Gikuyu, Embu and Meru ethnic communities in urging them to rise and take arms against colonial authority. An example of a corrupted Christian tune is 'I will praise only the Lord' which the fighters claimed: 'I will praise only Gikuyu and Mumbi':

---

[5] The first liberation struggle refers to the period of the struggle for independence in Kenya. This started in the 1920s up to 1963 when Kenya attained political independence.

I know not any other thing in my life
I will all the days of my life
Praise Gikuyu and Mumbi all the time.

This is a manifestation of the hard-line stance assumed by the majority of the Gikuyu in remaining faithful to their traditional African religion. Gikuyu and Mumbi are the father and mother of the ethnic group. Mythically, they lived at Mukurue wa Nyagathanga in Murang'a District of Central Kenya the holy shrine of Agikuyu (Kenyatta 1938).

Through feedback from sympathizers, the authorities gradually began to realize that the songs were 'treacherous' and 'seditious'. By using colonial decree they proscribed the singing and dancing of any song-narratives in Gikuyu land. Indeed the colonial administrator as censor had become, in Marx's words, 'plaintiff, defendant and judge combined in one' (cited in Jansen 1988: 85). In 1952 the colonial administration declared a state of emergency in Kenya. The colonizers defended their unpopular actions in the name of advancing civilization among 'barbaric' and 'murderous' human beings. In terms of the emergency regulations, Gakaara, an ex-freedom fighter, was imprisoned from 1952 to 1962 for writing and composing songs in Gikuyu language (wa Thiongo 1981; Gakaara 1988). Nevertheless, the Gikuyu community continued to sing these songs surreptitiously. For example in the forest the Mau Mau guerrillas sang:

We went to the battlefield happily
Then returned to our base happily
Our journey was quite good to and fro.

The Kenyan Nationalists engaged the British colonial administration in an unprecedented bloody armed struggle without any assistance from the outside world. Even after the colonizer declared a state of emergency for seven years, the song genre acted as a medium of linking various oppressed Kenyans whether guerillas in the forests, detainees in detention camps or the secluded Gikuyu masses in concentration camps. As Wachanga (1975: 13) states:

Many anti-government songs were written and sung. Many of them were written by Kinuthia son of Mugia of Kiambu. One book of collected songs translated into English was confiscated by government and mistakenly attributed to Stanley Mathenge (a Mau Mau General). Prior to reading the words of those songs the government had not realized that our movement was so militant and anti-government.

I have previously emphasized the important role of Mau Mau songs in Kenya's struggle for independence (Mwangi 2002: 64). I noted how 'The *Mwomboko* spirit of doing things together in calculated moves was manifested in the Mau Mau armed struggle'. An example of this is the song-text, 'Parents Do Not Worry':

Our parents do not worry about us
A child is born and may yet die in infancy
Tell the masses to be firm and be hopeful
As we forge ahead to stamp out colour bar.

The struggle for freedom and land in Kenya was guided by dialogue conducted by political activists around the country. The colonizer dismissed dialogue and chose high-handedness. This only further hardened the architects of the struggle for freedom. The censorship of Mau Mau songs did not deter the resolve, vision and mission of the people of Kenya. As a result of this ongoing struggle Kenya finally gained independence from Britain in 1963.

The postcolonial era: The rise of popular Benga⁶ song-narratives and the fangs of censorship

In the aftermath of independence, the new Kenyan government headed by Jomo Kenyatta did not regard music as problematic. However, the only licensed radio station was the Voice of Kenya (VOK), established according to the Corporation Act chapter 221. In Part III of the Act, the Chief Librarian was permitted to select staff members to constitute a Censorship Board that vetted and banned the playing of objectionable music referred to in this chapter.

The Censorship Board became an important means of maintaining the postcolonial government's hegemony in the face of various negative socio-cultural and political problems. Resistant musicians composed songs to check the excesses of Kenya's post-independent regime. This led to anti-establishment protest music, particularly in the form of Benga Beat in the early 1970s. For example, after the mysterious assassination of a government minister, Joseph Thomas Mboya composed and performed a song urging the government to bring the assassins to book (africabooks@world.att.net). The Kenyatta government made use of the broadcast censorship provisions to censor Tom Mboya. The song could no longer be broadcast. In addition, the government prohibited the record disc from being sold in music stores.

In 1975, the Benga composers were up in arms again when a veteran freedom fighter Kung'u Karumba disappeared under mysterious circumstances. Karumba had previously promised that those who had lost their loved ones in the armed struggle would receive financial compensation from the post-independent government. His proclamation appeared to contradict the government's stand so he was assassinated. The government alleged that he had gone to Uganda on a business venture. Popular musician Daniel Kamau refuted this government

---

⁶ Benga is popular modern dance style which emerged in Western and Nyanza Provinces of Kenya. It is now a popular national beat which is very popular in the whole country especially in the rural areas.

explanation in the song 'Where Did Kung'u Karumba Disappear To?' The song was banned from broadcast on 2 February 1975.[7]

The government of Kenya used draconian measures to punish musicians who opposed it. Such musicians were arbitrarily arrested and fined for incitement and infringement of the laws of the land. The string of assassinations continued, climaxing in the death of the populist politician, Josiah Mwangi Kariuki (*Daily Nation* [Kenya] 26 March 1975). Once again popular Benga musicians Daniel Kamau and Joseph Kamaru led other musicians by questioning the credibility of Kenyatta's regime in protecting the lives of its citizens. Kamaru's song 'J.M. Kariuki' says:

> Ooh J.M. Kariuki, he was loved and had offspring
> Was loved and adored by children and adults
> Was found in Ngong Hills split like timber.

In the song Kamaru alleged that whoever ordered J.M. Kariuki's assassination would one day be rolled in a bee-hive watched by the entire population, as had been the traditional Gikuyun method of punishing thieves and witches. This Benga song-narrative angered those in power who immediately censored it (on 20 June 1975) through the Kenyan Broadcasting Corporation (KBC) Censorship Board. According to rumours and articles in the local press, it was alleged that the composer was arrested and taken to the president's home. Together with other so-called errant musicians he was reprimanded and whipped by the president himself who then ordered the confiscation of their record discs and musical instruments (*Society Magazine* [Kenya] May 27 1983).

The government termed any music that accused it of culpability in such crimes as seditious, outrageous, obscene and unsuitable for the consumption of the music-buying public. The censorship of 'J.M. Kariuki' type political songs suggested that the government was fearful of the response such songs would evoke amongst the population. The records quickly sold out. Even people without record players bought them and kept them as socio-political souvenirs.

Apart from political songs with an anti-government theme, songs deemed obscene and anti-religious were censored by the VOK and later the KBC. In so doing the broadcasting censors integrally connected sexuality and religion. As Macmillan (1983: 514) has noted: 'Obscenity prohibition had early associations with blasphemy and seditions label: it was in other words concerned with the enforcement of political/religious orthodoxy as evidenced in a particular brand of sexual morality'.

The censorship of music referred to in this chapter (as banned) was not listed in the government gazette as one would expect. Rather, music banned by VOK or KBC is found in a hand-written file system which is still treated as confidential. Librarians on duty were simply asked to stop playing such music on air.

KBC's censors periodically prohibited the broadcasting of love songs deemed obscene. However, the songs were nevertheless played in music stores in Nairobi and other urban centres as well as in the rural areas. Among these songs were 'Nana' and 'Mwithua' by Daniel Kamau, banned by KBC on 8 February 1977. In 'Nana' the singer says:

> *Nana* my love why leave me at this hour of the night?
> Yet I have religiously undressed so as we sleep
> You have left me crying sweetly all alone
> Come back my love Nana lest I die of cold.

The broadcast censors proclaimed that such 'bedroom' literature corrupted the minds of the youth and other members of the society. Yet these lyrics are fairly tame compared to Marvin Gaye's number, 'Sexual Healing!' which the KBC General Service radio station played regularly. This would suggest that it was not necessarily the words which offended the censors, but more than likely the musician. Despite the broadcast ban, sales figures for 'Nana' were very high – the ban had only served to whet the public's appetite. Daniel Kamau claimed in the *Daily Nation* newspaper (13 July 1982) that it was an all-time hit surpassing his previous compositions. Undeterred by the censorship incident, he came up with 'Mwithua' (Scratching), a song in which a lover urges his/her counterpart to scratch all parts of his/her body including the private ones to save him/herself from dying of the hunger of love. This song too was censored as it was deemed obscene.

In 1985 Joseph Kamaru recorded a controversial Gikuyu traditional circumcision song entitled 'The Mono-Eyed Thing' which is a symbolic allusion to a woman's private parts. This was viewed as obscene and an embarrassment to the sanctity of womanhood. The song was censored and the KBC Censorship Board gave a stern warning to the composer on 9 November 1985. The censored music became more and more popular in entertainment circles and the revellers demanded more and more of this type of artistic dispensation.

On a religious level, the Christian song 'The Water is Bitter' performed by Ismail Ng'ang'a and the Gathaithi Choir was also deemed unfit for public consumption and banned by the broadcast censors. The song is full of biblical allusion to the bitter water at the 'Well of Marah'. It reminds us of the Song of Moses in Exodus (15: 22-25) as the Israelites were in exodus from Egypt to the promised land of Canaan. The song-narrative by the popular Gathaithi choir echoes the biblical message: 'When Moses was in the wilderness of Marah/The water became bitter and undrinkable'. The song-narrative satirizes the corrupt practices emergent in post-colonial Kenya. The vice threatened to tear down the young nation in the 1970s through to the 1980s and 1990s. Nepotism, sectarianism and tribalism were the hallmarks of Kenya's first republic's administration.

Despite the threat of censorship, record companies continued to produce and sell controversial records. The subsequent censorship of anti-establishment songs angered music consumers who regularly bought copies of records banned from airplay and then sang the music vigorously in their homes, churches, and work places as well as in the streets.

The latter postcolonial era: The rise of social, political and economic protests in the 1980s and early 1990s

When the so-called founding father of the nation died in 1978, his deputy Daniel Arap Moi took over the reins of power. In 1982 rebels from the Kenya Air Force staged a *coup d'état*, which pre-empted another one alleged to have been planned by Charles Njonjo, a former Attorney General and also a Minister for Constitutional Affairs. The disgruntled elements were protesting misrepresentation in Government operations in all spheres of development. After the abortive 1982 *coup d'état* Moi's system was characterized by tribalism, nepotism, dictatorship, political mismanagement and ineptitude among a host of vices. This prompted the citizens to protest against the excesses of the so-called Nyayo era rule.

In 1984, John Owino a musician from Luo Nyanza Province, came up with the song 'Baba Otonglo' which angered the government. 'Otonglo' means ten cents or money in the Luo language. This song-narrative is a form of allegory of the Kenya National Budget normally read every year in the month of June. The song also popularly known as 'Budget ya Nyumba', 'House Budget', is synonymous with the socio-economic problems attributed to Kenya's national budget. The head of the house (in other words, the Head of State), Baba Otonglo (Father of Money) struggles to make ends meet so as to keep his family together. However, his poor managerial skills and lack of insight and vision lands him in economic turmoil month in and month out, year in and year out.

The song-narrative was viewed as belittling the Head of State and it was consequently censored and the state's security agents confiscated copies of the record discs found in the music stores. However, there was an outcry as the majority of Kenyans identified themselves with the never-ending problems of 'Baba Otonglo'. The music dealers continued to sell the song on the black market. The cathartic effect generated by the social context of the song-narrative made it a sort of national anthem of the time.

The rise of illiteracy, poverty, peasantry and exploitation in the 1980s prompted music composers to question the status quo. One musician, John Ndicu, came up with the song, 'Nonginya Turiote', 'We Must be Consumed by the Hot Sunshine'. The song discusses the problems of poverty and unemployment as real threats to the survival of ordinary citizens.

> We must be consumed by the scorching sunshine.
> It is sad and tearful
> When your child demands land yet you don't even have a plot
> It is sad and tearful too
> That a university graduate today becomes a tout of a public service vehicle (*matatu*)

Censors from the KBC working for the interest of the autocratic Kenyan government viewed the song as an irritant and obscene voice of discouragement and banned it on 4 December 1987.

The state censors at KBC and the Criminal Investigation Department (CID) assigned the task of policing Kenyan popular music, normally interpreted free expression to be a challenge to the unpopular government. Artists were and, even today to some extent still are, more often than not viewed as enemies of the state. This assertion is usefully illustrated by the popular religious song, 'Muthini wa Nga', 'God's Pauper'. The singer, Joseph Mwaura, explores the themes of poverty, misery, suffering and suppression of the pauper dispensed by the mighty affluent members of society. He says that God's pauper lives every day because of the grace of God but not of that of the rich or the government. He asserts that in court cases between paupers and rich people, the former rely on God as an advocate while the latter use money and influence to buy justice. The KBC censors were not amused and promptly censored the song 'God's Pauper'. The Kenyan populace resisted by demanding that it be aired on government broadcasting stations as its message was relevant to Kenyan's contemporary society. The citizens learnt it and sang it in churches, buses, taxis, *matatus*, homes and work places across the land.

The latter postcolonial era: The clamour for 2nd liberation[8] and political pluralism in Kenya, 1989-1992

In this period the government viewed any voice of opposition as dissension. Dissidents were arrested and their rights violated at the infamous Nyayo House torture chambers. The non-partisan church in Kenya took a firm grip on opposing the profusion of untold suffering prompted by Moi's dictatorship. President Daniel Arap Moi feared losing power through the upcoming clamour for a multi-party democracy. He regularly made political pronouncements to castigate not only the dissidents but also the voices of church leaders.

Yet Kenyan composers continued to criticize the government's excesses through the song genre. In 1990 the assassination of Dr. Robert Ouko, the former Minister for Foreign Affairs and International Cooperation, prompted many local musicians to compose songs on the issue. Musician Sam Muraya was arrested immediately censors realized that his song 'The Death of Ouko' was creating shock waves among the populace. His musical instruments were confiscated by the state and KBC banned his song. In 1995 he was forced to flee Kenya and seek asylum in the U.K. This is after he released yet another catchy and sensitive number, 'The Tribulations of Molo' once again criticizing the Kenyan establishment. The song asserted that the government was involved in ethnic

---

[8] The 'Second Liberation' refers to the period between 1989 and 1992 when patriotic Kenyans sacrificed their lives to challenge Moi's misrule in Kenya.

cleansing in parts of Kenya. Songs about the arrest and detention without trial of fathers of the second liberation (ex-ministers Kenneth Matiba, Charles Rubia, Jaramogi Oginga Odinga among others) abounded in the early 1990s. The song-narrative, 'Matiba's Tribulations' by Kimani Thomas, emerged as a popular political stinger which the KBC government censors banned on 16 December 1994. Once again this led many music enthusiasts to find copies of the music and, after learning its words and rhythm, sing it with zeal.

In the 1990s Joseph Kamaru composed the song 'Bewitching the Nation'. This is an allegory of a politician who goes around the country campaigning and politicking to keep himself in power despite his term of office being over. All the state institutions are on the verge of total collapse and a heightening gloomy atmosphere is spelling out doom. By means of allusion the composer alleges that this political leader is actually bewitching the nation so that no other leader is given the opportunity to rule the country while he is still alive. KBC censors banned the song and CID officers interrogated Kamaru and stopped the distribution of the song in music stores.

Conclusion

This chapter shows how the colonial and post-colonial governments have used censorship laws and other repressive strategies to suppress the freedom of speech and association dispensed through the music mode of expression. Throughout these periods, anti-colonialist and anti-neocolonialist movements have engaged regimes through the use song, dance and poetry (Wa Kinyatti 1980).

In the post-colonial era this culture of resistance has grown and has given hope to the people that one day oppression and exploitation will end. Freedom of expression has increased in recent years. In 2002, almost the whole Kenyan nation danced to a religious tune turned into a political opposition anthem, 'Yote Yawezekana Bila Moi, ('All is Possible Without Moi'). The Kenya African National Union (KANU) tried to counter the euphoria to no avail. The current (2005) National Ruling Rainbow Coalition's campaign during the countdown to 27 December General Elections was boosted by the use of folklore materials and most notably music. As one classical song says: 'Music Alone Shall Live' and no amount of censorship of Kenyan or African music is likely to stop artists exploiting the tools of their trade in fighting for equitable development as well as the rights and dignity of humankind.

References

Daily Nation Newspapers Ltd (Kenya) 1975. 'JM in Zambia'. March 26: p. 1.
Finnegan, R. 1970. *Oral Literature in Africa*. Nairobi: Oxford University Press.

Gakaara, W. 1988. *Mau Mau Author in Detention: an Author's Detention Diary.* Translated from the Gikuyu by Paul Njoroge. Nairobi: Heinemann.

Gecau, K. 1995. 'Popular Song and Social Change in Kenya.' Media, Culture and Society, Volume 17. 557-575.

Good News Bible. 1994. 2nd Edition. United States of America: The United Bible Societies.

Jansen, S.C. 1988. *Censorship: The Knot that Binds Power and Knowledge.* New York: Oxford University Press.

Kanogo, T. 1987. *Squatters and the Roots of Mau Mau 1905-1963.*London: Heinemann Kenya.

Kenyatta, J. 1938. *Facing Mount Kenya.* Nairobi: Heinemann Kenya Ltd.

Kyle, K. 1999. *The Politics of the Independence of Kenya.* Basingstoke: Macmillan Press Ltd.

Leakey, L.S.B. 1954. *Defeating Mau Mau.* London: Methuen and Co. Ltd.

Macmillan, P.R. 1983. *Censorship and Public Morality.* Craft Road, London: Grower Publishing Limited.

Mwangi, P.M. 2002. 'The Poetics of Gikuyu *Mwomboko* Poetry: A Case Study of Selected Performing Artistes'. Unpublished M.A. Thesis, Kenyatta University, Nairobi.

Oboler, E.M. 1980. *Defending Intellectual Freedom: The Library and Censor.* London: Greenwood Press.

Stapleton, C. and May, C. 1987. *African all-stars: the pop music of a continent.* London: Quartet Books.

The Ministry of Information and Broadcasting: The Kenya Broadcasting Corporation Act 1990. Chapter 221. Revised Edition, Printed and Published by the Government Printer, Nairobi. pp 11-12.

Wa Kinyatti, M. 1980. *Thunder from the Mountains: Mau Mau Patriotic Songs.* Nairobi: Medi-Teki Publishers.

Wachanga, H.K. 1975. *The Swords of Kirinyaga: the Fighting for Land and Freedom.* Nairobi, Kampala and Dar es Salaam: East Africa Literature Bureau.

Wa Thiongo, N. 1981. *Decolonising the Mind.* Nairobi and London: Heinemann.

Internet Sites

http://www.africabooks@worldnet.att.net
http://www.theroc.org/aboutroc/roc 10.htm
http://www.theory.org.uk/effects.htm
http://www.v-day.org

Chapter 11

One Hundred Years of Censorship in Ghanaian Popular Music Performance

John Collins

Introduction

Censorship of the arts is one of the mechanisms that central social groups of a society use to consolidate and control social, political and bureaucratic power or 'hegemony', a word coined in the 1940s by the Italian Marxist Antonio Gramsci. Furthermore, Gramsci believed that the ruling-class control of a society is never permanent and that it has to continually repress or moderate anti-hegemonic impulses emerging from the masses: through trade unions, labour parties, independence struggles, youth movements, ethnic and other sub-cultures. Popular culture is another important arena where these hegemonic/anti-hegemonic struggles are worked out. On the one hand there is the hegemony of the ruling group with its 'repressive', and 'centripetal' approach that includes artistic censorship. On the other hand there are the 'emancipatory' and 'centrifugal' tendencies towards free expression and the creation of new identities within the emergent popular culture.[1]

The most important Ghanaian popular performance styles are collectively known as 'highlife' which first evolved as a fusion of local African and imported western and African-American performance elements in the coastal cities of Ghana from the late nineteenth century. In turning to the topic of the censorship of Ghanaian highlife I focus on areas of repression that have emanated from four differing areas of central hegemony over the last hundred years, as Ghana has witnessed a transition from British colonial rule to various forms of post independence governments.

The chapter therefore examines first the attitude of the British colonial authorities and missionaries to local popular performance up to independence. Secondly, it turns to the negative attitude to popular music by traditional African authorities. Thirdly, the chapter looks at political censorship of popular songs by the post-independence governments of Nkrumah and others. It concludes on the

---

[1] For Gramsci see 1971. For 'repressive' and 'emancipatory' see Ensenburger (1974) and for 'centripetal' and 'centrifugal' see Carey (1975).

current controversy over the lyrics of newer forms of highlife which the older generation sees as morally indecent.

As will be shown, the types of censorship applied ranges from bans on performances, arrests of artists, the de-throning of chiefs, destruction of music records, criticisms in the mass media, the banning of songs on radio, the re-writing of indecent lyrics and the curbing of songs and indeed whole music genres used by political opponents both in the modern and traditional sectors.

Colonial/missionary censorship

The British colonial system in Ghana became fully established after the ending of the slave trade in the early nineteenth century and particularly from the 1870s when the British imperial army launched a series of wars against the inland Ashanti kingdom that consolidated British rule throughout the whole country, then known as the Gold Coast. The colonial rulers and white missionaries wanted to turn Ghanaians into punctual, disciplined and 'civilized' workers for the new colonial economy and utilized music to help do this: particularly the martial music of regimental bands, refined classical orchestral concerts, 'highbrow' theatre and Christian hymns and anthems to counteract 'pagan' drumming and dancing. Ironically these imported styles were subsequently initially utilized by coastal, Ghanaians to create their own acculturated or trans-cultural styles of music, dance and drama, such as highlife and a local popular theatre known as the concert party.

Objections by colonial authorities to these Ghanaian popular performance forms that began to emerge in the coastal towns from the late nineteenth century first concerned music played by local 'adaha' fife-and-drum and brass bands. This was an early form of highlife that evolved from trained local regimental musicians influenced by the Afro-Caribbean music of six to seven thousand West Indian soldiers who were stationed at Cape Coast and El Mina Castles in the 1870s. They were there to help the British defeat the powerful inland state of Ashanti. In 1888 Reverend Minister Kemp described the sound of drum-and-fife bands as 'tormenting', and warned that the danger of allowing Sunday school processions to be led by them would 'ultimately lead to the ballroom, the heathen dance and other worldly amusements'.[2] In 1908 the District Commissioner of Cape Coast, A. Foulkes, put a curb on the five local brass bands of the town by forbidding them to play their 'objectionable native tunes or airs' as these led to competitive quarrelling, obstruction of roads, drinking and dancing.[3]

Despite these objections, coastal brass band music and its associated marches and dances spread like wildfire into the southern areas of Ghana during the early

---

[2] See Boonjazer-Flaes and Gales 1991, pp. 13 and 20 and f/n 20, 22 and 38: quoting from Kemp's Nine Years in the Gold Coast, London McMillan 1898 (see also Boonzajer-Flaes, 1999).

[3] Ibid., p. 14 f/n 23.

twentieth century. However the negative attitude of the colonialists to local brass band music continued, as is evidenced by a comment by Presbyterian missionaries in 1913 that the brass band playing at a festival in the inland Akan town of Akropong were thinking 'more of sardines and cigarettes than their souls'.[4] In 1923 the Father Bergi of the Bremen mission in Ghana's south-eastern Volta Region wrote that brass band (and other local popular music styles) were 'loosening' the morals of young people and 'making them unfit for work'.[5]

This negative attitude of the churches was partly a result of a failed attempt to use brass band music and its associated drills and marches for proselytizing and getting local people used to the 'necessities of industrial time'.[6] Many of the protestant missions established brass bands at the end of the nineteenth century but discovered that the musicians they trained would, behind their backs, invariably 'backslide' and play and dance to the popular songs of the local bands. Indeed during the 1930s the missions practically dropped the use of brass bands altogether and the Christian use of brass bands really only started up again after the Second World War, particularly with the Catholic Church and some of the Africanized Christian sects.

Appearing a little later than local 'adaha' brass bands, but in the same Cape Coast area, were popular music forms created by coastal West Africans, fishermen and sailors such as 'asiko' (or 'ashiko') and 'osibisaaba' that involved a combination of light percussion instruments and sailors' instruments: in particular the guitar and accordion.

From port towns pan-West African asiko music became popular in southern Ghana and in 1908 the Basel Mission in Krobo-land confiscated the drums of one such group for playing 'obscene songs'.[7] Osibisaaba was a contemporary music style to asiko and was created by Fanti fishermen. From the Fanti coastal towns of Cape Coast, Takoradi and Winneba it quickly spread into southern Ghana. In 1909 the police commissioner in the inland town of Nsawam took two Akan men to the local court and jailed them for playing osibisaaba, as according to Akyeampong (1996:61), it was a banned dance associated with social protest. The very same year the colonial authorities in Accra called the osibisaaba circle-dance in which men and women dance indecently 'objectionable'.[8] And in 1910 the Bremen

---

[4] Ibid., p. 21 and f/n 39: quoting Smith 1966: 137 'The History of the Presbyterian Church in Ghana 1835-1960', Ghana Universities Press, Accra.

[5] Ibid., p. 22 f/n 41 quoting a circular letter by Bergi 17 April 1923:5-7 in the Archives of the Norddeutsche Mission, Bremen. These popular music styles included sibi-saba (that is, osibisaaba) dancing, its associated saneko drumming, and brass band playing (and local variants such as kainka).

[6] An expression coined by Terence Ranger (1975:13) in connection with the European mission bands training of East Africans in late nineteenth-century Zanzibar.

[7] See Veit Arlt unpublished m/s 2002: f/n 29 quoting from the Basel Mission Archives D-1 90.

[8] Information from Joe Gazari of the Ghana National Museum quoting Ghana National Archives file ADM 11/1/884.

missionaries were complaining that osibisaaba (or 'sibi-saba') was spreading 'like wild-fire' and its texts included songs on the topic of pregnancy, marriage, 'concubines' and 'doing it slowly or the bed will break'.[9]

In spite of all these protestations against osibisaaba, this guitar and accordion dance music continued to spread into the cocoa rich areas of southern Ghana. By 1927/8 recordings of this music (by George William Aingo and Kwame Asare's Kumasi Trio) were being made by European companies, for as a result of lucrative cash-crops, many Ghanaians, even farmers, could afford wind-up gramophones. By the late the 1930s tens of thousands of these 'native recordings' were being sold on shellac 78 rpm records. In fact the sales of these vernacular guitar songs from Ghana and elsewhere in West Africa were so profitable that the record company HMV/Zonophone sold 181,484 of them in 1930, whilst this British company and German Odeon sold eight hundred thousand of these records before the Second World War.

The Second World War put a temporary halt to this lucrative Ghanaian record trade as the production of records almost ceased in most countries due to the raw materials (shellac) being used in the war effort. However the war did hasten the movement towards independence: especially after 1948 with the independence of India and the shooting in Accra of Ghanaian ex-servicemen marching for back-pay and the subsequent lootings of European and Lebanese shops. This wartime impact was reflected in the Ghanaian popular arts. One example actually involves Ghanaian serviceman Bob Vans (personal communication 1974) and six other Ghanaians who were members of the West African Frontier Force fighting with the British in Burma and India against the Japanese.[10] In Burma and India between 1943 and 1946 these Ghanaians and other West African soldiers established a West African Theatre to entertain the troops, and on returning to Ghana after the war Bob Vans and his colleagues set up the Burma Jokers concert party. However, in the critical year of 1948 they changed this to the name 'Ghana Trio': nine years before 'Ghana' became the country's official name at independence.[11]

Other concert parties were also involved in the nationalist struggle, for instance from the late 1940s to early 1950s the Axim Trio concert party staged a number of pro-independence plays such as 'Nkrumah Will Never Die', 'Nkrumah Is A Mighty Man'[12] and 'Nkrumah Is Greater Than Before'[13], whilst Bob Ansah's concert group

---

[9] Information and translations of 21 songs from Prof. Mary Esther Kropp-Dakubu referring to three letters written by German missionaries in 1910 now in the Bremen Staats Archives, index number 7,1024, 2, 41 folklore item 19.

[10] 65,000 Ghanaians experienced military service during the Second World War (Fage, 1966) of which six battalions fought in Burma (Aboagye 1999).

[11] The name Ghana for the British Gold Coast colony was an idea first muted by the nationalist Dr Y.B. Danquah to bypass the factious issue of 'tribalism' (that is, using a local ethnic name) by suggesting naming the country after the ancient kingdom of Ghana in present day Mauritania-Senegal.

[12] Personal communication with Bob Johnson in Teshi-Nungua, 20th March 1974.

staged 'We Shall Overcome', 'The Achievement of Independence' and 'The Creation of Ghana'. Ansah was also twice arrested by the British authorities and questioned about his plays. This censorship of popular theatre also occurred around the same time in the nearby British colony of Nigeria where there had been a general strike after the war. There the pioneer of Yoruba travelling theatre, Hubert Ogunde, had some of his anti-British plays banned. In 1946 Ogunde was cautioned by the colonial police for his play 'The Tiger's Empire'. In addition, he was fined and his theatre in Jos banned because of his 'Strike and Hunger' production, about the 1945 Nigerian General Strike. In 1950 his play, 'Bread and Bullets' about the Enugu coal strike was banned in Kano, and Ogunde was arrested for sedition (see Clarke 1979).

Many Ghanaian highlife and other popular musicians also supported the early nationalist cause[14] and what Ensenburger (1974) called the anti-hegemonic 'emancipatory' mode. In one particular case concerning a song called 'Freedom For Ghana' dedicated to the 'Honourable Kwame Nkrumah', the British became so worried as to whether or not the lyrics were subversive, that Colonial Office minutes were written on the matter.[15] This song was a calypso recorded by HMV in London in 1952 by the Trinidadian George Brown and a mixed group of Ghanaian and West Indian musicians. Nkrumah's Convention Peoples Party (CPP) ordered twenty thousand copies of the song. The West Indian Black Nationalist, George Padmore, was the correspondent for the Ghanaian newspaper at the time and wrote on the matter and provided the lyrics of the contentious song. The chorus goes 'Freedom is in the land, friends let us shout long live the CPP, which now controls Africa's destiny'. The song text also refers to CPP leaders such as Nkrumah 'from his Ussher Fort cell' and continues 'they called us veranda boys, they thought we were just a bunch of toys, but we won the vote at midnight hour, came out of jail and took power…the British MP Gammans was rude by his dog-in-the-mangerish attitude, but like an ostrich we know this man can go and bury his head in the sand'.[16]

---

[13] Gold Coast Evening News entry of 5 July 1950, which also said that the proceeds went to Nkrumah's Convention Peoples Party funds.

[14] Examples include the Ga pianist Squire Addo, the highlife Tempos dance band leader E.T. Mensah (Collins 1986 and 1994) and the guitar band highlife musicians E.K.Nyame (Collins 1985), Kwaa Mensah, S.S. Ahima and I.E. Mason (songs with John Collins/BAPMAF popular music archives, Accra).

[15] File number CO/554/595 from Mr. Maurice Smith to Mr. Williamson, saying that although the song makes 'offensive references to old-fashioned British Imperialism' there is 'nothing seditious' about it.

[16] Sekondi Morning Telegraph 5 February 1952. Other nationalists referred to are Gbedemah, Botsio, Kwesi Plange, Edusie, Appiah and Casely-Hayford.

The censorship of popular and neo-traditional music and dance by African traditional authorities.

While the British colonialists and missionaries were concerned with the establishment and maintenance of their hegemony and were hostile to emergent local popular performance, traditional ethnic authorities were concerned with preserving their control in the face of western influences. So there are also cases of chiefs, elders and other traditional authorities being antipathetic to both acculturated popular music and dance and even to some neo-traditional performance genres: these being traditional type drum-dances created in the twentieth century but influenced by popular performance.

For example, local traditionalists often disliked guitar highlife that began to spread from the coast into southern Ghana in the 1920s. Veit Arlt (2002: f/n 49)[17] notes that this was the case in the Krobo area of south-eastern Ghana whose paramount chief, Mata Kole, believed highlife music caused 'bad habits', 'disobedience', 'laziness' and 'even songs of reproach against chiefs'. Similarly, Akyeampong (1996: 62) refers to an attempt by elders to de-stool (that is, de-throne) a young Omanhene (chief) of Bekwai Ashanti in 1920 for drunkenness, holding a guitar in the hands and wearing western clothes.

It was because the highlife guitarists of the early twentieth century played their instrument in low-class dockside bars and in rural palm-wine drinking bars that this instrument became associated with drunkenness and was held in particularly low esteem. This negative attitude also applied to Ghana's pioneering highlife or 'palmwine' guitar group, the Kumasi Trio, that in 1928 made some of the earliest highlife recordings (for the British Zonophone label). The leader of this group was Kwame Asare (Jacob Sam) who had to run away from his home in Cape Coast to play guitar, as his father thought only 'ruffians' played guitar (Collins, 1996:3). According to Beattie Casely-Hayford (1987) this group originally comprised young Fanti cocoa brokers working for a British trading firm that stationed them in the small inland Akan farming-town of Apedwua.

The low repute of this guitar band was compounded by two other factors that made both traditional and western educated Ghanaians disapprove. Firstly, Yaa Amponsah, the sister of one of the musicians, taught the men of Apedwua to dance the highlife in western ballroom style where men and women hold each other. In traditional Akan dancing it is not considered decent for men and women to touch each other in public. Furthermore, Yaa Amponsah was collecting coins from the men she taught ballroom dancing, which led to assertions by the town elders that she was a wayward 'good-time girl' or prostitute.

The second factor that lowered the repute of the Kumasi Trio was that the lyrics of their most famous highlife song dedicated to and named after 'Yaa Amponsah'

---

[17] Veit Arlt is quoting Ghana National Archives file ADM 11/1/884 Case No 29/1924, Suppression of Indecent Dances by Chief Mata Kole to the Volta Region District Commissioner, 2nd August 1926.

was itself considered to be indecent by many Ghanaians as it contains the lines translated from Akan 'even though we are married let's remain lovers.... nothing can stop my love for you, not even if your mother threatens to douche me with pepper and your father with an enema of boiling water' (Ghana Copyright News, 1990: 5). Indeed, the Ghanaian art/choral composer, Ephraim Amu, who was training at the Presbyterian Training College at Akropong in 1927 was shocked when the British principal wanted Yaa Amponsah to be sung by the students, as Amu who considered it to be 'a vulgar street-song usually sung by drunkard, labourers, lorry drivers and low-class people: a song never to be sung by a Christian or educated person'. As a result Amu composed English words acceptable to local students that go 'half-past four is a good time to go home and play, too much learning is boring, we all want some time to play' (Ghana Copyright News, 1990: 5).

Despite all this moral indignation over the 1928 Yaa Amponsah record, it was an enormous hit in Ghana, especially with the rural communities and urban poor. This song was subsequently recorded by many other bands (including in Nigeria), and its melodo-rhythmic structure has become the template for many highlife compositions right up to the present day.

As noted above, the emerging twentieth century new traditional music styles influenced by westernized popular music were also often frowned upon by elders. New or neo-traditional genres were usually created from pre-existing 'recreational' forms of traditional drum music associated with youngsters and youthful age-sets. These recreational styles of traditional music, being linked to generational change and identity, were therefore faster changing and more open to foreign influences than the more slow-moving ritual, ceremonial and court music. Consequently, the more conservative traditional leaders and village elders often ostracized these new forms of traditional music.

Two early examples, both from the 1930s, of such 'modernized' recreational genres were konkoma music of the Akans of southern Ghana and simpa music of the people of Dagbon in northern Ghana. Konkoma was a 'poor-man's' version of the local Akan 'adaha' brass bands that did away with expensive imported brass instruments and made do rather with local drums and voices. It was associated with the youth of the period who were considered by traditional authorities to be 'rascals' (Casely-Hayford 1987), 'school-drop-outs' (Sackey 1989) and 'ruffian boys'.[18]

Simpa evolved in the Dagbon traditional area when local recreational music became acculturated with imported western and southern Ghanaian performance styles, (gome, concert parties and highlife). Simpa music has always been associated with the young and since its inception simpa gatherings have been

---

[18] The latter term is by A.M. Opoku, personal communication 7 Sept 1900. Ironically it was this very youthful nature of konkoma that decided the British to use it (for recruiting purposes and army route-march songs) during the Second World War.

considered by older people as improper places for young boys and girls to meet (Collins 1986: 36).

A later example of a youthful recreational reviled by the elders is the Ga kpanlogo drums-dance of the 1960s - which became the focus of youthful identity and protest. It was created in 1962 by Ga youth from the fishermen's Bukom area of Accra who were both influenced by local music and imported western rock 'n' roll and the twist. Because of the exaggerated pelvic movements that the kpanlogo dance borrowed from 'Elvis the Pelvis' and Chubby Checker, the older generation (and executives of the National Arts Council) initially opposed this new traditional genre, claiming that the dance was too sexually suggestive. On some occasions kpanlogo performers were even caned by the police, with their drums being seized and sometimes the musicians being put in the cells for a few days. This inter-generation dispute was only resolved in 1965 when Nkrumah's CPP organized a display of 50 such groups, and the kpanlogo drum-dance was officially endorsed.

Political censorship since independence

As discussed previously, many highlife musicians supported Nkrumah's early nationalist cause, which is why this leader put such an emphasis on fostering the popular (as well as traditional Ghanaian performance) through setting up numerous state and para-statal dance bands and concert parties.

However after independence in 1957 there were some highlife compositions that were critical of (or were considered to be critical of) the CPP government in power. A very famous example is E.T Mensah's 'Ghana Freedom Highlife' that was recorded at the Decca Studio in Accra in 1957. In celebrating Ghana's independence this song mentioned Nkrumah and some of the non-CPP nationalist leaders (J.B. Danquah and Dr. Busia). After the song's release E.T. Mensah was told by two enraged CPP Ministers, Kofi Baako and Krobo Edusei, that Nkrumah was annoyed with having his name linked with what he called 'detractors'. As a result and on the 'repressive' hegemonic instructions of the CPP government, Decca Records in London had to blot out the offending names on the master tape, destroy 10,000 copies of the record and reprint new ones (Collins 1986: 27).

Towards the end of the Nkrumah era (that ended in 1966) initially staunch supporters of the CPP released songs critical of the government. One was 'Ne Aye Dinn' (Hold It Well) by E.T. Mensah and his Tempos band and another was 'Aban Nkaba' (Government Handcuffs) by the concert party leader Bob Cole. (Dadson, 1991). However it should be noted that the songs that were critical of Nkrumah and his CPP government were not usually in the form of direct political protest but were rather oblique, disguised or wrapped up in some way as a parable, proverb or allusion. For instance, E.K. Nyame recorded several such highlife songs in the latter period of Nkrumah's rule. One was 'Nsu Bota Mframa Dzi Kan' which includes the lines 'if the rain falls the wind will blow first... so I'm warning you like the wind'. This became the slogan of the anti-CPP National Liberation Movement that opposed

Nkrumah's socialist policies. E.K Nyame followed this up with 'Ponko Abo Dam A, Ne Wura No Dze Ommbuo Dam Bi' which is based on the Akan proverb that translates as 'if the horse is mad it does not mean the owner is mad'.[19] Another well-known concert party highlife musician, K. Gyasi (of the Noble Kings) released the record 'Agyimah Mansah' in 1964 about a ghost mother lamenting the plight of her children. President Nkrumah personally questioned Gyasi about the lyrics, and the composer claimed these were based on a dream he had had and were not a political reflection by 'Mother Ghana' on the state of the nation. Nevertheless the song was banned from government-controlled radio. At the time all radio and television stations were controlled by the government until the mid-1990s ,when independent commercial stations were first allowed. There are now about ten television stations,and 100 commercial and community-based FM radios stations in Ghana.

After the 1966 military coup by the National Liberation Council (NLC) that ousted Nkrumah's CPP government the two performance unions, the Ghana Musicians Union and National Association of Entertainers, were dissolved due to their links with the CPP. Furthermore the musical entertainer Ajax Bukana, a staunch supporter of Nkrumah, (in fact his 'court jester'), was actually arrested by the police immediately after the coup and questioned for several days (Collins 1996: ch. 6).

After the 1966 coup anti-Nkrumah songs continued to appear for a while. An example is the African Brothers highlife record 'Okwanduo' (Wild Ox) which includes a refrain by a hunter that goes 'you are gone but woe to your brethren'. This, Bame (1969) believes, refers to the general public desire that although Nkrumah and many of his supporters had escaped, those who remained in the country should be punished. An even better known highlife of the prolific African Bothers famous guitar band is the 1966 song 'Ebe Te Yie' (Some Sit Well) about big animals pushing smaller ones into the cold. Although this song was considered to be a general attack against the political and economic elites that had emerged after independence, when Ampadu was officially questioned on the matter he claimed the lyrics were based on a fable his father had told him. This song, like K. Gyasi's 'Agyemah Mansah' discussed earlier, suggests that the public may change the meaning of a song to fit current views and retrospectively give a highlife song what Van der Geest and Asante-Darko (1982: 33) call a 'secret political meaning'.

The regimes that followed Nkrumah's were also subject to critical highlife songs. Following a brief period of civilian rule from 1969 led by Dr. Kofi Busia, another military coup took place on January 13th 1971 led by Colonel Acheampong. The highlife record by Kofi Sammy's Okukuseku's concert band entitled 'To Wo Bo Ase, Efidie Wura Beba' (Be Careful The Owner Will Come) was continuously played on the day of the coup, and in fact became the slogan for it. By the mid 1970s, however, this same highlife song was banned from radio and television as its message, which contains the lines 'be careful enemy, the one who will beat you has not yet come', also

---

[19] Personal communication with the late E.F. Collins of the University of Ghana.

began to be applied to the increasingly unpopular Acheampong regime that became notorious for its 'kalabule' or corruption.[20]

A song by the prolific African Brothers released in the early 1970s called 'Afe Bi Ye Nhyira, Afe Be Ye Asan' was also interpreted as an attack on this military regime, as the title means 'some years are a blessing whilst some years are full of trouble'. More openly critical was the Konadu's concert party band record 'Yedo Wo' (You Are Born With It) that reproved Colonel Acheampong for his failed 'Operation Feed Yourself' project and this highlife song was consequently banned from radio airplay (Van der Geest and Asanti-Darko 1982: 31/2).

There are also cases of neo-traditional music forms being censored or banned by the government authorities for political reasons, including the previously discussed simpa music of the Dagbon traditional area in northern Ghana. In the post-colonial era the genre became politicized when simpa groups began supporting either of two sides of a long-standing dispute over chiefly succession. In 1969 major violence erupted in the Dagbon traditional area and as a result the Ghanaian army moved in and a six-month ban was imposed by the police on what they believed were inflammatory performances of simpa music (Collins 1985: ch. 5). In this case government hegemonic control was therefore utilized in a 'centripetal' way (Carey 1975). In addition, Chernoff (1979: 212-13) mentions another acculturated recreational percussion genre that swept though the youth of Dagbon in the 1970s called 'atikatika' which was periodically banned by the local and national authorities as the children sang witty songs related to the Dagbon chieftaincy dispute, as well as criticizing local school-masters and businessmen.

Another example of political censorship concerns the previously discussed neo-traditional recreational kpanlogo drum-dance music of the Ga youth in Accra that in the early 1960s was criticized by Ga elders and by executives of that National Arts Council. Its performers were even caned and arrested by the police. This harassment was not only due to the previously mentioned generational gap between the Ga elders and youth, but also because early kpanlogo was popular with the fashionably dressed young 'Tokyo Joes'.[21] These were the rough political Ga activists and supporters of Dr. Busia's United Party who sometimes used kpanlogo rhythms in their anti-Nkrumah and anti-CPP songs. Another factor contributing to this official harassment of kpanlogo groups may have been the fact that the content of the short dance-dramas that were often part of a kpanlogo session, were sometimes anti-establishment and critical of such government officials as health inspectors (see Collins 1994).

---

[20] Even popular literature took on an anti-Acheampong stance and Barber (1987: 40) mentions mid-1970s' comics from Kumasi whose superhuman hero was a combination of the 'Spiderman' of American Marvel comics and Ananse-the-Spider of Akan folklore and who from a jungle hide-out supports the masses suffering under a military regime.

[21] Information of police harassment and 'Tokyo Joes' from Jones Attuqueyifio, personal communication 30 May 1979. Also see Salm 2003.

Despite popular performers throwing their weight behind the early nationalist struggle, within a few years of Ghana gaining independence (in 1957) performers of highlife bands and of neo-traditional genres (influenced by highlife) started to become critical of the various governments. In other words their anti-hegemonic messages were directed away from the colonial authorities towards their own Ghanaian governments.

Moral censorship in recent years

Here I will turn to what might be called the hegemonic attitude of the older generation towards the popular music styles created by the youth, usually expressed as moral indignation over the lyrics of the songs that dwell on the theme of sexual love. Although the lyrics of the older (pre-1980s) styles of highlife were not generally on the topic of romantic love[22] some popular highlife love songs of the past were considered immoral. These songs were generally composed by people who were in the twenties or thirties and an early example is the previously discussed 'vulgar street song' song 'Yaa Amponsah' composed by a group of young cocoa-brokers in the 1920s, the lyrics of which were cleaned up by the school-teacher Ephraim Amu. Another that was banned by state radio was 1950s song 'Se Wo Ko Na Anny Eyie A San Bra' (If You Go And It Doesn't Work Out, Come Back) by the then youthful E.K. Nyame which was frowned upon (but not banned) by older Ghanaians as it explicitly mentions a wife's desire for her husband to kiss her on the mouth, a foreign custom that at that time was not considered something to be mentioned openly. A few years after the prolific highlife composer King Bruce formed his Black Beats band in 1952 two of his Ga songs were banned from state radio. One was 'Telephone Lobi' (Sweethearts) which Bruce explains is 'a bit risqué, especially where the man says he wants to see the women in the flesh'. Another was his highlife 'Srotoi Ye Mli' (There Are Varieties In Everything) about differences in things like wine, vegetables and fruits. Although it was not Bruce's intention, when the general public people heard words in the song like 'sweet' and 'not so sweet', 'heavy' and ' light' they thought the song was about sex - and thus the song was censored from the state airwaves.[23]

A more recent example of a popular song banned from the airwaves include the 1980s highlife by A.B. Crentsil with its obvious sexual innuendo about 'Moses' using his rod to open the 'Red Sea' that is bordered by a 'black bush'. Another is

---

[22] Of 280 guitar band and dance band highlife songs (mainly on shellac record from the 1930s to 1960s) in the John Collins/BAPMAF music archives collection that have been translated in English, 41 (that is, about 15 per cent) are on the theme of love, most of the rest are on enemies and witchcraft, socio-political commentary, moral advice, orphans and family problems, money 'palava', sickness and death.

23 Both these quotes for songs are part of an unpublished manuscript that King Bruce and John Collins wrote between 1987-89.

the 1999 hit 'Abiba Yeah, Wa Donkoto Ye Fre Me', (Abiba, your lovely motions sweet me) by the up-and-coming highlife star Rex Omar, which mentions (in Akan) the word 'vagina'. This was even banned by some of the private FM radio stations which had begun to spring up in the country during the mid-1990s.

Since the mid-1980s two 'techno' varieties of highlife have been created by young people: namely a disco/drum machine style known as 'burgher' highlife,[24] followed in the mid-1990s by a vernacular rap known as 'hiplife' (that is, 'hip-hop highlife'). The lyrics of both these genres are predominantly on the topic of romantic love and often involve sexual innuendo. It is largely the older generation of Ghanaians that dislike these new styles of highlife, with their imported hairstyles, baggy clothes and 'gangsta-rap' attitudes. As a result of pressure from older members of the public some burgher highlife and hiplife songs have been banned from radio, both the government- and privately-owned ones. An example of a banned burgher highlife was the immensely popular 2000 release by Daddy Lumba called 'Aben Wo Ha' (It is Cooked) which is a thinly disguised song about women being sexually excited. In the case of hiplife music the lyrics are not only sexually explicit but also often misogynist. Indeed, hiplife is mainly a macho affair and there are only one or two female rappers, for example Abrewanana. Meanwhile female singers dominate the local gospel highlife that has emerged since the 1980s, creating a literal gender split in contemporary Ghanaian popular dance music. Some examples of the sexually explicit lyrics of hiplife include 'Police Aba' in which Nsiah Piese raps on the topic of women being sexually attracted to a policeman's baton, and 'Abuskeleke' by Sydney, which deals with the latest female fashion of baring the waist. Other hiplife songs that, according to the Ghana Showbiz newspaper editorial 'Hiplife Shame' (13 January 2001) promote promiscuity and teenage sex include Appiah Fordwour's 'Gyese Edu' (person's name), Cool Joe and Michael Dwamana's 'Te Bi Di' (Take and Eat), Max Kofi's 'Akadaa Ketewa Bi' (Youngster), Kaayire Kwame Appiah's 'Nketewa Do' (Small Love) and Lord Kenya's 'Bokoboko' (Slowly). Yet another recent example is Tic Tac's hiplife song 'Philomena' which criticizes the current imported female fashion of allowing genital and under-arm hair to grow. The song was associated with a dance in which the dancer scratches his or her pubic area.

Philomena Kpintinge (Lady's name)
Philomena change your ways, even though you look fly,
Let me say this as our grandparents have been saying it - bushy hair is threatening and fearful,
Excuse me I am afraid, when it is shown we will definitely fall down
When we inhale we will vomit, when it's shown to white-man they will go crazy
I have been told there is something under cover, hidden in a cloth

---

24 This was created in the early 1980s by Ghanaian expatriates living in Germany, particularly Hamburg.

It is hair isn't it? It is fearful unless a caterpillar road-grader levels (that is, shaves) it
CHORUS Philomena Kintinge yeye, hair hear, hair there, hair everywhere.
(Extracts translated from the Twi by Emmanuel Gyan)

Not only are some hiplife songs occasionally banned from FM radio stations but
there have been a number of newspaper reports commenting on them. A few mention
that these local rap songs give the youth a voice, but most accuse hiplife of being
'lewd', 'profane' and 'degrading' to women.[25] Indeed, in December 2002 the
Executive Director of the Ghana branch of the International Federation of the Women
Lawyers (FIDA) stated that some hiplife lyrics 'debase femininity and the bodies of
women … (and) constitutes violence against women on the airwaves' (*Ghana Times*,
12 December 2002). FIDA threatened high court actions against some radio stations
and disc jockeys. Both FIDA and the Musicians Union of Ghana (MUSIGA) have also
asked the Ministry of Information and the Ghana Media Commission to closely
monitor the local FM stations for indecent lyrics. But as the journalist William Asiedu
(*Mirror*, 28 December 2002) commented, hiplife songs that are banned or 'come under
fire for spawning immorality amongst the youth…make good sales throughout the
country… and become instant hits and chart busters'.

Conclusion

From what has been written here it can be appreciated that censorship in Ghana
over the last hundred years has involved popular artists being repressed by various
hegemonic institutions that include colonial administrators and police, Christian
mission houses, post-independence governments, modern bureaucracies and the
Ghanaian national army.

A more continuous and cyclical generational form of hegemonic control over
youthful popular (and neo-traditional music) has emanated over the years from
both the traditional authorities and the older and more conventional layers of the
general public in any period. These include the suppression of young highlife
musicians by some traditional rulers in the early twentieth century, the traditional
elders disdain for youthful simpa, konkoma and kpanlogo in the 1930s, 1940s and
1960s, the moral indignation of the older generation of urban Ghanaians over some
of the highlife records of E.K. Nyame and King Bruce in the 1950s and 1960s,
right up to the current dislike of hiplife and its associated youth sub-culture by the
parents of today.

The sanctions used by these hegemonic agencies and conservative generational
groupings have been varied. Performances have been censored, such as the curbs
put on 'obstructive' and 'objectionable' brass bands in 1900 Cape Coast by the

---

25 Examples include Mirror 16 December 2000 and 28 December 2002; Ghana Showbizz
31 January and 14 June 2000, and 13 January and 22 February 2001; Ghana Times 12
December 2002.

colonial District Commissioners, followed by the ban on the 'indecent' and 'obscene' osibisaaba dance requested by missionaries. Then in the late 1940s came the questioning of concert party leaders by colonial authorities for their anti-British plays. After independence there was the police harassment and caning of kpanlogo groups linked to the anti-Nkrumah political opposition during the early 1960s and the six-month government ban on northern simpa music during the 1969 Dagbon Chieftaincy dispute.

There have also actual arrests of artists over the years. These range from the jailing of guitar players by the colonial police during the 1920s, to the harassment of young kpanlogo drummers by the Ghana police of the late Nkrumah period and to the police detention of Nkrumah's personal musical 'jester' Ajax Bukana after the anti-Nkrumah coup of 1966.

Forms of political censorship have been imposed on recorded music: such as the 'subversive' Independence Highlife commented on by Padmore in 1952 that so worried the British Colonial Office in Accra, or the ten thousand copies of E.T. Mensah's Ghana Freedom Highlife destroyed on the order of Nkrumah in 1957.

Songs have also been banned on radio and television by the various post-independence governments that totally controlled the airwaves until the mid-1990s. These included political songs by both guitar band and dance band highlife musicians, as well as supposedly political highlife songs that the general public re-interpreted and gave a political meaning to. Likewise songs containing lyrics with a strong sexual innuendo or content, like today's burgher highlife and hiplife have, in more recent years, been criticized in the newspapers and banned by state radio as well as by some of the new commercial FM radio that have appeared over the last ten years or so.

A new Copyright Bill that is going before the Ghanaian Parliament in the near future might lead to a further form of censorship in Ghana. If passed the Copyright Bill will oblige Ghanaian performers (and painters, writers, film-makers, designers, and so on) who wish to commercially utilize their own indigenous folklore, to pay advance fees or taxes to the government[26] and also seek permission from the government before proceeding with creative enterprises. The hegemonic 'repressive' and 'centripetal' implications of this idea are too frightful to imagine: while this new bill has not been ratified yet and is thus a topic for a future paper, it suggests that battles over music censorship in Ghana are likely to continue.

References

Aboagye, F. (Lieutenant Colonel) 1999. *The Ghanaian Army*. Sedco Publication, Accra.
Akyeampong, E. 1996. *Drink Power and Cultural Change*. Oxford: James Currey.
Arlt, V. 2002. 'The Scholars Dance'. Paper presented at a meeting of the Swiss Ethnomusicological Society, Basel, 8 December.

---

[26] To be precise, the Ghana Copyright Administration and National Folklore Board.

Bame, K. 1969. *Contemporary Comic Plays in Ghana: A Study on Innovation and Diffusion and the Social Function of an Art form.* M.A. Thesis, Faculty of Graduate Studies, University of Western Ontario, Canada.

Barber, K. 1987. 'Popular Arts in Africa'. *African Studies Review*, Vol. 30, No. 3, September, pp. 1-78.

Barber, K., Collins, E.J. and Ricard, A. 1997. *West African Popular Theatre.* Indiana University Press/James Currey.

Boonzajer-Flaes, R. and Gales, F. 1991. *Brass Bands in Ghana.* Unpublished manuscript.

Boonzajer-Flaes, R. 1999. *Brass Unbound.* Amsterdam: Royal Tropical Institute.

Carey, J. 1975. 'A Cultural Approach to Communication'. *Communication*, 2, pp. 1-22.

Casely-Hayford, B. 1987. 'The Highlife Song Yaa Amponsah'. Lecture at 4th International Conference of IASPM held in Accra, Ghana between 12-19 August.

Chernoff, J. 1979. *African Rhythms and African Sensibilities.* Chicago: University of Chicago Press.

Clark E. 1979. *Hubert Ogunde: The Making of Nigerian Theatre.* Oxford: Oxford University Press.

Collins, E.J. 1985. *Music Makers of West Africa.* Washington DC: Three Continents Press.

Collins, E.J. 1986. *E.T. Mensah the King of Highlife.* London: Off The Record Press, republished in 1996 in Accra: Anansesem Press.

Collins, E.J. 1992. *West African Pop Roots.* Philadelphia: Temple University Press.

Collins E.J. 1992. 'Some Anti-Hegemonic Aspects of African Popular Music'. *Rockin' The Boat: Mass Music and Mass Movements* R. Garofalo (ed.). South End Press, Boston, pp. 185-194.

Collins, E.J. 1994. *The Ghanaian Concert Party: African Popular Entertainment at the Crossroads.* PhD Dissertation, SUNY Buffalo.

Collins, E.J. 1996. *Highlife Time.* Anansesem Press, Accra.

Collins, E.J. 2002. 'The Generational Factor in Ghanaian Music'. *Playing With Identities in the Contemporary Music of Africa,* M. Palmberg and A. Kirkegaard (eds) Helsinki: Nordic African Institute/Sibelius Museum Apo, Finland, pp. 60-74.

Dadson, N. 1991. 'We the Artists of Ghana'. The Ghanaian Mirror newspaper, 22 June: p.11.

Ensenberger, H. 1974. *The Consciousness Industry.* Seabury Press, New York.

Fage, J.D. 1966. *Ghana: a Historical Interpretation*, University of Wisconsin Press, Milwauke, Madison, London.

Ghana Copyright News. 1990. 'Ephraim Amu: The Story of Yaa Amponsah', Issue 1 March p.5.

Gramsci, A. 1971. *Selections from Prison Notebooks.* Lawrence and Wisehart, London.

Ranger, T.O. 1975. *Dance and Society in Eastern Africa 1890-1970.* London: Heinemann.

Sackey, C. 1989. 'Konkoma: A Musical Form of Fanti Young Fishermen in the 1940s & 50s in Ghana West Africa'. *Mainzer Ethnologische Abeiter Band*, Berlin: Dietrich Reimer Verlag.

Salm, S. 2003. *The Bukom Boys: Subcultures and Identity Transformation in Accra, Ghana* PhD Dissertation for the University of Texas, Austin.

Van der Geest, S. and Asante-Darko, N.K. 1982. 'The Political Meaning of Highlife Songs in Ghana'. *American Studies Review*, Vol. XXV, No 1.

Yankah, K. 1984. 'The Akan Highlife Song: A Medium for Cultural Reflection or Deflection?' *Research in African Literatures*, Vol. 15. No. 4, Winter, University of Texas Press, pp. 568-582.

Chapter 12

Where the Shoe Pinches:
The Imprisonment of Franco Luambo Makiadi as a Curious Example of Music Censorship in Zaïre

Graeme Ewens

Introduction

The circumstances surrounding the imprisonment of Franco Luambo Makiadi in 1979 for singing, and selling recordings of, obscene songs are set against the background of President Mobutu Sese Seko's policy of Authenticity in Zaïre (now Democratic Republic of Congo). Franco was considered to be a stalwart supporter of Mobutu and held the country's highest civilian honour. He was the country's most prominent citizen (after the president himself) and, since his debut in 1955, had become respected and admired across Africa as a composer, guitarist and bandleader. Although he had occasionally spoken out in veiled criticism of Mobutu's regime and received press criticism for earlier obscenities, Franco had avoided serious repercussions but was eventually penalized for overstepping the bounds of good taste. This article is based on material originally published in the author's biography of Franco, *Congo Colossus* (1994), augmented by additional research conducted some ten years later. The material is gathered from personal interviews with members of Franco's band, TP OK Jazz, including some who were charged or imprisoned with him, and anecdotal observations from meetings with Franco himself. Published interviews with Franco and comments by observers of Congo-Zaïrean culture have also been consulted.

The Voice of Authenticity

The regime imposed in Zaïre by the President/Founder Mobutu Sese Seko, who ruled the ex-Belgian Congo from 1965 to 1997, had a cultural dimension which reflected policies and techniques taken from Sekou Toure's rule in Guinea and Chairman Mao's cultural revolution in China. This form of totalitarian socialism was most evident in the policy of Authenticity, which called for the country's citizens to resist European 'colonial' influences and make a 'recourse' to authentic African values. This included a strong moral element intended to engender national pride and unity in the face of declining global standards of propriety.

As a ruler, Mobutu inspired fear in his people, rather than respect. The omnipresent iconography – flags and lapel buttons of the party-of-state (with its neo-fascist flaming torch logo), printed presidential textiles with his and his wife's image, and the presidential portraits which loomed over any office or public space – signified the cult of personality surrounding him. Mobutu had renamed the country Zaïre, along with the currency and the major river. The capital Léopoldville became Kinshasa (after the ancient name of the original village, Nshasa). Membership of the Mouvement Populaire de la Revolution (MPR) party was compulsory for Zaïrean citizens and in 1972, after returning from a visit to China, the president called for the observation of Authenticity. Amongst other diktats, a dress code was imposed, prohibiting men from wearing western suits and ties and restricting women to modest African style wrappers and blouses. All citizens were obliged to take on new 'African' names in place of their original Christian names which were considered to have colonial connotations. Regardless of rank or title, individuals were to be addressed as 'citoyen' and 'citoyenne'. Eventually large businesses were effectively nationalized and control was handed to the president's cronies. Compulsory community singing was introduced for employees of government agencies and these newly nationalized companies. 'Happy are the people who sing and dance', the president declared,[1] implying that there was something suspicious about those who did not participate.

The state-owned broadcaster transmitted only indigenous music, except on rare occasions and, under Mobutu's reign of fear, there was pressure on clubs or bars not to play much Western music. This helped to elevate the already internationally-popular, home-grown Congolese rumba to a high peak and the people of Kinshasa (Kinois) found common ground in the world of popular song, which often resembled a soap opera both in terms of the subject of compositions and the well-publicized relationships of leading musicians. The leading chroniclers/characters were Franco and OK Jazz on the roots-rumba front and Tabu Ley, Dr Nico and African Fiesta from the self-professed international school of Congolese music. Coming up behind, were the first of the new generation bands of the Zaïko Langa Langa family, whose lyrics and demeanour were more like those of western pop groups than traditional sages.

In keeping with griots (oral historians and praise singers) from many other parts of Africa, Congolese musicians had learned to couch their social commentary in metaphor, euphemism and layers of hidden meaning. Narratives about love affairs, family arguments and petty jealousies were often used as formats to criticize the regime – or so many of the listeners believed. Deprived of the chance to participate

---

[1] Declaration by President Mobutu at Boma on 2 September 1973 (Lonoh 1990: 59).

in the political process, many citizens politicized the minutiae of daily life and even the most apparently non-controversial lyrics could be construed as political comment. The popular topic of domestic or familial strife, for example, could be seen as referring to internal squabbles among the extended family of the country's rulers and administrators. Kinshasa was a city so rife with rumour and gossip that the rumour mill, known as Radio Trottoir (Sidewalk Radio), was often the most reliable source of information in the absence of a free press.

Not surprisingly, many of the country's principal musicians had works that were banned from the government-owned radio or TV networks or for sale to the public at various times of their careers. The Commission Nationale de Censure was set up in 1967 as an office within the Palais de Justice at Gombe, Kinshasa. For some time during the mid- to late 1970s, the commission was overseen by Kengo wa Dondo in his role as Attorney General. In 1976 he set up a special committee to monitor the lyrics of recorded music, comprising government appointees, clergy and music business people. 'Motivated by the rhetoric of radicalization, the commission took its work seriously', wrote the American author Gary Stewart. 'By early 1977, dozens of songs by various groups had been interdicted by the authorities' (Stewart 2000: 226).

However, according to one musician who became active in the new generation guitar groups of the mid- to late 1980s, there was another sector of the community of which musicians had to be aware: their own neighbours. The functionaries of the sole political party, the MPR, worked out of local offices in the zones of Kinshasa under the respective Commissaire de Zone. Their function ranged from arbitrating in community disputes to maintaining party morale and keeping an eye on whatever behaviour might be considered subversive or anti-social. A guitarist with one of the top youth bands at the end of the 1980s still wished to remain anonymous 15 years after leaving Zaïre to settle in Europe. He recalls that zealous members of the youth wing of the party, the Jeune Mouvement Populaire de la Révolution (JMPR) would listen to musicians rehearsing (which would usually be clearly audible in the street outside their rehearsal space). Anything contentious would be relayed to the party functionaries. 'The commissaire de zone would send the gendarmes to come for you', recalled the guitarist, 'and when you went to see him he would usually just ask for money. If you were singing anything that might be thought political or obscene, you had to change the lyric' (Interview 2003).

Yet another sector of society which had varying degrees of influence on the cultural scene was the church, specifically the Catholic Church, which, in one of the most notable episodes, managed to get one musician excommunicated by the Vatican. That was Verckys Kiamuangana Mateta, the ex-OK Jazz saxophonist, composer, bandleader turned producer, whose song 'Nokomitunaka', released in 1974, caused grave offence by daring to criticize God for unfair treatment of black people (Tchebwa 1996: 314).

Skirmishes with the censor

Early examples of songs that were withdrawn from public circulation for political reasons during Mobutu's Second Republic included the Grand Kalle's 'Independence Tcha Tcha Tcha'. This was a light, dance party number with a catchphrase that had a timeless quality, but it was also a song of the world, celebrating the bright lights of civilization and linking the fledgling free peoples of Africa with the rest of the planet. On Mobutu's taking power the song was banned from the airwaves, not because of its internationalism but because most of the names praised by Kalle had by then become unmentionable. Similarly, Tabu Ley Rochereau's song 'Molele' was in praise of a political figure of that name. When the song was originally released Molele was onside with the MPR but later, when he criticized the regime and came to be seen as a rebel, the song was banned and the disc withdrawn.

In a socio-cultural context there were several songs about prostitutes (bandumba), a class of woman which many musicians found intriguing. Two songs performed by Franco and OK Jazz spoke more in praise than condemnation: Franco's own song 'Quatre Boutons' (Four Buttons) and 'Cherie Bondowe', composed by Mayaula Mayoni, the guitarist and ex-professional footballer, both provoked popular discussion and official disapproval in the 1970s.

Throughout Mobutu's regime musicians had been liable to restrictive punishments for a variety of offences, imposed directly by government ministers, the censor or the state-appointed executive of the musicians' union. Congo-Zaïrean musicians had a long-standing habit of feuding in public and carrying on disputes through the dialogue of song. Among the most memorable were those between Franco and his errant vocalist Kwame; Franco and Tabu Ley; Franco and Verckys; Joseph Kabasele and Dr Nico; Tabu Ley and Dr Nico; Zaïko Langa Langa and Zaïko LL Familia Dei. Internal feuds were most often over power struggles in the band, 'artistic differences' or girlfriend rivalries. Franco's conflict with his ex-collaborator Kwame spilled over into a series of accusatory (but metaphoric) songs from each party aimed at the other. These disputes created such public interest that politicians frequently became involved on one side or the other and, in several cases, groups were suspended by the union from playing at home, or blocked from travelling abroad because they had brought their profession into disrepute. Tabu Ley was once suspended for turning up late for a presidential concert, and other bands suffered after individual musicians misbehaved on foreign tours. Additionally a band's siege, or home-base dance venue might be shut down for a period.

Franco takes a step too far

One case that generated great interest involved Franco Luambo Makiadi, one of the most honoured citizens of Mobutu's Zaïre, and a man who stood out from the generally high artistic level of Congolese musicians. He was an immensely popular and charismatic figure, known, loved and danced to by young and old across Africa in a way that no other musician was. His formal title Grand Maître (Grand Master) was most often borne by judges and legal dignitaries. As Zaïre's favourite son, Franco was the musician/composer often considered to be closest to Mobutu. He also liked to provoke and agitate people and was often criticized by the party-sanctioned press for some kind of impropriety. While some people undoubtedly hated him, most accepted the essential ambiguity that surrounded Franco and which probably preserved his life and career.

Thanks in part to the impetus of Authenticity, which had inspired Franco to produce some of his best work, the guitar wizard also achieved a reputation as a man of letters and a master satirist – later described by the Congolese writer Sylvain Bemba as the 'Balzac of Congo-Zaïrean music', after the nineteenth-century French author of La Comedie Humaine, which depicted the appetites and passions of the new social classes born of the French revolution (Bemba 1984: 32).

The new bourgeoisie had been created virtually overnight when Mobutu nationalized hundreds of private and multinational businesses. He appointed people from his party hierarchy and imposed them on all the essential industries, from agriculture, mining and manufacturing through distribution, infrastructure and service providers in what had been an efficient and profitable economy. At the same time as establishing elite and middle classes this move also created a system of behaviour that observers believe is unique to Zaïre/Congo. Each business was headed by a President Directeur-General (PDG), who ruled, in effect, like a village chief. Polygamy was euphemized in the expression for a mistress, 'duexième bureaux' (second office). All this was taking place behind a screen of moral righteousness that saw miniskirts and wigs officially banned in public. Franco was the keenest observer of this milieu, which provided raw material for his social commentaries.

He was also the president of the musicians' union UMUZA and, in 1975, he called a grand 'reunion' or assembly of 350 band representatives in Kinshasa to lay down the official line on censorship: in short, composers were advised to self-censor their lyrics before presenting them to the commission (Stewart 2000: 225). However, just a few years later, Franco memorably overlooked his own advice. When playing at home for his own constituency, Franco was invariably outspoken and the shows at his club, the Un-Deux-Trois, were becoming decidedly controversial. Although he was by that time virtually an unofficial ambassador for Zaïre, and holder of the country's highest honour, the Order of the Leopard, Franco was not beyond criticism, or the law.

His self-confidence was legendary, however, and he once described his own role as to 'see things with the critical eye of God', obviously believing in his own omniscience. He also described himself to the journalist Nzunga Badi as 'Just an attentive observer of the mores of our society' (*Antilles Afrique*: June 1983, p17). But for all his professed objectivity, Franco the citizen could not avoid the consequences of his actions.

Franco had often sailed close to the wind with his political allegories, and his satirical wit had already begun to annoy some important figures who took personal offence at his more topical social critiques. Although Franco never named names specifically, it was usually assumed that his criticisms were directed at particular individuals. He often said that was nonsense; he sang about generalities, but if people wanted to identify themselves with the villains in his little dramas that was their problem. In fact, in the mid-1960s he had been arrested and questioned over the content of a song called 'Luvumbu Ndoki', about a sorcerer who sacrificed victims, which was understood to refer to a series of executions ordered by the newly installed President Mobutu. This time however, Franco pushed the authorities, and his own luck, a bit too far and in a bizarre example of popular justice he ended up in prison. But the cause was not overtly political and there was no question of anyone misinterpreting the offending lyrics. It was a simple matter of bad taste.

In 1978 Franco released a cassette with three songs that caused outrage in the press and shock among his fans. The tapes were sold on the streets of Kinshasa by vendors at 'an exorbitant price' (Mbamba 1992: 93). One of the tracks was about the sexual shortcomings of a character named Falanswa, but it was the two numbers that carried European women's names that provoked most controversy and led to Franco's temporary disgrace. The songs 'Helene' and 'Jacky' each featured women of easy virtue in episodes described by one of his peers as 'the equivalent of a porno film'. The obscenities can still shock the worldly Kinois, who found the songs outrageous. The topics ranged from oral and anal sex to Jacky's disgusting habit of feeding excrement in a bowl of soup to one of her boyfriends.

The Kinshasa press denounced Franco in front-page stories which criticized him heavily for leading his audience into a world of obscenity. When the Attorney General, Kengo wa Dondo, and reportedly the president himself, heard these songs, there was official outrage. On his return from playing in Europe, Franco was called to explain himself. He denied the songs were obscene but his inquisitors ruled that, as it was a moral issue, they should put it to his mother to decide whether the lyrics were acceptable. According to Franco's aide and saxophone player, Rondot Kasongo wa Kosongo, Franco pleaded with them not to play the cassette to her but nonetheless she was summoned to be the arbiter of her 40-year-old son's fate (Interview 1993).

The mother, Mama Makiesse, was predictably shocked and Franco was duly arrested and tried, along with several members of the band, under Article175, paragraph 4 of the penal code which decreed: 'whoever sings, reads, recites, makes heard or pronounces obscenities at gatherings or public occasions in front of several people and in a manner understood by those people, will be punished by a period of penal servitude from eight days to one year and a fine of 25,000 zaïres or to one of those penalties'.

Franco and some of his companions appeared before the Supreme Court on October 16, 1979 to answer the charges. The singer Ntessa Dalienst, who was one of the few musicians to escape being incarcerated, recalled the trial:

> The musicians were imprisoned because they were badly defended. Franco had said to the judge: "I am to blame. It is me who sang the song. Me who composed the offensive words. So don't blame the group. I have been doing this since 1956, and that is what has made me". It is true he had asked me to sing on the song. I sang, of course, but the important thing is that he composed the song. When I sang with him I didn't utter one obscene word. "Mwana oh, mwana oh, Jacky, Kitoko na yo ya nyama" (This girl Jacky, she is a natural beauty) ... me, I stopped there. The prosecutor then posed the question that as I knew what Franco was singing, why did I not advise him against it? I told him that Franco had just stated that he had begun all this in 1956. When I met him he was already like that. What can I do? I cannot condemn him. It is you who want to condemn him. (Interview 1993)

Dalienst also added that these songs were 'imaginary but real': 'Kitoko na yo ya nyama – you have the beauty of an animal (graceful as a gazelle)' is not as innocent as it may sound. One interpretation is that slaughtered bush meat bleeds, as does a virgin when deflowered.

Prison sentence

Franco was indeed condemned, along with ten of the 20-odd OK Jazz musicians. They were sentenced to two months' imprisonment and Franco was reportedly ordered to hand back his medal for the Order of the Leopard (although this account has been disputed). Ntesa Dalienst managed to defend himself competently enough to evade the punishment, as did some of the other musicians, who regrouped at the band's rehearsal studio.

Those taken to the feared Makala prison in the heart of Kinshasa were seven guitarists: Simaro, Mackos, Thierry, Flavien, Jerry, Gege, Papa Noel; two horn players, Kapitana and Musekiwa, and only one singer; Checain. Most of them had played no part in composing or even performing the condemned songs. One of those musicians explained that after a few days, Franco's presence in the jail proved disruptive, with many visitors coming to see him from outside and from among the inmates. Franco was moved to Luzumu prison in Bas-Zaïre, outside the capital. Twenty-two days later the band members were released from Makala by a presidential act of pardon, although Franco was detained for a further 11 days, before being freed on medical grounds after he had been taken to hospital with a fever (Interview with Mangaya 1993).

Franco's arrest had taken place during one of his more turbulent and provocative periods, when the PA speakers at the Un-Deux-Trois club were blasting hard-core pornography over the peaceful neighbourhood in the zone of Kasavubu, to the displeasure of many respectable residents. The operators of that club and two others, the Jukebox and Petit Jean, were also prosecuted for the same infraction.

Some contemporary observers believed, however, that there were deeper, more fundamental reasons for the authorities' actions. As Olema Dephonvapi noted in 1984: 'Since 1974 his [Franco's] theme has been to discuss social and political problems. "Cherie Bondowe" included the monologue of a prostitute. "Toyeba Yo" (We Know You) denounced the exploitation of the masses by administrators and the police. "Ba Beaux Frères" (Brothers-in-law) accuses the intellectual elite of corrupting morals. It is probably following the success of his new songs, inaugurated with "Cherie Bondowe" in 1974 that Franco was imprisoned.'

If Olema's supposition is correct it puts a different perspective on Franco's perceived role as a stooge of the state, as these songs were recorded at around the same time as some of his most militant and 'authentic' activities. He had recorded a string of 'revolutionary' party songs and, following his participation in educating the country about Authenticity, Franco had been rewarded by Mobutu with the presidency of the musicians' union UMUZA, as well as being handed control of Mazadis, the country's main record pressing plant. Now, he had to resign the union presidency.

Restraint of creativity

Franco seemed to want things both ways, however. He freely accepted Mobutu's largesse but was not ready to compromise his position as an 'attentive observer'. As he later complained to Nzunga Badi of *Antilles Afrique*:

> There is a censor, which is normal and justifiable. His main function is to suppress licentious gossip. But where the shoe pinches is that the official existence of the censor restrains creativity in general and forces the artist into self-censorship. In France for example, when a musician has a mind to say 'merde' (shit) he says it, provided it is in a given context. Often a musician is condemned by default, without having the occasion to defend his point of view. And in any justice without defence, the accused remains vulnerable and risks being unjustly convicted.

Here it was not so much the word 'merde' as the context which incurred the censor's wrath. The lyrics were later described by one of Franco's contemporaries as 'infantile, the sort of thing no adult person would normally say. He was not just saying "shit"; it was as if he was actually shitting in public' (Interview with Se Sengo, 1993).

Shortly after his release from prison Franco had the chance to snap back at the man who had sanctioned his prosecution when Kengo wa Dondo was first appointed Prime Minister and then swiftly demoted. Franco's song 'Mokolo Tonga Abotoli Tonga Na Ye' (aka Tailleur), was taken to be a satirical commentary on this event, according to the Zaïrean popular music press. The lyric concerns a tailor who lends a needle to someone and then ask for its return; this was taken to refer to the president withdrawing Kengo from his post. When he was asked in the interview by Nzunga Badi (*Antilles Afrique*), Franco denied the song was about any particular individual but the fact that he was spending more time outside Zaïre suggested to many observers that Franco was not on the best of terms with the country's leaders. He denied that he was living in exile, although he had bought a house in Brussels and an apartment in Paris where he spent much of his time.

As if to make the point that he had no one to fear in Kinshasa, Franco recorded a song for the local market titled 'Na Mokili Tour a Tour' (As The World Turns) in which he asked sarcastically if he was really expected to leave the town where he belonged. 'Stop provoking me', he warned in the song. 'Must I leave Kinshasa, the town where I grew up?' He saves his most cutting put-down for the casual aside: 'Luambo used to know Mbelekete'. Mbelekete was a legendary name in the social history of Kinshasa's working classes and market traders, known by repute to people who were not yet born when he was active in the 1950s. He was a street character, clown and cycling exhibitionist in the 'quartier Far West' where Franco grew up, and the implication was that Mbelekete was more famous than a certain unnamed person (presumably Kengo wa Dondo) who was seeking to make his name in politics. Nevertheless, Franco did spend the best part of three years in Europe before returning to haunt the Prime Minister in his own home.

Recalled but not reformed

In 1987, after several years consolidating his international status and launching a series of social commentary songs in a prolific period of album releases, Franco was recalled to Zaïre to play for an official function. He gave his excuses to promoters in London whose shows he had to cancel, citing the need to perform for the president at Zaïre's Independence Day celebrations. In fact, he had been needed at another function: the birthday party of the daughter of his old adversary Kengo wa Dondo, who had now apparently made up his differences with the Grand Master.

According to one of his inner circle of musicians that event was particularly bizarre and showed that Franco had not forgiven the politician. He embarrassed his host and the guests by playing the controversial song 'Tailleur', not once but twice. When Kengo decided to join in the joke and possibly regain some loss of face, he requested Franco to play the song for a third time. But that was just too much for the Grand Master who passed his guitar to Simaro Lutumba, the OK Jazz vice-president, and walked out of the party (Interview with Kasongo, 1993).

During the intervening years since his imprisonment, Franco had taken on the role of a moralizer. He released several albums containing songs that criticized women for their shortcomings – usually in dealing with relationships with their men folk and/or female in-law relatives. 'Tu Vois?' aka 'Mamou' was one of the most cutting satires – and one of his finest compositions. The theme of this song was a conversation between two women, a divorcee with children and her married friend, Mamou, who had accused her of being a prostitute and trying to break up her marriage. In fact, Mamou is the hypocrite who has been using her friend as an alibi to cover her own adventures as she cheats on her husband. Around this time Franco was accused of taking a brutal approach to women's problems but women were the most critical and staunch members of his audience and he had to please them first with tenderness or ironic humour before getting to his point. The parts he sang most earnestly were often voiced in the words of women. However, in the title track of that same album he also launched a savage tirade against an unnamed man in 'Tres Impoli' (Very Impolite), which read like a catalogue of rude or offensive behaviour. The following year he released the epic song 'Mario', spread over two LPs, which denounced the lazy, dishonest and opportunist behaviour of a young man living in Europe. Several other songs addressed these topics from both sides of the gender divide, suggesting that Franco might possibly have been purging himself. However, his most functional and morally correct composition was 'Attention na Sida' (Beware of Aids), released in 1987.

Not withstanding the lyric content, both 'Jacky' and 'Helene' had been strongly structured compositions with classic OK Jazz arrangements pushing home their overtly erotic message. As if Franco did not want to waste one his most memorable motifs, the solo guitar pattern used in the former song was revived for 'Attention Na Sida'. By the time of its release Franco was suffering from a debilitating illness which, although he denied it, was almost certainly related to HIV-Aids. He played what was to be his final gig in Holland in September 1989 and died the following month – almost exactly ten years since the day of his infamous court appearance. Mobutu's hold on the vast country began to unravel soon after. Many listeners argue that the once dominant force of Congo-Zaïrean music started its decline at the same time as Franco's star began to wane. There was certainly no other composer waiting to take over his role as 'attentive observer', 'provocateur' or social commentator.

Conclusion

Franco was an enigmatic and often contradictory character. A high profile artist with quasi-diplomatic status in Africa, he was also known as The Sorcerer and Yorgho (Godfather) with many of the associations attached to those sobriquets. The self-proclaimed provocateur had a wicked, even perverse, sense of fun and a singular attitude to personal morality, and he did appear to live by a code of his own. Whether or not he approved of Mobutu (who came from a distant region and ethnic group), Franco was a pragmatist and he played the president's game. But he also liked to play games of his own. In releasing those obscene songs, he might have been peddling pornography, satirizing a prominent figure or just aiming to shock or provoke for artistic or commercial purpose. As Franco used to say, his songs only told half the story – the listener had to fill in the rest. And the same should probably apply to any attempt to understand his motivation.

References

Badi, N. 1983. 'Franco et L'OK Jazz', *Antilles Afrique*: June, p 17.
Bemba, S. 1984. *50 Ans du Musique Congo-Zaïre*. Paris: Présence Africaine Dephonvapi, Olema. 1984. 'Société zaïrois dans le miroir de la chanson populaire' in *Canadian Journal of African Studies* vol 18/1.
Ewens, G. 1994. *Congo Colossus*. Norfolk, UK: Buku Press.
Lonoh, Malangi Bokolenge. 1990. *Négritude, Africanité et Musique Africaine*. Kinshasa: Centre de Recherches Pedagogiques.
Stewart, G. 2000. *Rumba on the River*. New York: Verso.
Mbamba, Toko W. 1992. *Autopsie de la Chanson de Luambo Makiadi Franco*. Paris: Uhuru Universal Collection.
Tchebwa, M. 1996. *Terre de la Chanson*. Belgium: Duculot.

Discography

All tracks by Franco and TP OK Jazz

Jackie, Helene, 1979. Cassette, un-numbered, informal release.
Ba beaux frères, 1978. LP, African/Sonodisc, 360 105.
Tailleur,1981. LP, Le Quatre Siècle Vol 3, Edipop, POP 03.
Tres Impoli, 1984. LP, Edipop, POP 028.
Mario, 1985. LP, Choc, Choc, Choc, CHOC 004/005.
Attention na Sida, 1987. LP, African Sun Music, ASM 01.
Cherie Bondowe, 1974. 45rpm, African, 91 016 (Zebi 001).

Interviews with the author

Anonymous interview, London, 2003.
Interview with Rondot Kasongo wa Kasongo, OK Jazz saxophonist and aide/personal assistant to Franco, Brussels, 1993.
Interview with OK Jazz vocalist Ntessa Dalienst, Brussels 1993.
Interview with ex-OK Jazz guitarist and fellow inmate Gege Mangaya, Brussels, 1993.
Discussion with ex-OK Jazz musician Mose Se Sengo, Fan Fan, London, 1994.

Chapter 13

For a Song –
Censure in Algerian Rai Music

Malika Mehdid

Foreword

One day in 1994, at a time of conflict and deep political unrest in Algeria, Matoub Lounes, prominent cultural activist, singer and composer of Kabyle music, was abducted by a group of Islamist militants who held him prisoner for a two-week period. To the great relief of his numerous fans, he was released unharmed, but not before being threatened with reprisals if he continued with his musical career.

That year, during Matoub's abduction, other dramatic events took place. Probably the most sensational was the execution-style assassination in Wahran (Oran), the capital of western Algeria, of the singer, song writer and composer cheb Hasni,[1] the rising star of the rapidly expanding movement of popular music known as rai and the one who, without doubt, enjoyed the largest following among the country's youth.

Hardly another year had passed before a new wave of grief engulfed the music scene as the news quickly spread, that Rachid Baba Ahmed had been assassinated. He was a famous music composer and producer who, along with his brother Fethi, was credited with the technological innovations which paved the way for the successful emergence of the new rai movement. They also launched some of rai's best-known artists on the national and international stage, notably chebs Khaled and Anouar, and the duo cheb Sahraoui and cheba Fadela.

A few months later, music fans nationwide were again shocked by devastating news concerning cheb Aziz, another star of popular music, who lived and worked in Constantine, the capital of the eastern region. Late one evening, as he left a party where he had performed, he was ambushed by an armed gang and was abducted. The next day, when his mutilated body was found, he joined the terrifyingly long list of victims of the conflict.

By a tragic twist of irony, Matoub Lounes, who had incredibly survived the ordeal of abduction, and subsequently settled in France where he resumed his

---

[1] The term 'cheb' (feminine 'cheba') meaning 'a young person' or 'young' became a title associated mostly with rai singers in the wake of the success of their music in the early eighties.

musical activities, returned to his native Kabylia a few years later. Here, in 1998, adversity eventually caught up with him again, this time for a final act: one morning, during a car journey to the village, he was ambushed by unidentified snipers, shot and fatally wounded.[2]

Music and Censure

These atrocities vividly reflect the turmoil which beset Algeria during the recent crisis. Although this crisis affected all areas of Algerian society, this chapter focuses specifically on the manner in which rai, a popular music style from the western province, was affected. What is offered is a brief overview of the historical development of this musical tradition, which regards the violent and virulent suppression of rai in particular (as illustrated above) as an epitome of many traditions, voices and instances as well as of legacies of repression, which contributed to constructing rai as a perennial object of censure. Evidently, the issue is also one of censorship, whether formal or informal. However, it is argued that activities of censorship, which may be both related and distinct, may be subsumed under the broader notion of censure or even 'censureship' for two main reasons. First, censorship is regarded here as one of a number of repressive states, which produced this complex musical movement through a specific temporality and spatiality in a telling way. Secondly, it is the noted presence and material impact of censorship, which is of particular interest in the present context.

Censure is thus defined here as a set of overt or covert practices and societal pressures which abrogate, appropriate or transform a cultural production, diachronically and synchronically, through social structure, representation or discourse in which it becomes subject to more dominant aesthetic forms that are essentially socio-cultural norms.

The musicality of rai has thus been shaped by meaningful moments, marked by both progress and decline through censure, and presented here within a suggestive chronology in which they are not so linear but rather complex, intricately interconnected and overlapping.

Rai and Censure: Colonial Instances

The French military conquest of Algiers in 1830 and the subsequent colonial occupation of the country marked a major watershed in Algeria's modern history. Under colonial rule, native Algerians were invariably treated as second-class citizens in their own land. They were subjected to a formal regime of racial and religious segregation, which impacted negatively on the arena of aesthetics and cultural expression as a whole. This regime involved a continuous demise and

---

[2] For more insights into Matoub Lounes' life and work, see his autobiography, *Rebelle* (1995).

marginalization of indigenous culture through restrictive measures and policies. These restrictions were intended to control and regulate cultural practices according to prevailing norms and values, which demeaned the colonized culture and subordinated it to European culture.

Censored Performances/Censored Voices

During the colonial era, a variety of mechanisms were used to manage indigenous cultural manifestations, as shown by the examples below. Bezza Mazouzi (1990: 109) for instance, discusses an Algerian traditional dance choreography known as Arfaoui, usually performed by men. This particular war-like dance used to involve the use of a rifle as a prop; a tradition that had disappeared by the early twentieth century after the colonial rulers had banned it. In order to continue their artistic practice which otherwise would have ceased, the natives replaced the rifle with a wooden cane, an adaptation still current today but with only a few suspecting its colonial origin.

With the establishment of French civilian rule over Algeria after 1870, territorial divisions were defined and managed across the country through a strict regulatory system for allocating or withdrawing special passes and permits. This system had implications for travelling musicians' ability to perform. Even as late as the mid-twentieth century, artists who wanted to tour towns and villages around the country had to apply for authorization from local councils. In some cases, requests were turned down, as the following colonial administrative archival evidence reveals:

> A female singer, Rekia G. from Oran and her flute players, Belkacem S. from Bou Saada, Kaddour D. from Tafraoui and Lakhdar H. from Mostaganem have not been granted an authorization because suspected of affiliation and collaboration with 'trouble makers' from the PPA [the Party of the Algerian People]; Tahar S.N.P. from Bechar who performs with three musicians and three female dancers and Ahmed B. 'who resides in the middle zone of the shanty-town of Sidi Hasni', are not authorized as well as Halima G. from Temouchent because of 'sexual misconduct'. (cited in Daoudi and Miliani 1996: 63)[3]

Colonial public officers thus used an arsenal of rules and other devices to demarcate and police ethnic and racialized boundaries. Beyond the delineation of racial space, a paramount concern was to identify and stop performances deemed unfit or 'misplaced' and to keep 'agitators' and other categories of colonial misfits at bay. Therefore, in the case of artists suspected of being pro-nationalists and by implication 'trouble-makers' in the eyes of the colonizers, as illustrated in the above quote, censorious interventions allowed the circumvention of possibilities for organized or individual cultural resistance. It is argued that these interventions constituted a form of censure.

---

[3] Quotes and citations used throughout (except for the last citation on the final page) are my own translations from the French.

It is worth noting that these censored cases, while representing only mere fragments of a vast written record about colonial policy at work, indicate the extent and the nature of the control exerted on native cultural performances by the colonial authorities. As such, they underscore the more typical politics characterizing imperial relations of domination and subordination. By generating its own sets of debased images of colonized culture and subjects, this regime of authority used in turn these representations to legitimate its treatment of them. Sometimes the images in question involved attaching notions of strangeness or deviance (or both) to the behaviour of indigenous artists, for instance, in reinterpretations of some cultural and ritualistic activities. This was especially the case for women, whose actions were redefined in sexually suggestive terms or even as outright prostitution. In addition, native practices and bodies were criminalized, reconstructed as potentially threatening and dangerous as in the case of the 'disarmed' Arfaoui male dancers or the performers discussed above. Reduced to being 'other', natives, including performing artists, became mere objects of management through containment.

Overall, throughout the colonial era, negative pressures were exerted on musical activities through a variety of mechanisms, ranging from straightforward interventions claiming to regulate the cultural sphere through rules and regulation, to less blatant forms such as the segregation of native artists and musicians confined to their communities in a movement of spatial and symbolic ghettoization which, over time, led to the downgrading of musicians' artistic expression. However, it is argued here that these effects of censure were ultimately embedded within the imperial edifice itself which stood as the absolute structure of control and power imposed on the Arab-Berber population, over many decades of direct rule. And so it appears that various forms of suppression, broadly identified as (part of) colonial censure and therefore constitutive of the very experience of coloniality, entailed the destruction of native cultural forms.

A Colonial Birth: Modern Rai

Bouziane Daoudi and Hadj Miliani (1996: 38) argue that modern rai comprises a wide variety of musical forms and styles from the Wahran province where its history closely intertwined with that of an old classical poetical tradition, melhun or sung poetry. It appears that these music styles, deriving from the dominant rural musical tradition of badawi, evolved into an independent urban and popular musical movement that grew considerably under the impact of colonialism, developing specific features distinct from existing genres. More specifically, these new and shifting urbanized styles, still attached to badawi, also known as 'zendanis' and developing within the more humble milieus, seemed to escape the canon of legitimate musical practice (Daoudi and Miliani 1996: 39). This musical development was firmly established by 1920, a period which some scholars pinpoint as the period during which modern rai arose (Daoudi and Miliani 1996; Mazouzi 1990; Mezouane 1992).

Miliani (1983) had previously contextualized the history of rai within the upheavals and socio-economic changes triggered by colonialism during the nineteenth century, followed by a large-scale urbanization movement and the resulting impoverishment of the native population. Large numbers of the colonized, especially in the rural hinterland, were made destitute as a result of colonial expropriations and dispossessions. Miliani thus argued that music, in its lyrics, delivery and rhythmic mode, came to embody the very forms of the material conditions experienced by the colonized, mainly poverty and marginality. In the process, it became increasingly destructured and less poetically rich, its lyrical material more visibly referenced, thematically and linguistically, within the popular vernacular as well as the everyday forms of expression and concern of ordinary people existing at the bottom of the social order of the colony.

Inter-war Modernizing Rai

During the period between the first and second world wars, rai underwent further processes of change associated with colonial forms of modernization that characterized subsequent periods. In many scholarly accounts, this period is deemed of crucial significance in the history of Algerian music, with major transformations taking place. These include the use and spread of the gramophone, the introduction of the piano, trumpet and other Western instruments and the prevalence of foreign music styles, modern 'Oriental' (mainly Egyptian and Lebanese) as well as Western. Daoudi and Miliani (1996: 47) described the era as a period of 'cultural effervescence' with the traditional badawi undergoing, on the one hand, intensive urbanization, more of its singers performing in the city and, on the other, increasing numbers of recordings of indigenous music being released on gramophone.

In 1935, for the first time, the main radio station, Radio-Alger, played up to five hours per week of concert-form Arab music (Daoudi and Miliani 1996: 57). Listeners mostly met up in coffee bars and smoking parlours since very few native Algerians actually owned a radio.

Anti-colonial Rai

In the face of a growing anti-colonial resistance movement in the post-First World War period, the French increasingly relied on repressive measures to stifle any expression or movement suspected of enunciating nationalist ideals. In a context marked by episodic political confrontations, power struggles intensified in both the political and cultural arenas. Musicians, poets and singers were perceived as potentially subversive and increasingly became the object of scrutiny. If their lyrics criticized the colonial system or their behaviour in any way gave cause for concern to the local authorities, they suffered harassment, the banning of their performances or themselves from certain places or even imprisonment and deportation to far away islands.

For instance, in 1936 the colonial authorities banished composer and performer Abdelhamid Ababsa from the town of Tlemcen, after he sung a patriotic song entitled 'Fidaoun El-Djazair' (resistance fighters of Algeria) during a performance in the town centre (Cheurfi 1997: 10). In the same city lived another musician,

Abderrahmane El-Kebir. He was also an activist in the local cell of a nationalist party, the MTLD (Movement for the Triumph of Democratic Liberties). Once the local police force became aware of his involvement with the nationalist movement, they subjected him to constant harassment, which eventually led him to leave the area (Cheurfi 1997: 197).

Such semi-official procedures were part of a wider routine harassment policy targeting artists. However, police aggression intensified parallel to the growth of anti-colonial resistance. In the process, many promising and flourishing careers were wrecked and many livelihoods destroyed.

By the 1950s, as nationalist activity intensified in preparation of the final onslaught, colonial rulers shifted to a dual strategy in dealing with performers in an effort to undermine their influence over an indigenous population in a state of mass mobilization. While they pursued an even more aggressive policy against artists suspected of dissidence, they also made conciliatory gestures towards performers in general, in an effort to co-opt them through provision of larger media access (television and radio), recording facilities and opportunities to tour Algeria and France. In others words, censoring interventions were shifting, involving tactics of both punishment and appeasement.

As a consequence of the new policy, a platform was set for the best-known performers. The decade thus witnessed an upsurge in musical activity as some musicians took advantage of the opportunities on offer, among them some precursors of the new rai movement such as cheikha Remitti and Ahmed Benzerga. However, in opposition to the colonial government, in 1954 the FLN (National Liberation Front) declared a war of independence to end French occupation in Algeria. Musical action supporting the aims of the liberation movement increased, although some composers resorted to using allusion and allegory to avoid the censorship of songs written in favour of the revolution. At the same time, as noted by Daoudi and Miliani (1996: 77), the FLN issued instructions to musicians to tone down their activities, a directive especially aimed at those performing in cabarets, whose actions the nationalist leaders particularly condemned, and which signalled the puritan orientation of the revolution. Thus, these new ideological impositions compounded by the dramatic atmosphere of the war itself had eventually led to suspended activity in the music scene; many performers left the television platforms, concert halls and coffee houses, and marched straight into the heart of the blazing battle, enrolling as freedom fighters within the ranks of the FLN. Many, such as Blaoui Houari and Ahmed Saber, were caught and jailed, others were executed on the guillotine or assassinated, as was the case with Charef El Houes, a flute player, murdered by the French military in 1957 (Cheurfi 1997: 21). Still many more were killed in battle. A few others, among them Ahmed Wahby, joined the resistance quarters based on the eastern border in Tunisia, and enrolled in the music bands set up there by the FLN for the duration of the war (Daoudi and Miliani 1996; Cheurfi 1997).

Rai and Censure: Post-colonial Instances

With the declaration of independence in July 1962, a new stage in Algerian history opened up; an era which may be periodized in a succinct form, as a series of key events that marked the thwarted nation-building process of the newly independent country in a movement concomitant to the development of rai.

Independent Rai (1962-1965)

The French left behind a landscape devastated by years of war, yet the public mood remained jubilantly confident. Young people, experiencing new freedoms and shifting identities, developed a particular taste for music and celebrations. Urban youth in particular eagerly joined the spirit of the swinging sixties emanating from Europe, dancing to the tunes of rock, yeye, the twist and other sounds such as rhythm and blues, jazz and soul as these swept the region, leaving their mark on a nascent generation of performers (Daoudi and Miliani 1996). A simultaneous massive rural exodus meant that a growing proportion of the urban population identified with the more indigenous and peasant cultural roots, which helped intensify the fusion of these forms with the more urban-based cultural legacies and musical arrangements (Virolle-Souibes 1988: 54). As had traditionally been the case, sometimes these urban rhythms were mixed with some of the prevalent foreign musical arrangements and sounds or musical influences of the day.

However, a degree of anarchic creativity was noted within the newly appropriated national institutions for cultural production and distribution: former producers, publishers, television and radio personnel, who were mostly European settlers, departed, leaving the culture industries (both public and private) barely functional.

Pop Rai (1965-1978)

The post-independence euphoria was soon over, as an 'iron curtain' descended on Algeria. In June 1965, a coup-d'état ushered in a new political regime which resumed leadership on the basis of a radical political ambition: over the following decade, a new society was to be built, inspired by a socialist-authoritarian model and a populist Arab-nationalist ideology.

This new regime, austere in outlook and politics, attempted to reshape the socio-cultural field through a series of formal and informal policies and recommendations; incidentally, some of these were not too dissimilar in their effect from those associated with former colonial rule. For instance, the convergent treatment which public authorities meted out to artists critical of the established order, such as the case of Abdelaoui Cheikh, a composer, who received a six-month jail sentence for declaring his opposition to the new rulers. Another was the famous 'raist' and artist-rebel Ahmed Saber, who suffered imprisonment for his repertoire of satirical songs denouncing the regime's abuses of power.

During this early period of independence, popular culture was the most targeted object of the new political regime in its systemic effort at inducing revolutionary change. Accordingly, features and expressions it deemed unorthodox were curtailed. But, in some respects, its rigid and reductive ideological approach to cultural matters only served to sharpen the already polarized structures of cultural production and consumption inherited from colonialism, consequently driving parts of popular cultural expression back to the very ghetto from which it had broken free with the advent of independence.

More specifically, some forms of cultural performance were banned, like women's singing in restaurants and cabarets, which helped create and sustain a gender-differentiated social space and cultural practice. This prohibition inadvertently created a space for the emergence of male singers endowed with particularly feminine voices, such as the young Boutheldja. Soon, restrictions on the sale of alcohol and beer were introduced; a problem over which cheikha Hab Lahmar lamented in one of her songs (Virolle-Souibes 1988: 54) and which recalled a ban imposed by colonial authorities on the sale of wine and alcohol in Muslim public places a few decades earlier. In addition, this new restriction intruded on a hard drinking, non-conformist culture in which rai had been steeped during its modern history.

This dual push for cultural 'purification' and restoration may also be illustrated by other instances, for example the curtailment of religious ceremonies held outside the remit of established religious practice represented by the mosque such as the age-old popular cult of saints, a widespread practice among women. Proponents of Islamic doctrine denounced it as bordering on heresy, especially after musicians restored some of the older entertainment elements associated with these public celebrations, which, in the form of traditional food banquets known as 'waada', were sometimes accompanied by music and dance. Their gradual demise effectively deprived rai of an important space for celebration (Benkheira 1986: 87; Virolle-Souibes 1988: 54).

Despite these setbacks, musicians were still intent on playing music and, throughout the 1960s, Wahran buzzed with old and new sounds. Artists experimented with the vast array of tunes at their disposal, doing so through practices of creative adaptation, syncretism or improvisation. During this time, some 'raists' made crucial changes to orchestra. According to Mazouzi (1990: 92), Belkacem Boutheldja introduced the accordion in replacement of the zamr, a traditional flute to which it was nearest in sound, while Sghir Boutaiba later altered the physical shape of the accordion to further adapt its sound to the traditional melodic system. Another attempt to modernize the music without creating dissonance with native forms of musicality was made by Messaoud Bellemou when he introduced the saxophone into rai music. Boutheldja and Bellemou later conjugated their efforts into a vital partnership, jointly releasing a record in 1974, marking the effective birth of pop-rai, which encapsulated the musical trends of the moment.

However, some of these interventions in the name of so-called modernization were problematic, as they took place at the expense of traditional instruments, their use and value reduced in the process. And, as stated by Mazouzi (1990: 93), the door was now open to the introduction of all kinds of new instruments without aesthetic justification.

Nevertheless, Daoudi and Miliani (1996: 109) argue that the new instruments radically transformed the genre, to the point that lyrics were reduced to the status of a mere vehicle. As a result of this successful transformation of the style of rai, the sale of vinyl records soared. In an otherwise rather lethargic and amorphous national scene, the work of these artist-pioneers brought about a cultural revival. However, such development had taken place, unaided by any structure of promotion or support, therefore remaining largely unknown and uncelebrated outside of the confines of the western province. More strikingly, not a single piece of music by rai performers of that period was broadcast by any of the radio stations across the country nor any rai performance or concert ever screened by the state television before 1988. As unequivocally put by Daoudi and Miliani (1996: 94), the musicians from that seventies 'modernizing generation' of rai would 'practically never be allowed to cross the invisible Rubicon line set between them and the Algerian media networks which were all, at the time, under the control of the state'.

Thereafter, rai continued to evolve as an independent artistic form, outside any state or financial sponsorship, national representation or media coverage, given the covert forms of ostracism which characterized its treatment in the hands of the 'priests of high culture', mostly cultural policy-makers and theologians who determined the value of various cultural manifestations within the spheres of officialdom and beyond. In that sense, the music and its performers were censored in forms that were not so much direct as symbolic, being ignored by the media, concert promoters, intellectual elites and the political establishment.

New Rai (1979-1994)

With the death of the socialist leader Boumediene in 1978, many hoped that a more liberal era would be heralded in. Indeed, the single ruling party somehow slackened its grip on society, but the lack of liberties and a growing mismanagement of the economy heightened the already rampant socio-cultural tensions.

During the following year, in 1979, amid a stifling atmosphere resulting from the legacy of the Boumediene years, an ordinary gesture by an eighteen-year-old female vocalist, Fadela Zelmat, standing and performing a song in a cabaret in Wahran, had the surprising effect of a catalyst in the world of popular culture, sending a swift wind of freedom blowing through it. As she sung her song entitled 'Keyti Ma H'lali Noum' (I cannot get to sleep anymore) on the theme of a woman longing for the presence of an absent lover, this performer broke a taboo and flaunted a banning order: that of women performing in public places of entertainment. Fadela, like the cohorts of singers about to emerge, sang the blues of a post-war generation of young people, feeling out of place in their own society. In so doing, she managed to capture the mood of an era. She also helped open the way to a more typical female presence within the world of rai, singing the despair of the condition of women's lives as they had become trapped in a web of social hypocrisy and a culture of machismo (Daoudi and Miliani 1996: 94). This event thus probably provided the context for the birth of what critics identified as 'second-wave rai' with a new breed of performers suddenly becoming more visible and vocal. They broke ranks with their elders, bursting on the music stage with a renewed dynamism fuelled by frustrations born of a deadlocked socio-political arena, their songs conveying distinct new yearnings for freedom and self-affirmation and reflecting their more immediate preoccupations and desires. According to critics, 'second-wave' rai effectively emerged in that period, with Kabyl music, among the most innovatively dynamic of cultural expressions in the country. As a consequence, the course, form and content of popular music were again radically transformed.

Most rai music researchers have elaborated on the modest social backgrounds of many of the singers. They have often experienced family tensions and struggles for survival and, with the exception of a few, have received only limited schooling and no formal musical training. This, combined with the relative lack of proper enforcement procedures in the regulation of the music industry, made artists and vocalists vulnerable to exploitation by unscrupulous publishers, especially in the form of detrimental contractual conditions. Pirating, plagiarism and unauthorized duplications of cassettes were rife. It was reported that some record sellers in Algerian cities and even in the Paris quarter of Barbes literally made copies of cassettes 'under the counter'. The recording conditions were also often marked by mediocrity (Benkheira 1986; Schade-Poulsen 1999; Virolle-Souibes 1988). Despite these stark production conditions, rai still attracted a growing number of hopeful singers wanting to make records while their performances in private family parties and nightclubs still remained an important part of their activities.

During the 1980s, more instrumental changes were introduced, as a number of Western instruments were adopted, such as the synthesizer and electric drums. These modifications further enhanced the appeal of the music among the young. Furthermore, the explosive growth of cassette sales since the late 1970s favoured a nation-wide distribution of the music, making it widely available and helping to circumvent the undeclared 'official' suppression of rai music and its isolation within the country, as well as dissolve the one-party state monopoly on the circulation and diffusion of cultural goods as a whole (Benkheira 1986: 174).

As a result, during the early 1980s, a wave of 'rai-mania' swept the country, eventually forcing the media and the cultural and political establishments to take notice of this 'musical phenomenon' and appreciate its irresistible vocal presence and the cultural significance of its huge impact on the young, who constituted the bulk of the population. During this period, a number of grassroots protest movements emerged across the country with rai music developing alongside them. Faced with such growing public dissent and calls for political reforms from various sections of civil society (the young, the feminists, the Islamists, the Berberists and others), a group of liberal policy-makers soon took charge of the formal cultural sphere where they opted for a more creative approach, increasing the budget to the public entertainment sector, especially with regard to the promotion of musical activities. They hoped to improve the standing of the state in the face of a dismal socio-economic and cultural policy record in a calculated attempt at diffusing the simmering popular anger, but by doing so, they embraced populist strategies somewhat reminiscent of earlier attempts at the appeasement of artists by the colonizer. Not surprisingly, many observers interpreted such a shift of policy as a crude 'co-optation' or recuperation of music by political forces (Virolle-Souibes 1989: 56).

Nevertheless, despite this shift, the tendency to sideline rai and other forms of popular expression as valid cultural manifestations initially prevailed until it became apparent to all that rai was the overriding popular music of the day. For instance, during a major musical festival, officials failed to invite a single rai star but throughout the concert, the audience called for cheb Khaled (Daoudi and Miliani, 1996: 87). Thereafter, an attempt was made to 'instrumentalize' the tremendous popularity of Wahrani rai through the launch of a lavish programme of activities, including the sponsorship of large music concerts. And thus, in the mid-1980s, a number of music festivals unwittingly served as an opportune framework for a formal consecration of rai as 'legitimate' popular culture. Furthermore, rai was even presented as 'national music' with national representation controversially bestowed on it alone (to the exclusion of other musical styles) during official celebrations held in Paris in 1986, and sponsored by the Algerian authorities (Mezouane 1992:176).

During the second half of the 1980s, rai became a thriving 'world music' genre, in the wake of a wide popularity achieved beyond Algeria, and a successful but not necessarily smooth transition into the French cultural scene, that is, beyond the diasporic space where its representation was confined to community-based radio stations such as Radio-Beur and cultural activities associated with minorities. In Algeria itself, a comparable scenario was unfolding as the integration of rai music into the wider cultural landscape continued, with the first national radio broadcasts of rai songs and concerts being aired in 1988.

Around that time, a hit song released by cheb Hasni (1987), entitled 'Barraka' (the shack), performed in duo with cheba Zehouania, and which, despite its immense popularity among the young, was deemed 'scandalous' by some quarters, as its lyrics invoked in unambiguous language the sexual attraction which two lovers felt for each other. On hearing the lyrics of this song blasted from the loud sound systems used by record shops, some Islamists requested from the shop-owners that they lower the volume, a rather exceptional gesture at the time (Daoudi and Miliani 1996: 106). However, beyond its manifestation as a not so ordinary 'street-level' act of censorship, the move was perhaps symptomatic of more fundamental pressures tearing the Algerian fabric. As the uproar about the song and the debates that ensued captured some of the rampant anti-rai feeling still persistent in society, they also revealed the depth of underlying tensions. Therefore, it seems that the song marked a politico-cultural turn while, at the same time, it pinpointed a significant moment of fracture.

In October 1988, week-long riots broke out and ultimately led to politico-institutional change. Under the impact of these riots, but also as a result of a long-standing struggle by civil society, the immediate post-riots era soon witnessed a democratization of the public sphere. This saw the introduction of crucial reforms, including the advent of a multi-party system and a liberalization of the economy. However, in spite of all the changes reshaping social space and the growth of its popularity rai, as a popular musical genre, continued to be the object of renewed pressures. Yet, during this more liberal period, it was the media and concert promoters who voiced the most criticism, mediated via concerns expressed over questions of musical ethics, textuality and poetics as well as conditions of production (Mazouzi 1990: 91). But more direct forms of censure also persisted with the effect that musicians were, all the while, exhorted to 'purge' their lyrics of words, expressions and themes deemed vulgar (Mezouane 1992: 67). As a result, publisher Baba Ahmed noted:

> Before, I used to let the chebs free to sing lyrics of their own choosing. Now, I am more careful. When they sing some vulgar expression, I say: 'stop!' If they ignore the instruction, I simply cut out the bit in question, later, during the mixing. (quoted in Virolle-Souibes 1989: p.60)

Consequently the rai musical movement underwent further changes. Virolle-Souibes (1989: 59) pointed out that 'a new wave of more pragmatic and less tempestuous chebs and chebettes' arose who seemed 'to be motivated by style or material inclination'. In support of her comment, she quotes the words of a local reporter who had also noted a defensive attitude among rai performers:

> The most brilliant chebs have become quite shrewd and calculating. During the celebration of a festival organized by the Cultural Association for the city of Oran, neither Khaled, Saharoui nor any other singer for that matter wanted to sing the hit of that 1987 summer, 'We Made Love in an Old Shack' [also known as 'Barraka']. Yet, at party times, everybody would enthusiastically use the tunes of this record as a sing-along. (Mokhtari cited in Virolle-Souibes 1989: 59)

It is argued here that these artists' relationship with their audiences, on the one hand, and with the structures of musical production and distribution within the private or public sector, on the other, surely indicated a level of ambiguity due to the confusions and tensions of a cultural field being radically transformed by changing aesthetic and socio-political currents. And, as noted by observers, even while adopting tactics to avoid stigmatization, musicians and composers refused to conform to specific ideological agendas or socio-political interests and thus produce songs on demand. However, their own sense of identity as 'cultural workers' and social actors was then being challenged in unprecedented ways within a rapidly fragmenting society so that they had to learn to navigate new and troubled waters to ensure their own survival and the preservation of their musical practice. It was becoming increasingly evident that new threats were looming, with a lingering hostility still felt towards them by a society slowly developing more conservative cultural tastes and inclinations under the growing impact of an emerging and omnipresent religious fundamentalist movement. The Islamists' influence in society being quite pronounced, it helped spread with efficiency their uncompromising views about the meaning of culture and cultural forms. Their rejection of music (in particular) as a legitimate cultural expression, found an outlet in their disapproval of rai, as they repeatedly accused the singers of corrupting the youth, causing social ills and the collapse of public morality. This led to a consciously self-imposed censoring attitude among musicians; some of its 'unconscious' effects may probably be witnessed in a new style that later emerged within this period, labelled 'sentimental rai'.

Sentimental Rai (1990-1994)

In the early 1990s, the rai scene grew stronger as increasing numbers of hit records were produced. A new style emerged, known as 'sentimental' or 'lovers' rai', which appealed to the tastes of new categories of listeners: families and women in particular, many of whom, in the past, had tended to be put off by the sexual aggressiveness of the lyrical content of 'hard rai' songs. By contrast, the new romantic musical streak was identified as proper or 'clean rai'.

However, despite new freedoms acquired by the press, the arts and civil society, the post-riots era, after 1988, remained a deeply troubled period with growing social tensions and a political scene dominated by a growing militant Islamist movement. The situation became even more volatile after the unexpected sweeping victory of the FIS (the Islamic Salvation Front), the largest Islamist party, in the 1990 local elections. By early 1992, civil strife had broken out, following the victory of the FIS in the initial round of national elections that were abruptly cancelled by an intervention of the army. Violent forms of confrontation then ensued between the army on the one hand and members of the AIS (the Islamic Salvation Army), the armed wing of the FIS, and other militant groupings of various denominations, on the other.

The impact of a strategy of terror followed by some Islamist militants was devastating for the whole population. The situation was particularly bad for artists and intellectuals, as the Armed Islamic Groups (GIA) had declared war on them. One of their most notable victims from the Wahran music scene was the producer Rachid Baba Ahmed. Others, such as cheikha Djenia, had their houses burnt down. However, it was the event of the assassination, in autumn 1994, of the star of 'sentimental rai', cheb Hasni, which would punctuate, in the most dramatic manner, the historic passage of the rai musical movement.

Post-rai (1994-2000s)

The event of cheb Hasni's death constituted a seminal moment in the history of popular music, as it signalled the end of the road, at least provisionally, for the significant journey of rai. In the words of Daoudi and Miliani:

> In September 1994, the assassination of cheb Hasni, the most popular singer of rai 'second wave', symbolically marks a temporary conclusion to this phenomenon which, over a period of twenty years, has given, without any contestation, a new impulse to the practice and history of music in Algeria. (cited in Daoudi and Miliani 1996: 35)

During this 'voyage', popular culture and music grew considerably, deeply transformed in varied aspects of production, consumption, identity formation and changing subjectivities; transformations which amounted, in their breadth and social impact, to a cultural revolution.

The shocking killing of popular performers such as cheb Hasni filled the darkest pages in the history of Algerian music. Understandably, the acute socio-political crisis during the remaining part of the decade, combined with the effects of militant Islamism and the atmosphere of fear generated, further reduced the space for the production and reproduction of rai songs (Daoudi and Miliani 1996: 34). As a result of the unfolding national tension, some of the more prominent artists resorted to leaving the county for indefinite or temporary exile, a process that eventually gave birth to new forms within diasporic rai. Those performers who stayed adopted self-censorship as a strategy of survival. In other words, in the years that followed, they repositioned themselves within a fast changing field, faced as they were with growing dilemmas, born of the ideological and armed pressure exerted by radical Islamism, political uncertainties and the economic imperatives that rai had been experiencing within rapidly expanding nation-wide and international markets.

Finally, it has become evident that some of the processes involved in censure paradoxically find both an additional enemy and new supportive links through the economic within both local and trans-local contexts, as popularization and commercialization provide new sources of pressures as well as offering possibilities for renewal. For instance, within an international perspective, as global record companies acquired some control over rai music, producing and staging it for a wide trans-national market, rai became more visible and less silent within Algeria as well as globally. More specifically, for instance, rai albums produced by Western companies acquired superior technical qualities while some melodic 'authenticity', at least within earlier productions, has been maintained (Mezouane 1992: 92). Yet, such a process has not been devoid of contradictions, integrating its own repressive registers into the music and reformulating them within shifting definitions of censure and even censorship.

Furthermore, beyond the historical events discussed above, there is a new post-rai period to account for new developments in rai within Algeria, spaces of diaspora and elsewhere. This entailed the emergence of various musical modes. Originating in rai or inspired by it, endless forms of fusion and musical hybrids developed while, at the same time, they somehow re-enacted an ambivalent relationship with the earlier mode of Wahrani rai, implicitly setting to compete against it. From this, a question arises as to whether such new developments, opened up by worldwide music distribution, have now bestowed on rai some assured centrality derived from its influence which is not just locally or regionally based, but which also reaches out on the global stage. The answer is by no means settled, as it may be argued that this musical style has never enjoyed a position of centrality throughout its entire history. For over a century, it evolved on the periphery of an imperial and post-imperial culture and survived relentless dislocations and appropriations as well as systematic suppressions, within it and around it. Furthermore, such an historical process may not have been discontinued with the integration of this music style into mainstream Algerian culture and its transition into the world music stage, but only taken on new forms.

Resistant Rai

As evident from the critical positions so far reviewed, politics and processes of modernization have contributed, in different contexts, to drive rai out of the ghetto. However, as Virolle-Souibes (1989: 56) correctly argues, instances of resistance to rai – which amount to its censorious treatment – so far articulated through many voices, have also become more diverse and displaced. In other words, anti-music and more specifically anti-rai pressures have certainly remained persistent, translating an endemically adverse treatment of indigenous popular cultural forms.

Overall, negative conditions of reproduction compounded by the adverse effects inherited from earlier formations and changing conditions of marginality have shaped the world of rai and contributed to structuring this music in specific ways, distinct from mainstream and other regional cultural productions nationwide. More specifically, those conditions have ultimately determined this cultural expression, in a sense, as an enduring subaltern form of signification and communication because rai remains, as succinctly put by Benkheira (1986: 87), 'the manifestation of a marginalized culture'. As such, this marginalized culture, which becomes 'expressed' and, more to the point, embodied by a musical movement such as rai has prevailed because it is, to a large extent, the product of a historically defined memory. Therefore, within fragments bequeathed by such collective memory, forms of marginality have not been erased but altered and transmuted into those musical tunes and rhythms which were, as allegorically put by critics 'hummed, all through a century, by the lips of those who had most suffered from the ravages of the (brutal) changes and (definitive) reconversions imposed on their universe' (Daoudi and Miliani 1996: 132). And, in turn, such a memory has become embedded in the sounds of what the poet Mahmoud Darwish (1984: 41) termed 'the music of human flesh'.

In the new millennium, Algeria has finally begun a slow and arduous transition into an era of recovery. However, to be effective, this process requires addressing, at all levels, the causes and effects of past ill treatments and of new socio-material injustices. This endeavour, for now, seems unlikely. Social space has remained fragmented and social progress thwarted by the impact of adverse socio-material and cultural legacies, those inherited from a colonial history and those born of post-colonial contradictions and conflicting encounters. The most deadly of these was certainly the unravelling of the Islamist movement in the 1990s and the bloody conflict that followed but also, subsequently, the persistence of forms of conservatism, authoritarianism and chauvinism within political culture, in addition to new pressures due to economic and cultural globalization. All these pressures indicate that the status and role of cultural expression in whatever form, but more essentially as music, remains, more than ever, both the ideal terrain for – and the underlying object of – an ongoing struggle.

Finally, the idea inferred throughout is that of a complementary relationship between notions of censure, censorship and music. Music impacts powerfully on listeners, which is why it attracts the attention of varieties of censors. In the process, musicians become the objects of attacks, whether these take the form of open aggression or institutional and symbolic violence. However, even if 'censureship' has the potential to undermine, marginalize or silence musicians and even kill them, it does not succeed in stopping the music.

References

Belhalfaoui, M. 1986. *Le Rai*. Colombes: Editions du Théatre Universel.

Benkheira, H. 1986. 'De la Musique Avant Toute Chose: Remarques sur le Rai', *Peuples Méditerranéens* 35-36, pp. 173-177.

Cheurfi, A. 1997. *Dictionnaire des Musiciens et Interprètes Algériens*. Algiers: ANEP.

Daoudi, B. and Miliani, H. 1996. *L'Aventure du Rai: Musique et Soci*été. Paris: Editions du Seuil.

Darwish, M. 1984. 'The Wandering Guitar Player', in A. al-Udhari (ed.), *Victims of a Map: an Anthology of Arabic Poetry*. London: El-Saqi Books.

Dernouny, M. and Zoulef, B. 1983. 'L'identité Culturelle au Maghreb à Travers un Corpus de Chants Contemporains', *Annuaire de l'Afrique du Nord*, pp. 3-31.

Langlois, A. 1996. *Rai on the Border: Popular Music and Society in the Maghreb*. Unpublished thesis. Belfast: Queen's University.

Lounes, M. 1995. *Rebelle*. Editions: Stock.

Mazouzi, B. 1990. 'La Musique Algérienne et la Question Rai', *La Revue Musicale* 418, 419, 420, pp. 7-119.

Mezouane, R. 1992. 'Génération Rai', *Autrement* 60, pp. 64-70.

Miliani, H. 1983. 'Culture Populaire et Contradictions Symboliques: les Représentations des Femmes dans la Chanson Populaire dite Oranaise', *Documents de Travail du GRFA/CRIDSSH Oran* 9, pp. 1-24.

Miliani, H. 1989. 'Une Esthétique du Fragmentaire: Dame Remitti et ses Enfants Putatifs', in A. Ben-Naoum (ed.), *L'Oralité Africaine: Acte du Colloque International d'Alger*. Algiers: Centre National d'Etudes Historiques.

Schade-Poulsen, M. 1999. *Men and Popular Music in Algeria*. Texas: University of Texas Press.

Virolle, M. 1995. *La Chanson Rai: de l'Algérie Profonde à la Scène Internationale*. Paris: Khartala.

Virolle-Souibes, M. 1988. 'Ce Que Chanter Veut Dire: Prélude à d'Autres Couplets'. *Cahiers de Littérature Orale* 23, pp. 177-209.

Virolle-Souibes, M. 1989. 'Le Rai entre Résistance et Récupération', *Revue du Monde Musulman et de la Méditerranée* 1: 15, pp 47-62.

Chapter 14

Concluding Comments on the Censorship of Popular Music in Africa

Martin Cloonan and Michael Drewett

Observations on popular music censorship in Africa

The chapters which comprise *Popular Music Censorship in Africa* have detailed some of the experiences of music censorship on the continent and brought new light to bear on issues of music censorship. Quite clearly the countries of Africa have many divergent histories to offer, dependent on regional contexts and historical periods, yet the countries considered in this volume are broadly united in their experience of imperialism and transition into a post-colonial age and all the concomitant difficulties and challenges. As Cloonan noted in Chapter 1, the documentation of popular music censorship in Africa has been generally neglected, especially in comparison to the many studies conducted in the USA, United Kingdom and Eastern Europe. It is therefore useful to consider the occurrence of popular music censorship in a cross section of African contexts as has been undertaken in the preceding chapters. The mixture of issues and case studies collected here illustrate a number of points which we would like to highlight in this conclusion.

The first of these is that once again censorship is shown to be a characteristic of *all* societies. It may change its shape, but it is ever present. For example, one of the most striking findings of this collection is that forms of music censorship which pertained in colonial societies were continued in various ways in post-colonial societies. Liberation organizations and colonial powers both had censorial agendas. Both wanted to drown out dissident voices, to check musical opposition. The tactics employed here – ranging from promoting other forms of music through to imprisonment and even to assassination – meant that musicians frequently needed some deft political footwork in order to retain their freedom of expression. On some occasions they used subterfuge in the form of *double entendres* in order to retain at least some freedom of expression. At other times they simply told it as they saw it.

This leads to our second observation, that one of the themes of *Popular Music Censorship in Africa* is resistance. Musicians in Africa were involved in both anti-colonial struggles and in battle with post-colonial governments (but as noted below, not all contests were with governments). At such times musicians have had to become active social agents, often seeking to speak on behalf of those who could not speak for themselves. In such cases musicians can be seen as resisting *all* forms of repression, including repression exercised by those who had previously been their comrades in liberation struggles. It may be overstating the case to say that African musicians are closer to their communities than might generally be the case elsewhere, but it is clear that their capacity to speak on behalf of the dispossessed has led them into resisting political oppression. This is true of both colonial and post-colonial societies.

The opposite side of this coin is that musicians can be co-opted. This happened in apartheid South Africa and is happening in contemporary Zimbabwe. In the former instance musicians were called upon to give credence to the apartheid regime by performing in South Africa and in the phoney homeland of Bophutatswana, and South African musicians in particular were urged not to participate in government propaganda songs. In the latter instance the promotion by the state of pro-regime musicians has led to the *de facto* censorship of others. However, the historical lesson of both these cases may be that those who choose or are coerced into co-option may pay a heavy price.

Another observation is that *Popular Music Censorship in Africa* once again shows that censorship comes in many forms. While Cloonan argued in Chapter 1 that Africa appears to have seen more overt political censorship than is generally the case in what he calls the west, it is also clear that music censorship in Africa is by no means the sole prerogative of governments. Other censorial agents – such as broadcasters, vigilantes, and liberation movements – are also prominent. Amongst the most striking cases were apartheid South Africa (Chapter 2) and Algeria (Chapter 13) in which musicians faced strong forms of censorship from organized political groups with different priorities than musicians' freedom to sing what they wanted to, wherever they wanted to and with whom they wanted to. The various examples discussed in this volume emphasize that music censorship in Africa is myriad, rather than singular.

It also clear that the process of music censorship is not simply an administrative one, no matter who executes it. Cloonan and Garofalo (2003: 3) distinguish between 'the narrower concept of censorship' and the broader concept of 'policing', which conveys 'the variety of ways in which popular music can be regulated, restricted, and repressed'. Yet when considering the situation in authoritarian regimes including many discussed in this book, the connection between censorship and policing is integral, which is why policing has received wide coverage in this volume. While Akpan (Chapter 6) stresses the need to go beyond the limiting (and inaccurate) view of Africa as solely a space of repressive state censorship, many of the African examples considered in this book illustrate the integral role which policing plays in the censorship of popular music. Censorship boards might ban music but it is often the threat of police or vigilante action (in the form of coercion and violence) which puts real fear into musicians. As Drewett (2004a: 13) has argued elsewhere:

In repressive regimes the world over, artists have refrained from certain artistic expression not simply because of censorship laws or the presence of censors, but because of the repressive repercussions of failure to submit to government dictates. It is certainly true of authoritarian states that policing gives censorship its teeth, enabling censorship to be far more daunting than it would otherwise be.

Popular Music Censorship in Africa leaves no doubt that this has often been the situation in Africa. As noted, the integral link between censorship and policing is by no means unique to Africa, as the situation in contexts such as Nazi Germany, Chile under Pinochet, the Soviet Union and the McCarthy era in the USA attest. Yet the repetition of relevant examples found in this collection brings home the point that the role of people (government agents and otherwise) willing to enforce censorship practices are key to the manner in which censorship has swept through both colonial and post-colonial Africa, and into the present day.

African popular music censorship in a post-11 September age

In the aftermath of 11 September 2001 the Bush government has attempted to convince the world that it is politically necessary and acceptable to erode civil liberties in the name of the war on terror. Popular music and musicians were not exempt from these attacks. As Eric Nuzum (2004: 151) reveals, Clear Channel responded by advising its programmers to remove 'lyrically questionable' songs from their play lists, while record companies and musicians responded to 11 September by withdrawing songs, album covers and music videos which similarly might offend the hegemony of the United States ruling elite. On a more coercive level, Canadian band Godspeed You Black Emperor were surrounded and arrested by gun-wielding members of the police and FBI because they pulled into an Oklahoma gas station with what (in an age of global terrorism) seemed to be two suspicious looking vans and an equipment truck (Moore 2003: 99). Although they were released after a few hours of questioning, the dangers of unquestioningly accepting arguments in favour of political correctness is evident.

An important parallel between the United States and African contexts, as revealed in *Popular Music Censorship in Africa*, is that arguments in favour of 'politically correct' censorship of popular music have begun to make inroads into the civil liberties of musicians in the twenty-first century. While the case in the United States has been against terrorism, in Africa there has increasingly been pressure to censor in the 'politically correct' interests of national unity and traditional values. Reading through the chapters of this book, it becomes apparent that calls for various forms of unity have their own censorial implications. In the context of liberation struggle unity might mean not singing the songs of the oppressor. In post-colonial regimes it might entail the singing of praise songs or songs attacking political opponents. It might also mean not criticizing other communities – as in the case of contemporary South Africa. Whatever the practice, the underlying motivation is to drown out dissident voices which might disrupt fragile unities. For those musicians who want to be true to their muse, rather than political expediency, confrontation appeared to be inevitable. This volume contains several examples of this, each with its own lesson to give. South Africa, for example, prides itself on possessing one of the most liberal constitutions in the world, yet as Gary Baines demonstrates in Chapter 4 this did not prevent its Film and Publication Board and state-owned South African Broadcasting Corporation from placing severe restrictions on the sale and broadcast of a song which was judged to be politically incorrect. In both South Africa and Zimbabwe (to name two examples) conservative popular musicians would like their governments to (re)introduce strict censorship over sexually explicit songs which they feel undermine their cultural values.[1]

Supporting the rights of those dissenting voices which do not uphold the politically correct hegemonic (and sometimes counter-hegemonic) positions does not necessitate the acceptance of a value free liberal position. We acknowledge that absolute freedoms cannot exist because one cannot have the right to do whatever one wants to do without impinging on others' corresponding freedoms to do what they want to do and their rights to be protected from harm. For this reason Jim McGuigan argues that 'absolute freedom of expression is a principle of intolerance', given that the notion of free speech 'is used to justify all manner of oppressive discourse, most notably sexist and racist discourses' (McGuigan 1996: 157). However, as Drewett (2004b) has argued, McGuigan conflates allowing the expression of a particular discourse with the acceptance of that discourse. It is argued here that supporting absolute freedom of speech does not necessitate the justification of oppressive discourse. On the contrary, freedom of speech allows oppressive discourses to be heard, but also allows for counter statements and arguments to be made, in an ongoing contest in which critical discourse is encouraged. This is preferable to a state-supported form of 'defensible' censorship whereby state censors get to defend censorship according to their own agenda. The post-11 September aftershocks are adequate warning of the dangers of such an approach. The argument put forward here (and similarly made by Drewett in Chapter 2, Craig and Mkhize in Chapter 3 and Baines in Chapter 4 and intimated in discussion throughout *Popular Music Censorship in Africa*) is that musicians should be permitted to voice issues through song so that public debate can be encouraged and topical issues openly dealt with, rather than hidden from public view as though they did not exist, only to rise again at a later stage in a more

---

[1] In a meeting with an official from the Zimbabwean Censorship Board at a Freemuse workshop in Harare April 2005, a number of neo-traditional Zimbabwean musicians asked why the Board was not censoring sexually explicit songs performed by young musicians who, it was argued, had no respect for traditional values. Similar sentiments were expressed about the South African situation at a Freemuse workshop held in Johannesburg, South Africa in 2001.

hazardous form. At the same time however, oppositional voices must be heard, so that ongoing contest between competing views can be expressed in public forums.

Certainly, the idea of taking forward the struggle for the freedom of expression is one which the authors of this book most want to stress. *Popular Music Censorship in Africa* is a contribution to the ongoing debate about freedom of musical expression. We have no doubt that battles over freedom of musical expression will continue in Africa as they will elsewhere. Africa has both particular and general lessons to give. It provides new insights, as well as re-affirming previous ones. To dip one's toe in the pool of music censorship as we have done here is to send ripples across it. We hope that readers will have felt those ripples and will want to contribute their own.

References

Cloonan, M. and Garofalo, R. 2003. 'Introduction', in M. Cloonan and R. Garofalo (eds), *Policing Pop.* Philadelphia: Temple University Press. pp. 1-9.

Drewett, M. 2004a. 'An analysis of the censorship of popular music within the context of cultural struggle in South Africa during the 1980s'. PhD thesis. Grahamstown: Rhodes University.

Drewett, M. 2004b. 'Is anything undesirable these days? Changing dynamics in Popular Music Censorship in Post-Apartheid South Africa'. Paper presented to the Ten Years of Democracy Workshop, UNISA, Pretoria, August.

McGuigan, J. 1996. *Culture and the Public Sphere*. London: Routledge.

Moore, M. 2003. *Dude, Where's My Country?* New York: Warner Books.

Nuzum. E. 2004. 'Crash into me, baby: America's implicit music censorship since 11 September' in M. Korpe (ed.) *'Shoot the Singer!'*, *Music Censorship Today*. London: Zed Books, pp. 149-159.

Index